Kafka and Kabbalah

KARL ERICH GRÖZINGER

KAFKA AND KABBALAH

Translated by Susan Hecker Ray

CONTINUUM / NEW YORK

1994
The Continuum Publishing Company
370 Lexington Avenue, New York, NY 10017

This edition has been suported by a grant from Inter Nationes, Bonn.

Printed in the United States of America

Library of Congress Cataloging-In-Publication Data

Grözinger, Karl-Erich
[Kafka und die Kabbala. English]
Kafka and kabbalah / Karl Erich Grözinger : translated by Susan Hecker Ray
p. cm.
Includes bibliographical references and index.
ISBN 0-8264-0659-9 (alk. paper)
1. Kafka, Franz, 1883–1924—Religion. 2. Judaism in literature. 3. Cabala in literature. 4. Cabala—Influence. I. Title.
PT2621.A26Z74614513 1994
833'.912—dc20 94-299
CIP

This entire literature is an assault against the frontiers, and if Zionism hadn't intervened, it could easily have developed into a new occultism, a Kabbalah. The rudiments are already there. On the other hand, it would take an incomparable genius to sink new roots into past centuries or to create the past centuries anew...

(Diary entry of January 16, 1922)

CONTENTS

1. Kafka and Judaism 1

2. *The Trial* and the Tradition of the Gatekeeper in the Kabbalah . . 15

3. When and How the Celestial Court Functions 33

4. The Ecstatic Ascent to Heaven 39

5. "No One Else Could Enter Here, for This Door Was Meant for You Alone" 46

6. The Gatekeeper Tradition as It Relates to the Description of the Court 51

7. The Status of Man vis-à-vis the Officers of the Court 53

8. The Human Face as a Reflection of Divine Judgment. 55

9. The Kabbalistic Depiction of the Celestial Courts—History as Judgment 61

10. The Incursion of Judgment into Human Life—Disease and Dreams. 69

11. "Women Have a Great Power"—The Feminine Element in the Hierarchies of the Court. 77

12. The Judgment Theme in Eastern Jewish Folktales—Kabbalah as Narrative 83

13. The Animal Stories 95

14. Divine Judgment via the Word—
"I Now Sentence You to Death by Drowning" 121

15. Language and Reality—
Writing as a Form of Prayer 127

16. "Josephine the Singer; or, the Mouse People" 141

17. The Aphorisms—
between the Two Trees of Paradise 165

18. Kafka Without End—
Yet Another Interpretation? 179

Appendix 190

Notes 209

Bibliography 219

Index 223

1
KAFKA AND JUDAISM

In the dual role of writer and thinker, Franz Kafka forged new directions for the German language as well as for world literature; he was also a Jew. Is this last fact of any significance, or can modern Kafka criticism simply state it and move on to the task at hand? After all, the reception of Kafka's work has demonstrated how adaptable it is to a number of interpretative approaches, all of which were able to make their point without emphasizing the Jewish component. More mindful of necessity than of silent scruple, critics usually kept to their own intuition, paying little more than cursory tribute to Kafka's Jewishness.[1] Fortunately, this is no longer the case in just about every modern representation of Kafka's life and work. Hardly any scholar today would fail to emphasize the significance of the predominantly Jewish atmosphere that surrounded Kafka, and this is essentially a sign of respect and recognition of the enigmatic and far-reaching references Gershom Scholem made regarding the kabbalistic influences in Kafka's work. Toward the end of his article titled "Ten Unhistorical Statements about the Kabbalah" (*Judaica* III), Scholem writes: "Although unaware of it himself, [Kafka's] writings are a secularized representation of the kabbalistic conception of the world. This is why many of today's readers find something of the rigorous splendor of the canonical in them—a hint of the Absolute that breaks into pieces" (271). In his book on Walter Benjamin, *The Story of a Friendship*,

Scholem quotes himself: "I said then . . . that one would have to read the works of Franz Kafka before one could understand the Kabbalah today, and particularly *The Trial*" (*Friendship*, 158). Without intending to minimize the astuteness of Scholem's insight, the fact is that references such as these remain extremely pale and colorless for most critics. The majority either restrict themselves to vacuous generalities or else proceed from an image of Judaism that bears no resemblance whatsoever to Kafka's Jewish milieu. Take, for example, the statement Bert Nagel makes in his informative chapter on Kafka's Judaism, where he claims "that the old commandant" of "In the Penal Colony"represents "the God of the Old Testament," and "thus there is undoubtedly something of the Old Testament God Yahweh in the fathers Bendemann and Samsa and in the commandant of the penal colony" (118). Or again, when he sees in Kafka the "author of Judaism": "The fact that Kafka not only identified himself as a Jew and took up the cause of Judaism, but, perhaps even more importantly, the fact that he still harbored the basic ideas of ancient biblical Judaism as well, all testify to a continuation of the Jewish heritage. Kafka's God is still the judgmental and punitive God of the Old Testament" (123).

Downright dubious is the most recent attack H. Binder made refuting a Jewish/kabbalistic element behind Kafka's thinking. Despite the extensive commonalities he has acknowledged as existing between Kafka and this background, he now speaks of a "contemptuous tendency" on the part of the Kabbalah vis-à-vis mankind; according to this trend, the world is supposedly a "creation of the devil." Binder also speaks of the "occultism" of the Kabbalah, which could not possibly have influenced Kafka. The Kabbalah is neither contemptuous of mankind nor is it a conspiratorial "occultism" in the vein, let's say, of the *Protocols of the Elders of Zion*. It is, rather, a widespread and widely read, generally accepted mystical theology, accessible to everyone, especially among Eastern European Jewry and Hasidism.

Observations like these not only exude the prejudicial Christian image of Judaism; they also persist in the absolutely erroneous idea that Judaism has remained unchanged in its two-thousand-year post-biblical history—as if there weren't a rich and multifaceted, philosophically diverse post-biblical body of Jewish literature and thought; as if the philosophy and ideology of Judaism were a static, monolithic block in terms of rational thought. To talk about *the* Jewish religion and way of life within a philosophical-theological context is one of the fundamental errors that grew out of an image of Judaism based on dogmatic or self-conceived ignorance. Already closer to the truth are the no longer rare references to the influences the Yiddish theater had on Kafka. The work of Evelyn Torton Beck did much to substantiate this fact ("Durchbruch," 204–23). In light of the entries in Kafka's diaries on the subject, this influence can hardly be contested.[2]

The very existence of these distinct and divergent views within Judaism forced Scholem, the Nestor of modern research on the Kabbalah, to repeatedly emphasize Kafka's particular relation to the Kabbalah and to Eastern European Hasidism. It also occasioned his provocative "dissident thoughts" "that admittedly do not deal with Kafka's place in the continuum of German literature—in which he has absolutely no place—but in that of Jewish literature" (*Friendship*, 212). Respect for the tremendous stature of Gershom Scholem requires just about every modern critic to acknowledge his view. Paradoxically, however, recognition of this influence frequently remains rather dry and sterile because many critics are unable to read the Hebrew and Yiddish sources and thus have no choice but to resort exclusively to secondhand information. This is all the more regrettable since it is precisely this aspect of the Jewish tradition that has so much to tell about Kafka, a fact one cannot fail to appreciate in light of the diary entry serving as the introductory motto for the present work.

This study proceeds from the basic assumption that Kafka could have been influenced by the Jewish, or better said, by a certain Jewish tradition. Is this approach justified in spite of the fact that he himself deplored his inadequate Jewish upbringing? He did so not only in his *Letter to My Father* ("But what kind of Judaism did I get from you!" [*Wedding*, 144]), but also in the much quoted statement: "I was not introduced to life, like Kierkegaard, by the heavily overbearing hand of Christianity, nor have I clutched the tip of the disappearing Jewish prayer shawl like the Zionists. I am end or beginning" (*Wedding*, 89).[3] Such laments on Kafka's part are best measured against the claims a writer of his sensibility with an interest in philosophic questions might make of any religious education and religious tradition.

However, we should not let this fact lead us to assume that Kafka had no knowledge or no Jewish experiences that might have colored his thinking and his writing. All of Kafka's texts—including his novels and short stories, but primarily his diary entries and aphorisms—reveal an extraordinarily detailed and sophisticated knowledge of things Jewish. He acquired this knowledge through his own studies, through conversations with friends, and through family life as well as through observations of Jewish life in Prague, especially in the synagogue. Granted, this was not a formal knowledge of rabbinical-halakhic rules of orthodoxy and of philosophical-theological speculation; what Kafka knew might better be described as a popularized Kabbalah and the Jewish traditions influenced by it.

Kafka was a careful observer and evidently a very attentive listener. His diaries reproduce what he saw and heard with an accuracy that lends his notes the authority of religious-historical source material. A comparison of these diary entries with the Eastern European Hebrew and Yiddish original works leaves no doubt about their reliability. One thing is clear: Kafka knew more about Judaism than his remarks on the subject would lead one to believe. What he gleaned from direct instruction and personal readings was substantial, but the experience of customs, gestures and everyday behavior rooted in various traditions cannot be overestimated. Visible objects like the *mezuzah* (the scroll on doorposts of Jewish homes), the *tefillin* (phylacteries or prayer boxes attached by leather straps to the forehead and arm of the worshipper), the prayer shawl, the thoughts accompanying acts of charity, the texts of holiday rituals practiced privately at home and publicly in the synagogue and so easily transmitted via conversations with friends—all of these things provided a knowledge-hungry person like Kafka with the fundamentals of popular Jewish religion and Jewish lore, and characterize Jewish behavior and thought much more profoundly than does a formal knowledge of ethical and philosophical works. However, such Jewish lore also creates a culture gap for the reader who is unfamiliar with this everyday way of life and who therefore overlooks it.

This reference to the Jewish traditions and attitudes intrinsic to Kafka must be accompanied by a warning against falling prey to the unjustified extreme of relegating him exclusively to this tradition.

The whole of Jewish intellectual history, spanning as it does thousands of years, is itself distinguished by the fact that the great Jewish thinkers took a creative approach to their tradition and constantly renewed it. What's more, they did so under the—at times profound—influence of non-Jewish cultural elements, which they absorbed, interpreted, processed and "Judaized" to the extent that they were ultimately perceived as a genuine part of Jewish tradition. This fact alone lends considerable support to Scholem's extreme position. Kafka did what many Jewish thinkers and writers before him did: he merged his Judaism with modern thinking and thus created a new form of Judaism, his own Judaism. If a large number of Kafka readers with ties to modern Christian or non-Jewish European cultural backgrounds feel directly addressed by Kafka and have a sense of being "at home" in his works, their response is by no means novel in Jewish intellectual history. Medieval Jewish philosophy with the Kabbalah in its wake, as well as Eastern European Hasidism have been as deeply influenced as has non-Jewish mysticism by the philosophical systems of medieval Platonism and Aristotelianism. In many respects these sources gave rise to a number of similarities vis-à-vis the corresponding Christian movements—one need only think of the neoplatonism of such Christian mystics as Dionysius Areopagita on up to Meister Eckhardt and the early Spanish Kabbalists of Gerona in the thirteenth century, the Ijjun Kabbalah, the Zohar, Moses Cordovero and Eastern European Hasidim.[4] The Christian Kabbalah of the fifteenth to the eighteenth century actually believed it could best express its own Christian religiosity with the help of the Jewish Kabbalah.[5] To this day, Princess Antonia's kabbalistic altar-painting in the modest church of Bad Teinach in the Black Forest remains a most impressive demonstration of this.[6] In many respects, medieval Jewish philosophy is a component of the broad rubric of European philosophy, and Maimonides (1135–1205) as well as Solomon Ibn Gabirol (1020–1057) may be named here as having exerted a direct influence on Christian scholasticism and mysticism, as well as Leone Ebreo alias Judah Abravanel (1460–1523) with his *Dialoghi d' amore*. Mention should also be made of the lasting effect Martin Buber had on the Christian churches, particularly his interpretation of Jewish history as an attempt to modernize Judaism.[7]

All of this is sufficient admonition against a pan-Judaistic understanding of Kafka. At the same time, however, it underscores the conviction that inattention to the Jewish side of Kafka's work, non-appreciation of its Jewish roots, runs the risk of misunderstanding his work. The scores of contradictory Kafka interpretations should serve as a warning as well as food for thought in this regard. Regardless of the way they present their material, one can no more truly understand Thomas Mann's *Joseph and His Brothers* or Joseph Roth's *Job* without a knowledge of their biblical counterparts than one can understand Kafka without a knowledge of the literary and narrative world that provided him with the motifs, thoughts, and overarching concepts he freely and creatively reshaped and reproduced in the western European mantle of modern German.

In each of these instances, every critical reader is faced with the task of recognizing the New as the new and the altered against the background of the Old. Kafka is not a Kabbalist simply because he appropriates kabbalistic traditions and transforms them. Exactly what he is, though, can only be defined by the person who accurately locates his points of departure. The *interpretation* of Kafka's works will remain primarily the task of future Germanists; my main purpose as a Judaist is merely to present the Jewish *background* for such interpretations. My presentation, therefore, will concentrate on those aspects of Kafka's works most reminiscent of the Eastern Jewish Hebrew and Yiddish traditions, and thus most evocative for anyone familiar with them. Beyond that, any locating of Kafka's position in the literary tradition is a task I gladly leave to the readers of this book themselves. My main objective is to help them see the Jewish elements that lie hidden beneath the surface of Kafka's texts. This problem applies less to the diaries, whose every page bears a Jewish stamp, and much more to the fictional texts. And yet, as far as the latter are concerned, one should not be misled by statements such as the one made at the 1990 Kafka Colloquium in Marbach, where one participant found great significance in the fact that the pivotal conversation in Kafka's novel *The Trial* did not take place in a synagogue, but rather in a Christian cathedral. After all, Kafka's diary entry, dated Yom Kippur, 1911, noted: "Altneu Synagogue yesterday. Kol Nidre . . . *churchlike* interior. Three pious, evidently Eastern Jews. In socks."

Kafka managed to divert his interpreters' attention away from the true background of his thinking and his storytelling by means of transpositions such as this into a Christian European setting. To what extent he did this will be shown in the following discussion of the kabbalistic parallels in *The Trial*. The Jewish element is obvious in the diaries, but it remains esoterically concealed in the stories and novels. It is this dissembling strategy, the avoidance of any concrete references, that has been observed so many times in Kafka's work and which is ultimately responsible for its ambiguity.

There are many echoes of kabbalistic elements and traditions in Kafka's works, but the Kabbalah itself, as might be expected, is not a homogeneous whole. By Kafka's time, this mystical-religious phenomenon already had a history of at least seven hundred years behind it. If one adds to that the ancient talmudic Hekhalot mysticism (the mysticism of the heavenly halls or palaces) which contributed essential presuppositions for what came to be known as medieval Kabbalah, we are talking about a history of eighteen hundred years. Each phase of the long history of Jewish mysticism left its own traces in the writings of later generations—traces that evolved in completely different cultural and intellectual worlds. Thus, in the course of the centuries, an in part totally heterogeneous conglomerate of conceptions and thoughts came into being, and not all authors attempted to reduce this body of thought to a more or less unified whole. Many of the later authors evaluated the traditions they received only eclectically, completely eliminating one aspect or another and frequently looking upon what they preserved from a completely novel point of view.

All of this must be kept in mind when speaking of Kafka and the Kabbalah. It also explains why Kafka will always betray affinities to one or another strand of the kabbalistic tradition, and in many instances to fundamentally different or even contradictory strands. Kafka himself was unable to study the often extremely difficult classical kabbalistic texts in the original Hebrew or Aramaic languages, but he had to have been familiar with certain popularized basic patterns. We know this because they played a role in the daily habits and in the popular teachings of the community. An enormous number of folkloric morality books and collections of homilies popularized the highly mystical theosophical, historiosophical and anthroposophical teachings of the Kabbalah.

These works were certainly available to the simple Jew, but they were studied primarily by the preachers in the synagogues and houses of study (*bet midrash*) in preparation of their sermons. Such moral writings and folk tales actually defined the general Jewish consciousness in middle and eastern Europe; they were the medium through which each individual living in this milieu received a body of specifically Jewish knowledge, as well as attitudes and world views. That being the case, we should not be surprised to discover parallels between this popular literature and a large number of motifs in Kafka's texts.

The following pages will present a brief discussion of the basic and distinctive features of kabbalistic thought that can be shown to have left unmistakable traces in Kafka's own thinking and writing.

One central, basic principle of the Kabbalah is the belief in the unity of all being. The visible world is linked to the invisible worlds of the divine and the celestial in the neoplatonic sense of a single chain of being, all tied together by means of the outflow of the emanation of divine light and life that produced and maintains all these worlds. However, whereas the neoplatonic and even the Aristotelian systems of the Middle Ages always represent the ideal world in some less tangible intelligible substances like the intellect, the world soul (sometimes represented by a trinity) and nature (as with the neoplatonists), or in the ten separate intelligences which are occasionally identified with the ten classes of angels in the ancient rabbinic literature (as with the Aristotelians), the intelligible world of the kabbalists is pictured as consisting of a vast number of mythologically conceived divine and celestial quintessences. At the apex stand the ten spiritual forces, lights, words or *sefirot*, frequently depicted in the shape of a tree but which are inextricably intertwined through the reflection of the ten in each individual one. Like the neoplatonic world of ideals, these ten spiritual forces form the basic pattern of all being, while at the same time they are depicted anthropomorphically, as it were, as a celestial family consisting of a father, a mother, a son and a daughter—with male and female components and loving and chastising aspects. The structure of the ten sefirot is repeated through the four stages of cosmic construction: the sefirotic world itself (this is the revealed God), the world of the Divine Throne, the world of the celestial angels and finally the terrestial, material world called earth. With reference to the biblical passage in Isaiah 43:7, these four are called the worlds of *Atsiluth* (emanation), *Beriah* (creation), *Yetsirah* (formation) and *Asiyah* (the world of making, or concretizing action). In their articulation they accord with the medieval philosophical interconnectedness of all being: the world of absolute intelligences, the world of the celestial spheres and the sub-lunar terrestrial world among the Aristotelians, or intellect, psyche, nature, and the sub-lunar world among the neoplatonists.

The Kabbalah took these basic rudiments of the medieval philosophical world picture and synthesized them in various ways with the ancient Jewish cosmological tradition as well as with gnostic elements. The result was often an opalescent, encyclopedic composite expressed on differing linguistic levels. The same idea might be depicted at one time in the traditional language and imagery of the Bible, at another with the imagery of ancient talmudic homiletics and mystical tractates, yet again in an anthropomorphic style quite gnostic in outlook, or else in verbal-onomatological, or linguistic, expressions. The most common descriptions relied upon a combination of all these approaches. At its base remains the one fundamental idea that every single phenomenon of this world—nature, heaven, the human form, language and bilbical literature—of everything that exists in this world, in other words, derives from the one divine pattern. That this pattern, in turn, can be recognized in everything means that it can be described by everything.

Another essential aspect of the Kabbalah is the fact that knowledge of the world and of God as well as the description of all the phenomena of being is not an academic acquisition; it has its own practical side and practical application. Knowledge of the essence of being enables humans to orient themselves and to intervene on their own behalf. Such intervention is considered at once as being of use to the Godhead as well as to the whole world. The entire kabbalistic system thus ultimately serves to assign man's place in this composite, to show him the potentials as well as the responsibilities of his actions and behavior in this universe and to place at his disposal the means to affect it. This is theurgy, the ability to affect the roots of all being in order to release a flood of blessings over the earth. By means of his contemplative practices and the actions that grow out of them, man is in the position to exercise a direct influence on the divine world. The ontological basis of this ability is the structural and fundamental unity of being, which directly and dynamically connects man to the divine worlds. Praying, studying the Torah, obeying the commandments and a person's every earthly activity are seen in this all-encompassing connection of reciprocal influence; a person's total behavior is an action *sub specie aeternitatis*. In this network, man is both actor and actum. His actions always have consequences in the world above and, sooner or later, they will elicit specific reactions from that realm.

Once we accept the assumption that Kafka was influenced by the kabbalistic ideas outlined above, we can look upon Josef K. and the surveyor in Kafka's *Castle* as men who know of the interconnected nature of the hidden and the revealed worlds and who try their hands at theurgy in order to intervene in the divine direction of things. The justification of a statement such as this will become evident only at the end of this book, after the reader has recognized the extent of the correspondence between Kafka's works and this aspect of Jewish thought. All the same, these theurgical attempts on the part of Kafka's heroes turn out to be failures. They run amok or become entangled in vicious circles on a low level, with the result that they are unable to attain their intended higher goal. The Kabbalah also knows this problem of futile theurgy and describes it in terms of prayers whose ascent is cut off. Such prayers remain hanging somewhere in the low levels of the ontological hierarchy and may even become imprisoned in celestial "attics" provided for this very purpose. These prayers share the fate of the man from the country in Kafka's parable of the same name. He had already failed to pass the test at one of the lower gates and thus could not continue his journey.

Like medieval neoplatonism, the Kabbalah understands the different levels of the world as a qualitative hierarchy. The celestial levels closest to the human world are that much closer to the quality of the terrestrial world than are the higher levels situated above them, and woe to the prayer and woe to the soul that do not penetrate to higher levels, for what happens to them is what happened to Kafka's two heroes, Josef K. and the surveyor K. They both have responsibilities, of course, the one with the court and the other with the castle, but what they see there is hardly different from their own miserable world. From a kabbalistic viewpoint, what Kafka depicts in these two great novels, *The Trial* and *The Castle*, is the crisis of the Kabbalah, the failure of theurgy, the inability of the individual to employ his actions to gain access to the ultimate authority.

A very similar but by no means so pessimistic a turn in the Kabbalah occurred in the mysticism of Hasidism; its formulation goes back to one of this movement's most prominent figures, Dov Ber, the Maggid (Preacher) of Mezhirich (1710–1772). As the chapter on Kafka's aphorisms will show, Dov Ber turned away from the activism of the theurgists and believed that a solution to the suffering in this world is to be sought in the exact opposite of activism: in the individual's renunciation of the desire to effect a change on his own. For Dov Ber, the highest form of humanity is the complete renunciation of human independence and human ego-consciousness. His is an understanding of the self that sees itself only as a vessel of the Godhead which, in absolute quietism, surrenders itself via self-annihilation in the nothingness of the Oneness of God—an attitude, by the way, that increasingly comes to characterize Josef K.

A variation of this hasidic renunciation of theurgy is its transference to the rebbe, the *tzaddik*. According to this, no longer is each individual called to theurgy; instead, the hasidic rebbe takes on the role of intercessor for his community. For Kafka, these are the advocates and the various other standbys in the court or the village. Josephine the Singer plays this role in Kafka's story of the same name (*Stories*, 186). Once again Kafka demonstrates the crisis, the inability of the helper to really be of any help; even though, on the lower level, the illusion of help is already helpful.

A further similarity between Kafka and the mythological cosmology of the Kabbalah is the idea that the invisible hierarchies not only extend into the already less attractive lower levels, but that this hierarchy reaches down into everyday life, into its most banal and even its dirtiest aspects. Every one of the different strands of the Kabbalah view the evil in the world as part of the one world that emanates from God and stands in His service. The only difference is that Kafka, more so than the mythological descriptions presented below, depicts the hierarchy of the worlds primarily on its lowest level. One could also say that Kafka relegates the kabbalistic descriptions of the hierarchy, be they of the courts or of the castle, completely to the human sphere. Even so, as a type of sociomorphic and anthropomorphic myth of world hierarchy—a myth, moreover, that never completely loses sight of the transcendent—they maintain a mythological language.

An additional distinctive feature common to both Kafka and the Kabbalah is the idea that the court and the authorities before which human life in its totality must answer are part of the hierarchies of being that permeate the world. They do not represent a single court of justice before the Throne of God. History is also understood against this background. Within this structural frame, history exists only as a cyclical oscillation between the divine poles of mercy and judgment. These two poles determine the whole of being from its highest level right on down to life on earth. Everything that happens on earth is a direct consequence of this cycle of justice and grace or of the suspension of judgment in mercy (the divine union) and of the reign of the court (separation). Human life and history, therefore, are nothing more than a pendulum swing between acquittal and judgment, between arrest and its postponement. Where theurgy succeeds, it exerts an influence upon the union and thus upon the well-being of this world. In this case the world escapes judgment via grace or arches over justice via love and an abundance of blessings. In the hasidic variant mentioned above, the hallowed state can only be attained through renunication of the self, for the continued existence of individuality is separation, is judgment. Here history is viewed as a pendulum swinging between separation and union, between ego and its sublimation in the Oneness of God.

Another branch of the Kabbalah that is important for Kafka but which contradicts much of the hasidic version is the one promulgated by Isaac Luria in the sixteenth century. Kafka took from it the inclusion of inanimate nature, of plants and animals, into the scope of human life. In this late form of Kabbalah, theurgy is understood primarily as a process of the purification of the soul. The soul of the First Man, Adam, was shattered during the Fall into untold thousands of divine sparks. Now, after its break, it must bring about collectively that which was actually the task of the First

Man with his macro-soul—namely, to reunite these sparks with their divine source and repair the cosmic break. This task can only be accomplished within the frame of an all-encompassing purification of souls, which every divine spark of the initial soul has to attain for itself via the route of transmigration, or reincarnation, in humans, animals, plants, and minerals. Only after this has succeeded will the individual souls return to Adam, who will then be able to complete the task he was once assigned. Thanks to this theory, non-human nature, too, becomes part of the course of human redemption, with the result that animals and "dead" things are looked upon in a totally different way.

This doctrine produced a great number of folk tales that articulated the new relation to the human environment and which, as we shall see, are closely related in many respects to Kafka's animal figures and inanimate life. Animals and other things are now no longer objects, but people dwelling in animals and in things.

Lurianic Kabbalah fully developed the ideas of animating nature and granting it a soul already well-known in earlier forms, and it culminated these ideas with the belief that the whole world is full of wandering souls and demons. The cause of all this wandering about is sin; to keep oneself away from sin becomes the dominant motif of this Kabbalah, and it has engendered a Judaism that, in contrast to the otherwise predominant Jewish attitude, was very pessimistic. Fear of the power of evil forces and an ever-present awareness of sin produced forms of asceticism and renunciation that were unknown to Judaism before and remain so afterward. Knowledge that the court of justice is permanently in session, knowledge that sin lurks everywhere and particularly in the form of sexuality, are themes that also characterize the sermons and the moral values Isaac Luria helped determine. This ascetic form of Judaism, terrified by the world and by sin, was known in Kafka's family, and his diaries attest to the fact that it was an occasional topic of conversation.

Kafka's aphorisms, on the other hand, express a completely different form of Kabbalah, namely the mysticism of the individual and the nothingness promulgated primarily by Dov Ber. This form seeks to avoid sin via the act of mystical union and the renunciation of all things of the world. Any doubt as to whether Kafka had direct knowledge of this mysticism is soon laid to rest by a study of his aphorisms. Even Josef K. ultimately chose this path: "I always wanted to charge into the world with twenty hands and, what's more, for a purpose that could not be sanctioned. That was wrong" (*Trial*, 269). This turn away from synergistic theurgy toward a passive acceptance of the world as it was seems to be the attitude that Kafka himself apparently achieved in his aphorisms.

Kafka's texts can thus be viewed within the context of a discussion already current in the Kabbalah in its own right. Common to all the positions touched upon in this overview is a conscious awareness of how interwoven individual human life is with the life of the visible environment and the invisible upper regions; an awareness that this earthly life in its most profound essence is dependent upon the invisible world, upon justification or condemnation before its limitations. Life and death, in turn, are dependent upon these limitations. Also common to all these voices is the fact that man's relation to the supernatural is decisively co-determined by his own behavior. This is where the commonalities end, however, for differences of opinion arise as to whether this behavior can be a theurgy practiced directly by the individual or representatively by the hasidic rebbe on behalf of others, or whether desisting from human activity must necessarily take the form of total passivity.

Kafka does not present a closed kabbalistic system; what he does offer is a wealth of commonly held ideas and basic assumptions. As we shall see, these need not be relegated to pure coincidence; rather, they can be looked upon as having influenced him via the many various contacts and reference points in his immediate surroundings.

2
THE TRIAL AND THE TRADITION OF THE GATEKEEPER IN THE KABBALAH

Gershom Scholem once wrote the following suggestion to Walter Benjamin, who at the time was considering writing an essay on Kafka: "My advice to you, too, would be to base any study of Kafka on the Book of Job, or at least on a discussion of the possibility of a divine judgment, which is what I see as the one and only theme in all of Kafka's writings" (*Friendship*, 212).[1] Regardless of one's reaction to this type of reduction of Kafka's works, one thing is clear: it is precisely the theme of the court of law that positions Kafka unmistakably within the Jewish tradition. However, I want to repeat that this use of the term "Jewish" has to be approached with some care, for throughout its long history Judaism has always and still does accommodate a plurality of views under its roof, and these views frequently conflict violently with one another. Less true in the realm of *halakhah*, the legal tradition, but all the more so in the philosophical-theological realm is the fact that Judaism was and is the arena of a great variety of possibilities that communicate with one another, more or less. This is why one would do well to identify the specific currents within Judaism with which Kafka was most familiar. As mentioned above, I believe the conclusion will very likely be that we are talking about a popularized folkloric form of the Kabbalah that manifested itself in sermons, in prayers and in the religious observations of daily life. This includes the narrative traditions of Jewish folk tales, especially those stemming from Eastern Europe. These latter traditions fall under the rubric of hasidic legends, but this term is not always appropriate because only some of them actually do deal with specific hasidic themes.

In an effort to make the skeptics or the unconvinced more receptive to these ideas, I would like to reverse the usual sequence and begin with the most obvious. In doing so I am fully aware that this approach goes against the scholar's expectation of a coherent and structured theoretical system that fixes every chapter to its proper place within the overall context of the topic under discussion. Nevertheless, I want to present the following thesis: *The Trial*, Kafka's most perplexing work, as well as the one most typical of his thought, bears the stamp of that type of Jewish morality literature most influenced by the Kabbalah, and it does so not only in its basic concept but in its structure and its outlook as well. In fact, the evidence is so strong that I do not think it too bold to base an entire interpretation of the novel on this similarity. However, I want to stress once again that any conformity should not prematurely ignore the differences that also exist. Kafka's *Trial* would not merit its ranking within the great tradition of Jewish literature if it did not offer something new and original under its garb of concurrence and harmony—if a completely new plant did not emerge from the well-tended beds of ancient gardens.

Kafka's authority in matters hasidic and kabbalistic was his friend Georg Langer. In the autobiographical introduction to his book of hasidic tales, originally published under the title of *Neun Tore*, Langer wrote: "I am gradually becoming familiar with the hasidic literature as well. The first book I read was *Reshit Hokhma* (*The Beginnings of Wisdom*), that kabbalistic textbook of asceticism, humility and abstention, full of glorious quotes from the mysterious Zohar. . . . *The Beginnings of Wisdom* is a work of the famous Kabbalist Eliahu de Vidas, who lived in Palestine toward the end of the seventeenth century[2]. . . . The Rabbi of Belz himself recommended I read it" (28f). This was a very accessible book, intended to admonish as well as to edify wide circles of readers and, as the reference to the Belzer Rabbi conforms, it was a well-known classic of edification literature in Eastern Europe even in Kafka's time. Traces of its influence can still be seen in the narrative tradition of that region's folk literature.

This comprehensive and as yet untranslated work of devotional literature contains a chapter under the rubric "The Fear of God" which discusses the significance of the celestial courts. What follows is an outline of the basic ideas, presented in the same sequence the author himself offers in seven pages. This deliberate reconstruction is meant to demonstrate the style and the structure characteristic of this type of kabbalistic judicial tractate. As we shall see, it will prove to be of some importance later on.

Eliahu de Vidas begins this chapter with the following words (Bl. 30b):

> [. . .] one must live in constant fear of the judgment hovering over a person every day and every hour, for this is how our sages[3] interpreted the passage in Job (7:18), where it says: "And that Thou shouldest remember him every morning, and try him every moment." Rabbi Yose's interpretation reads: Man is judged daily . . . Rabbi Natan, on the other hand, says: hourly. . . .
>
> [The Talmud][4] has other things to say about this as well: . . . if a man has fallen sick and is close to death, let them say to him: Make your confession . . . , for a sick man is like him . . . whom they lead to the place of execution. If he has defenders, he will be rescued, but if not, there is no rescue. And what are the mightiest advocates? Repentance and good works!

A few lines down the author continues:

> Judgment looms over the world every day, for the world was created in judgment [i.e., according to the principle of law], and this is its foundation. Therefore let man be ever watchful against sin, for he does not know when his judgment will begin. [It may happen that] he sits in his house and his judgment begins, or he leaves the house and goes outside and his judgment begins, and he does not know whether he will come back home . . . , for the judgment goes before him . . . . (Bl. 30c)

One of the many reasons why this court is always in session and can convene at any time is the fact that, as de Vidas stresses, every day everything can bear witness against a person, and this includes the stones and the walls of his house, the angels who constantly accompany him, his own soul, the Torah, and much, much more (*Reshit Hokhma*, c. 11, Bl. 29b–30a).[5]

> Beware all sorts of witnesses who daily testify against you. . . . Man should not say: 'Who could bear witness against me?' The stones of his house and the walls of his house testify against him. . . . Rabbi Shela says: 'Two angels accompany man and testify against him.' . . . Rabbi Hidka says: 'A man's very own soul testifies against him.' . . . And not only that, the members of his household also testify against him. . . .
>
> The words of Rabbi Shela concerning the two angels who accompany man and testify against him are to be understood in this way . . . : When a man gets out of bed, two witnesses stand before him and they go with him throughout the day. [The angels admonish and warn, because] when a man stretches out his hand toward the business of the world, the witnesses cry: 'Depart from evil, and do good' (Ps. 34:15). If he listens to them, all is well, but if not, then 'Satan stands at his right hand to accuse him' (Zech. 3:1), and on high [in judgment] they all testify to his sins against him. . . . [Even a man's most secret thoughts are brought before the celestial court, for] Rabbi Aha said: 'The soul reports everything a man does in secret, in the dark and in broad daylight. The books are read before the Holy One, blessed be He, and they tell of all men's deeds.'

This tractate from the book *Reshit Hokhma* lacks the humor one occasionally finds in hasidic judicial tales[6] (about which more will be said later on); it is rather more indebted to the severity of an ascetic Kabbalah. Kafka was also acquainted with this variant, as one of his diary entries indicates (*Diaries*, 133):

> My Hebrew name is Amschel, after my mother's maternal grandfather, whom she remembers as a very pious and learned man with a long white beard who died when she was six years old. She can recall how she had to hold the toes of the corpse and beg forgiveness for whatever transgressions she may have committed against him. She also remembers the many books

> that lined her grandfather's walls. He bathed in the river every day, even in winter, when he had to chop a hole in the ice to do so.[7]

Shortly before this (December 25, 1911) Kafka made an entry very closely related to the same topic:

> Circumcision in Russia. Tablets the size of one's palm bearing the imprint of kabbalistic symbols are hung throughout the house, wherever there are doors; these protect the mother during the period between the birth and the circumcision against evil spirits which are particularly dangerous to her and her child at this time. . . . Also as protection against evil spirits during the first seven days after the birth, toward evening on every day except Friday, the belfer (assistant teacher) brings ten to fifteen children, but never the same ones, to the mother's bed; there they recite the 'Shema Israel' and are rewarded with candy. These innocent five- to eight-year- olds are supposed to be particularly effective in warding off the evil spirits that become most insistent toward evening. . . . These evil ones are wildest the day before the circumcision, and therefore the last night is a vigil when everyone sits up with the mother until dawn. (*Diaries*, 132)[8]

As we shall soon see, according to kabbalistic texts this world of spirits is also part of that omnipresent judicial world of chastisement and accusation. Kafka's scattered remarks concerning these themes attest to the attention he paid to them as well as to his objectively accurate observation and information.

But back to the tractate *Reshit Hokhma* De Vidas does not mince any words in his effort to impress upon his readers the idea of an omnipresent celestial court in constant session. This court has the power to intervene in every-day human life at any time via disease and all sorts of other afflictions; its verdict can occasionally be postponed, or else it leads immediately to death. And this, the author insists, is because the world was created with *din*, with judicial justice. The renowned and legendary theologian and mystic of Prague, Chief Rabbi Judah Löw ben Bezalel (1525–1609) (still current in the Prague consciousness under the acronym

Maharal and famous as the creator of the golem[9]), saw God's sovereign powers over the world in His judicial authority itself. Even as late as Kafka's day the preachers in the synagogues of Prague most certainly referred to the sermons Rabbi Löw published on this theme, and particularly during the autumnal High Holy Days (Rosh ha-Shanah and Yom Kippur), when even the most hardened agnostics could still be expected to attend the synagogue. In one of these sermons[10] the Maharal said: "God's Kingdom [the tenth spiritual force in the Kabbalah] is His dominion over the world, and His dominion is the way of the Law. . . . He is the Judge and the Kingdom is His regulation."

Following his introductory description of the omnipresence of the celestial courts, Eliahu de Vidas turns his attention to the various forms of divine punishment. Not unexpectedly, these correspond to the respective transgressions in human behavior. He then goes on to discuss those measures the Divine Judge established in the world in order to instill a fear of God in man. These include thunder and bad dreams, among other things. As stressed in my earlier work on Kafka, they are not to be taken lightly, but rather as God's warning to mankind (*Reshit Hokhma*, Bl. 31c). Besides dreams and thunder, de Vidas says it is primarily the *shekinah*, the "Kingdom," namely the tenth spiritual force or *sefira* mentioned above, that serves as God's admonisher in the world, for this tenth manifestation is, according to the Kabbalah, the primary venue of the celestial court. In describing the judicial function of this tenth sefirah, Eliahu de Vidas inserts a quote from the Zohar[11], reproduced here in abbreviated form (III: Bl. 239a):

> There is a highest place, which lets [the light] flow forth and which ignites all [other] lamps . . . , and out of this place goes forth a tree for stilling thirst and providing sustenance. And this precious higher tree stands above all trees . . . , this one was and is and will be, nothing can be added to it and nothing taken away . . . , for this tree is the Torah and God fixed it as inviolable . . .
>
> But [after planting this tree] God set another tree below it . . . , He set it there so that whoever wants to go to the higher tree may only enter with permission. Whoever wants to enter, therefore, finds the lower tree and is afraid to approach unless he is worthy.

> For this [lower tree] is the Gatekeeper . . . and [God made him] so that the inhabitants of the earth will fear it and will not draw near, except those who are worthy to draw near—and no one else! So that men will keep the ways of the Torah and not deviate to the right or the left.

As we shall see, de Vidas uses his discussion of the celestial courts to describe the messengers of the court, its verdicts and ultimate execution via the sword of justice. Part of this theme is a representation of man before the Gates of the Torah, of man before the Gate to the Law which is guarded by a watchman. Rabbi Eliahu's depiction therefore rests upon the conventional kabbalistic identification of the sixth sefirah with the original divine form of the Written Law (the Five Books of Moses) and of the tenth sefira with the original divine form of the Oral Law, i.e., with the teachings of Jewish tradition. In other words, the celestial Oral Torah, which is the tenth manifestation of the kabbalistic sefirotic tree, is the guard along the path to the celestial Written Torah. Here, as custom has had it ever since the Kabbalah of the thirteenth century, including the Zohar, the ancient gatekeeper motif of the early hekhalot mysticism has been transposed to the original divine form of the Torah. Into this Torah a person can and should go, for that is his destiny; however, it is guarded by the gatekeeper, by the oral tradition. The Zohar and de Vidas as well depict both aspects of the divine Torah, i.e. the goal of the journey as well as the gatekeeper, as two trees. These are the trees named in Genesis, the Tree of Life and the Tree of Knowledge of Good and Evil. The Tree of Knowledge is the guard over the Tree of Life.[12]

To this Torah/gatekeeper tradition Eliahu de Vidas immediately appends another tradition closely related to it in a kabbalistic sense. He says:

> When a man wants to enter into Holiness, he immediately discovers several accusers. If he is not worthy, he is like a man who wants to come before the presence of the king: before he enters to see the king, he must pass through several gates, one after the other. Before every gate are set several watchmen, who guard over that treasure [of wisdom] so that no one may go in who is not worthy to enter. If it were not so, all sinners

> would enter into the secrets of the Torah. Therefore, if a sinner wants to enter in order to learn the secrets of the Torah, several avenging angels confuse him . . . , so that he does not arrive at a place which is not meant for him. If a man is good, however, all his accusers and chastisers become advocates, and they lead him into the preserved treasure. And about such [a worthy one] they cry: "Our Lord, here is a good, righteous and God-fearing man who would come before You and who has said to us: 'Open the gates of justice, that I might enter and praise the Lord!'"

This second traditional piece that de Vidas interpolates here thus adds to the Torah-gate motif that other doorkeeper motif frequently referred to in connection with Kafka. It is the idea of the heavenly halls which the mystic must pass through in order to appear before the Throne of God, a tradition that medieval kabbalists and kabbalists of early modernity took over from Jewish antiquity.

In the ancient Jewish hekhalot literature, passage through these halls was no more than a journey through concretely conceived celestial palaces. In the Kabbalah, on the other hand, this passage through the heavenly halls precedes the journey through the world of the sefirotic manifestations and can be interpreted simultaneously as a passage into the Torah, into the Law. When seen in this way, passage through the heavenly halls is one way to enter the wisdom of the Torah which leads to life, which leads to the Light of the Godhead.

A second important change with respect to the ancient Jewish talmudic hekhalot mysticism is the combining of this celestial world of halls with the idea of the court. The ancient mystical examination of the adept at the Gates of Heaven is now understood as judgment. It follows that the Kabbalah conceives of a person's path toward the true life as a path through various judicial instances. The path to life, to the Light of God, leads through hierarchically structured judicial authorities, one higher than the other. The individual instances are the keepers of the gates to the next higher hall.

The judicial authority of these celestial courts, however, is not restricted to the heavenly part of the human journey. It also operates on earth and affects the daily life of every person even before they themselves consciously undertake the ascent through the courts. Human life on earth is held to be the vestibule of man's judicial journey, even if most people fail to recognize this fact. Life on earth determines the success of the subsequent journey through the divine world of the Torah. It also determines how high human prayers will ascend through the judicial halls, for these prayers are the predecessors, as it were, of the individual's own ascent (more about this below). This is what allows the kabbalistic handbooks to depict the daily liturgy in the synagogue as a person's ascent through the heavenly halls, whereby the individual words or letters of a prayer represent the various celestial palaces.[13]

The author of our judicial tractate does not leave us in the dark as to why he inserts the gatekeeper tradition into this context of the omnipresent court. It is meant to instill in the reader a fear of the instances that could hold up his journey to life; these are the very instances whose messengers are already guiding him on earth. Toward this end, Eliahu de Vidas continues, the judicial instances rely upon such means of chastisment as thunder and bad dreams and diseases, which they send to afflict the living. Kafka's diaries reveal just how seriously he took his own dreams, particularly those having to do with his writing, which he considered the justification of his life (cf. *Diaries*, 225, 262, 274). Even Joseph K. occasionally refers to the strange and unaccustomed weakness that suddenly overcomes him in connection with the proceedings already underway against him (*Trial*, 107). According to de Vidas, when such judicial chastisements strike a person, he must "bow to the court that controls him, and he must not oppose it stubbornly; he may not mock these chastisements nor may he disregard them" (Bl. 31d). Joseph K. had to be told pretty much the same thing: "Good Heavens! . . . that you cannot resign yourself to your position." "Don't be so obstinate, no one can defend himself against this court; you must make a confession" (*Trial*, 13, 143). By interpolating the gatekeeper tradition into his judicial tractate, Eliahu de Vidas wants to direct his readers' attention to those authorities that punish him, but which, by doing so, simultaneously want to clear the path for him to the Tree of Life—unless, of course, he proves rebellious, in which case the gate remains barred to him. But we are getting ahead of ourselves.

After looking at the awe-inspiring celestial gatekeepers, our kabbalistic moralist comes to speak of the punishments the celestial court sends down to earth. Disease, thunder and bad dreams have already been mentioned. Eliahu de Vidas expands upon this topic (Bl. 32a): "Beware also, for the Holy One, blessed be He, has various messengers to execute judgment on men and to call in their debt."

Following the ancient talmudic tradition, de Vidas now enumerates "whole armies whom God has charged to call in the debts of mankind: wild animals, bears and lions, even such things or beings generally considered superfluous, such as snails, flies and fleas" (Bl. 32a). Among the divine messengers who bring chastisement, however, is also mankind. Every misery and every pain they inflict upon someone else is to be understood as a warning from the court—particularly those injuries inflicted by non-Jews. This also includes the actions of one's own Jewish compatriots as well as of those who do not intend evil and only involuntarily inflict pain upon another. De Vidas summarizes: "When people do evil deeds, they, the transgressors, are like the wild beasts, a scourge to strike (or: to whip) the people. When people disobey the Torah, they are marked, and the servants of the court recognize them," (Bl. 32a).

"Everything is part of the court," (*Trial*, 202) Titorelli tells Joseph K., completely in keeping with this outlook.

Exhortations of this kind are meant to insure that a person understands even the most insignificant event as a messenger of the court whose task is to admonish and chastise people during their life on earth. Having established this, the kabbalistic tractate addresses the final act of the whole process (c. 12), namely: death. The "day of death is the great judgment day, when man will be sentenced according to all his deeds." "The day on which a person departs from this world is the day of the Final Judgment, a day on which the sun turns dark," a day of darkness (Bl. 32b). What follows is one of the ways de Vidas describes this final event (Bl. 33a):

> Man goes through this world thinking it will always be his . . . , but as he continues to pass through the world, iron shackles are fixed around his neck, and before he repents, he is judged at the executioner's block along with the other accused.

> If he finds someone to defend him, he is saved from the court . . . , but if not, he is condemned by the court to depart from this world. If he lifts his eyes while still lying in the King's chains, he will see two [men] coming toward him. In his presence, they record everything he did in this world and every word that ever passed his lips. The man renders an account of everything and they write it down.
>
> [Finally]
>
> Alas this judgment and woe betide his deeds . . . for he is being judged while still in irons, and if no defender can be found, the King's executioner descends and stands before his feet, a sharp sword in his hand.
>
> The man looks up and sees the walls of a house blazing brightly in its glory. Then he sees him before him, all eyes, his garment made of flames of fire that flicker in front of this man. That's the way it is. Some people saw an angel in the market place and stood before him, while others did not see him.[14]

One is almost tempted to conclude this kabbalistic description of execution with Joseph K.'s demise: "Then the man opened his overcoat and took out of its sheath . . . a long thin double-edged sharpened butcher's knife, held it high and checked it in the light . . . [Joseph K.'s] eyes fell on the top floor of the house bordering the quarry. Like a flash of light the shutters of a window flew open, a distant and high man, weak and thin, suddenly leaned far out . . . Who was it? A friend? A good man? . . . someone who wanted to help?" (*Trial*, 321)

Are both instances a final shimmer of light and hope in the darkness of the great Judgment Day? The hope of a final advocate who might be able to postpone the verdict at the last moment?

This will conclude our summary of this popular kabbalistic tractate. It covers the omnipresence of the celestial court and its direct intervention as well as the judicial messengers and chastisements and concludes with execution, the death of the person. Inserted in the middle is the tradition of the gatekeepers before the Law and of the heavenly halls of the court. An impressive structure well suited for any synagogue sermon. Take, for example, the chapbook *Kav ha-Yashar*, originally written in Poland and printed in Yiddish and Hebrew, a book that went through between thirty and fifty editions since its initial appearance in Frankfurt am Main in 1705 and which treated this theme rather similarly (c. 39):[15]

> God has many envoys, and numerous accusers appear day after day in the celestial court on high, testifying against a man because of his sins and transgresssions.
>
> And yet, man pays no attention to this, for he has already heaped sin upon transgression and does not believe he will be called to judgment because of them, as if Heaven paid no attention to evil-doers.
>
> But the truth is that the Holy One, blessed be He, keeps His silence until the measure is full—and the judgment (*din*) becomes more and more severe and suddenly the sentence of wrath is loosed over this man like a storm wind. . . . Thus the court's verdict descends upon man unexpectedly; suddenly his whole body trembles, burns and becomes hot, and he falls on his bed. . . . Therefore, be not arrogant, for you see that the day of your death is near . . . and the celestial court is always in session; the advocates present your good deeds, and the accusers raise their objections. . . .

Sermons on this theme (another will follow below) were particularly common in the synagogues during the autumnal period of repentance and fasting surrounding Rosh ha-Shanah and Yom Kippur. Depending on the position of the moon within the solar year, these holidays begin in August with the Hebrew month Elul and continue until October, the Hebrew Tishri, and represent the annual judgment period of the Jewish religious calendar. Surely such synagogue sermons could still be heard in Prague during Kafka's day, when he used to attend occasionally.[16] It is common knowledge that even the most assimilated Jews find their way to the 'temple' during these High Holy Days, a fact Kafka also noted (*Wedding*, 115): "On the evening after Yom Kippur even the worst Jew doesn't go to the theater." Kafka was always aware of this judgment period, and this awareness was certainly an essential component of his otherwise, to his mind deplorably poor, Jewish upbringing. In his *Letter to My Father* he went so far as to say that he, his father, attended the synagogue four times a year, two of which were surely Rosh ha-Shanah and Yom Kippur, which Kafka describes on the very next page as the "High Holy Days." In a letter to Felice Bauer dated October 8, 1916, Kafka's mother wrote: "We observed the Jewish holidays like proper Jews. On New Year's we closed the shop for both days and yesterday, Yom Kippur, we fasted and prayed assiduously" (*Felice*, 721). That same year Kafka mentions the Feast of the Tabernacles (*Felice*, 732) in a letter to Felice, and on October 11, 1916, he wrote: "By the way, I hardly said a word about the New Year at home and nothing at all to you, all completely in keeping with the meaninglessness which this day holds for me now" (*Felice*, 723). (Note the "now"!) As early as September 1907 he mentioned the New Year in a letter to Hedwig W. (*Letters*, 42). However, Kafka not only noted the date of the holiday, but its content as well. On September 28, 1917 (two days after Yom Kippur, which fell on September 26 in 1916) he noted right after a reference to the meaninglessness of the previous year (*Diaries*, 333; *Critical Edition*, 839f):

> To death therefore would I consign myself. The remnants of a faith. Return to the Father. Great Day of Atonement.
>
> From a letter to F., perhaps the last (October 1). If I really examine my ultimate goal, it turns out that what I actually want is not to be a good person and meet the demands of the highest *court* [author's emphasis], but rather just the opposite, to survey the whole community of animals and men, to understand their basic preferences, desires, moral ideals, to reduce them to simple rules and then to shape myself as soon as possible in their mold so that I would become totally pleasing to all, and in fact (this is the perversity of it) so pleasing, that I might finally commit all the dirty doings inside of me openly without forfeiting their love, all the while still remaining the only sinner who won't burn.[17] All told, then, my only concern is the *human court* [author's emphasis] and what's more, I want to deceive it, but without deception.

Kafka was very taken by the theme, for this particular text turns up twice again in his notes and letters of those days, once in the October 1 letter mentioned above (*Felice*, 755) and again in a letter to Max Brod (*Letters*, 178).[18] On September 17, 1921 (New Year was September 22), he reflects: "I was never under the pressure of any responsibility other than the one that the existence, the look, the *judgment* [author's emphasis] of other people placed upon me," (*Wedding*, 220).

On September 15, 1915, he had already made the following observation about the upcoming Yom Kippur (*Diaries*, 298; Yom Kippur fell on September 18 that year, Rosh ha-Shanah on September 9): "Scene of the Polish Jews going to Kol Nidre [the opening prayer of Yom Kippur]. The little boy walking next to his father with the prayer shawl under his arms. Suicidal, not to go to the temple."

Two days previous, in other words, likewise in the midst of the penitential days between New Year and the Day of Atonement, the period characterized by a solemn air of judgment, Kafka visited the house of the Wonder Rabbi of Grod in the Prague suburb of Zizkov. Not coincidentally, on October 21, 1911[19] he attended a performance of Abraham Scharansky's *Kol Nidre* "at the Jews" (*Diaries*, 71), and on October 1 of that year he noted: "Yesterday in the Altneu Synagogue. Kol Nidre. Muffled murmurings like the stock exchange. In the vestibule a box with the inscription: 'A gift in secret pacifieth anger' [naturally in the eyes of the celestial judges, author's note]. . . . In the Pinkas Synagogue I was moved by Judaism more deeply than ever" (*Diaries*, 47f). Kafka himself seems to have had the habit of attending services at least on the High Holy Days; Max Brod also reports of a common visit to the synagogue he and Kafka made on September 17, 1909.[20]

Is it purely coincidental that, as Malcolm Pasley asserts, it is this same span of human life in judgment that Kafka concluded in one fell swoop during these very High Holy Days of 1914?[21] Rosh ha-Shanah, New Year, fell on September 21 (it began the evening of September 20). Yom Kippur, accordingly, fell on September 30 (Kol Nidre the evening of September 29). The start of the penitential period, which begins on the first day of the month of Elul, the first day on which the shofar was sounded in the Jewish city, was Sunday, August 23. On August 15 Kafka noted in his diary: "I've been writing for a few days now, may it continue. I am no longer as completely protected and enveloped in my work as I was two years ago; nevertheless, I have found some sense; my monotonous, empty, crazy bachelor's life does have a *justification*" (*Diaries*, 263; author's emphasis). And on August 21: "Perhaps it is right to postpone work on the Russian story until after the *Trial*. In this ridiculous hope, which obviously only deals with technical matters, I am once again working on *The Trial*" (*Diaries*, 271). "The Judgment" was also written in one sitting, this time during the night of September 22/23, 1912. Yom Kippur was September 20/21 (*Diaries*, 183).[22] Steinberg has also demonstrated that the story "In the Penal Colony" was probably written immediately before or immediately after the Yom Kippur holiday.[23]

Our summary of the judicial tractate Eliahu de Vidas included in his morality book *Reshit Hokhma* undeniably confirms the fact that the theme of a 'gatekeeper before the law' was current within the context of Jewish-kabbalistic judicial theology at least since the 16th century and that this popular book passed it on to the pious masses in Eastern Europe particularly. It is also a fact that those closest to Kafka knew of this tradition by 1915 at the latest, and most probably via Georg Langer, who began to study this work rather early in his career as a kabbalistic Hasid, which began in 1913.

It is also possible that Kafka met Langer even before 1915. In the foreword to the English language edition of Langer's book, titled *Nine Gates*, his brother, František Langer, wrote that Kafka became friends with Langer during the war and that both of them used to take walks together in Prague (xxiii). František Langer apparently does not know any further details concerning the beginning of this friendship, since he refers to Kafka's diaries on the subject. František was a physician stationed on the Eastern Front from the outbreak of the war until 1915, when he returned to Prague just in time to make his informed affidavit freeing his brother from military prison where he was being detained because of his strict Jewish way of life (refusing to eat the non-kosher military food, refusing to work on the sabbath, and particularly refusing to bear arms). As a result, Georg Langer was declared a "mental case" and released from prison (xviiif).

Around 1910 or 1911, Georg Langer turned more and more toward orthodox Judaism; he learned Hebrew and was frequently found "poring over borrowed Hebrew folios" (xiif). In 1913 he journeyed to the Galician *shtetl* of Belz to become an Hasid. He went back home for a brief period before 1914 and soon became the talk of the town, for, to the open embarrassment of his family, he returned dressed in the garb of an Hasid. His "Jewish friends in Prague" (xvii) provided him with kabbalistic literature, but he soon returned to Belz nevertheless. He was still there when the war broke out a few months later and, after a vain attempt to flee to Hungary with the rabbi, he received his draft notice. Obediently, Georg returned to Prague. He evidently never left again after his recruitment because he soon found himself under military arrest for refusing regular service on the same grounds as before. Given this history, it is not improbable that Kafka may have had some contact with this strange, repatriated Hasid, so recently on everyone's lips, around the time the war broke out, which is to say shortly after July 28, 1914. According to František, "Kafka evidently found Jiři a kindred spirit" (xxiii). The brother's information is not always precise, however: "After his discharge from the army, Jiři returned to the Rabbi of Belz and spent the rest of the war with him" (xix). Nevertheless, by September of 1915 the two of them were already such close friends that Kafka accompanied Langer to the wonder-rabbi in Zizkov (diary entry of September 14, 1915).

Kafka certainly had some knowledge of the mystical tradition of the journey through heaven as well as of the gatekeeper tradition connected with it already prior to his acquaintance with Langer. As early as 1911, again on October 29, (*Diaries*, 81; *Critical Edition*, 204), Kafka copied down a talmudic tale he had heard from Isaac Löwy. It is the main piece of talmudic evidence for the mystical journey through heaven and its gatekeeper tradition; ever since then, this talmudic tradition has served all subsequent Jewish mystics as the original paradigm of the mystical journey through the celestial spheres. There can be no doubt that Kafka soon questioned his friend Langer, the mystic, about it. Even Löwy would have told him more than Kafka noted in his diary (*Diaries*, 81; *Critical Edition*, 209): "Löwy: Four friends became great talmudic scholars in their old age. But each one had a particular fate. One went mad, one died, Rabbi Eliezer became a free thinker at the age of forty, and the oldest of them, Akiva, who postponed his studies until his fortieth year, was the only one to attain complete knowledge . . ."

Löwy told Kafka a version of the story that combined other talmudic tales, most of them from the same pages.[24] Such was the case with the legend of the late start Rabbi Akiva made with his studies and the relation between Rabbi Meir and Elisha ben Avuyah (Aher = heretic), whom Löwy mistakenly refers to as Eliezer here. According to the talmudic versions:

> Four men entered the Garden of Paradise, Ben Azzai, Ben Zoma, Aher [Elisha Ben Avuyah] and Rabbi Akiva.
>
> Rabbi Akiva said to them: "When you come to the glittering marble stones, don't say: 'Water, water![25], for it is written [in the Bible]: 'Whoever tells lies shall not stand before my countenance.'" Ben Azzai looked and died . . . Ben Zoma looked and went out of his mind. Aher cut the growth down [that is, he turned heretic]. Rabbi Akiva ascended in peace and returned in peace. . . .
>
> The angels wanted to cast Rabbi Akiva back, too, but the Holy One, blessed be He, said to them: "Leave this old man, he is worthy to betake of my honor." (Babylonian Talmud, Hagigah 14b-16a; Tosefta, Hagigah 2:3–4)

The commentary of Rashi of Troyes (1040–1105), appended to all editions of the Talmud and still considered authoritative today, gives the following, now generally accepted, understanding of this talmudic passage: "They ascended into heaven with the help of one of the Names of God," i.e., with the help of an invocation.[26] This means that by 1911 Kafka was already familiar with this central component of the mystical ascent to heaven, a fact that seems all the more significant since, as we saw before and will see again, it is precisely this same theme that was also a part of the High Holy Days.

In light of these findings, namely of Kafka's awareness of the High Holy Days and their theme of judgment which found its way equally to his diaries and his stories, we are surely justified in wondering whether Kafka might not have composed his own judicial tractate based on the traditional model precisely during those High Holy Days of the Jewish calendar reserved for repentence, self-reflection and judgment. We know from his diaries that he passed much of the summer of 1914 with thoughts of death and sought *justification* for his life in the writing of *The Trial*. And in the already quoted diary entry of August 15, 1914, he did have this to say about his work on that novel: "I've been writing for a few days now, may it continue. I am no longer as completely protected and enveloped in my work as I was two years ago; nevertheless, I have found some sense; my monotonous, empty, crazy bachelor's life does have a justification. I am once again able to carry on a dialogue with myself and no longer stare into complete emptiness.

Only in this way is there any cure for me" (*Diaries*, 263; *Critical Edition*, 548).

Obviously, the conformity between texts, themes, times and attitudes discussed so far can not be dismissed as pure coincidence. It not only raises the question but seriously suggests the possibility that *The Trial* ought to be understood within the context of Jewish judicial theology, and this totally apart from the other themes Kafka introduced into this novel from European modernism. It follows that these new themes, then, would have to be seen as a reinterpretation of this ancient Jewish theme heavily relying upon modern insights or sciences concerning man, his soul, society and whatever other theme one might also discover. We shall come back to the fact that the High Holy Days represent the annual period of divine judgment of man's actions, a judgment that decides his fate in the coming year, be it life or death, happiness or chastisement. The days surrounding Rosh ha-Shanah and Yom Kippur, however, are not merely a period of judgment; they simultaneously offer an opportunity to influence the verdict for the better by changing one's ways, by meditating, repenting, fasting, through prayer and ritual as well as through reconciliation with one's neighbors. Moreover, the autumnal judgment theme looks not only to the upcoming year, but far beyond that: it points to man's situation before God's Judgment Seat and the ultimate end of human life. Thanks to the Kabbalah, the latter is understood as a mystical "journey to heaven," a journey to the Torah or the Law, which is the main purpose of human life. It is a journey that is supposed to lead a person ultimately to the Light of God.

3
WHEN AND HOW THE CELESTIAL COURT FUNCTIONS

The concept of a continuous court which meets day and night without intermission and in various hierarchically arranged divisions forms an integral part of the kabbalistic ontology and is one contribution the Kabbalah has made to Jewish theology. The older, pre-kabbalistic, talmudic and biblical concepts of judgment, on the other hand, were oriented more toward the end point of individual or collective history. According to ancient Jewish thought, the judgment of the soul and its torture in the grave (*Hibbut ha-kever*) as well as the punishment of the soul in Gehinnom[1] (purgatory), which lasted twelve months at the most, come at the end of each person's life. They are conceived as the balance of that life, rather like the global final judgment expected at the end of time, which, ever since the days of the prophet Daniel, follows after the resurrection of the dead. In addition to these established judgment periods and at the latest by the end of the Mishnaic period around the year 200, ancient Judaism knew four annual, cyclically recurring judgment periods during which the fate and continuing state of a person's health in the coming year was decided. Whether a person would experience plenty or want, life or death, all depended upon the sins he committed (*Mishna Rosh ha-Shanah* 1, 2):

> The world is judged four times [a year]:
> at Passover regarding the barley harvest,

> at Shavuot regarding the fruit or the trees,
> at Rosh ha-Shanah (New Year) all the
> inhabitants of the world pass before HIM as
> at the counting of the soldiers[2] . . .
> and at Sukkot (Feast of the Tabernacles) they
> are judged regarding water.

The most important of these four annual judgment periods as well as the climax of the Jewish religious calendar is the New Year judgment that begins on the first day of the month of Tishri (falling somewhere between September and October) and continues until the 10th of Tishri, Yom Kippur, or even until the 21st of Tishri, to the circumambulations of Hoshanah Rabbah on the seventh day of the Sukkot festival. This celebration is hard to miss wherever there is an actively functioning Jewish community. It is marked by additional religious services, a penitential period during which everyone reconciles themselves with their neighbors, family and friends; it is a time when everyone tries to settle their debts and when the pious turn to various rituals meant to perfect their atonement. These rituals include the practice of *kapparah*, whereby the penitent swings white roosters in a circle above his head in a vicarious and symbolic atonement for sin, and even public lashings. On the afternoon of New Year's Day the congregation gathers in groups by a river or some other body of living water to take part in the ritual of shaking the hems of their garments free of sin, as it were. This is called *tashlikh*. It is as impossible to miss the sight of these celebrations as it is to fail to hear it in a Jewish community, for

> They sound the shofar during this month [i.e. Elul, the month before Rosh ha-Shanah; in other words, after the middle of August]; it starts on the second day of the new moon and is blown every day after morning prayer. . . . The reason for sounding it in this month is to awaken the people to repentance; for it is the nature of the shofar to awaken and arouse fear, as the Bible says (Amos 3:6): "Shall the horn be blown in a city, and the people not tremble?"

This is according to the popular Eastern European abridged version of Shulchan Arukh, the halakhic code of Judaism considered authoritative ever since the seventeenth century.[3] The shofar, this ram's horn whose blasts and quavers penetrate to the marrow of one's bones, characterizes the whole autumnal penitential period and reaches its climax on New Year's Day itself, the day the Bible calls simply a day of blaring.

Having presented this supporting material, I will now turn around and say that all such evidence attesting to Kafka's awareness of the holiday is actually superfluous; it is merely meant to show the intensity with which these solemn days descend upon every Jew from his earliest years onward.

The High Holy Days are also the period when the sermon, otherwise not necessarily a part of synagogue services, becomes an important element of the service, particularly on the sabbath between Rosh ha-Shanah and Yom Kippur. This is known as the Shabbat Shuvah, the penitential sabbath; tradition has it that even the community rabbi preaches on this day, which is usually not one of his official duties.

The Kabbalists naturally took over the ancient Jewish judgment periods enumerated above and integrated them into their system of a court constantly in session. The Talmud already describes the scenario surrounding the New Year's judgment in great detail, and just about every Jew regardless of how assimilated he or she may be is familiar with it in one form or another, not the least because it has found its way into the customary greetings heard on these days. In addition to a "Good Year", people wish each other a "Ketiva Tovah", a "Good Inscription" and "Hatima Tovah", a "Good Seal"—referring, of course, to the judgment inscribed in the heavenly books during these days between Rosh ha-Shanah and Yom Kippur. The Talmud says (Rosh ha-Shanah 16b):

> Three books are opened at the New Year:
> one for the truly righteous,
> one for the truly wicked
> and one for those who fall into neither category.
> The truly righteous are immediately entered
> and sealed for life.
> The truly wicked are immediately entered
> and sealed for death.

> And the intermediate ones remain in the
> balance from New Year until Yom Kippur.
> If they are deserving, they are entered
> for life; if they are not deserving, they
> are entered for death.
> Everyone[4] is judged on the New Year,
> and the sentence is sealed on Yom Kippur.

One element, central even to the ancient Jewish homilies on the judgment theme, is the idea that the individual is granted a preferential status at this time, which he can use to intervene in his running affairs from his position on earth. He does this by keeping the commandments, by repenting and reconciling differences with his neighbors and by observing the prayers and rites described above. However, there is one other, most effective way to bring about such an intervention, and that is by appealing to God that He might not look upon man's sin. All of this is based on an interpretation of the first two verses of Psalm 17, where it says: "Hear the right, O Lord, attend unto my cry; give ear unto my prayer from lips without deceit. Let my judgment come forth from Thy presence; let Thine eyes behold righteousness." In one of the much read anthologies of holiday homilies, one preacher puts it this way (Friedmann, 40:168a):

> The Israelites speak before the Holy One, blessed be He: Lord of the World, You sit in judgment and judge us, the accusers stand before You and the advocates stand before You.
>
> The latter present our good works and the former their accusations. Direct Your eyes solely upon the advocates, as it says in the Psalm: "May Your eyes see righteousness!" And the Holy One, blessed be He, says: "Upon your life, I will do so! Why? Because I want to exonerate you."

The way in which talmudic literature expresses the grace inherent in divine judgment frequently does not correspond to what a western European might expect. The ancient Jewish preachers occasionally use very bold images to express the certainty that man can have absolutely no vindication in the celestial court if one keeps to the strict rules of justice. If a person seeks acquittal in this court, one of the homilists suggests they would have to resort to some sort of 'foul play'. It was this awareness that moved the preacher to formulate the Jewish concept of *sola gratia* with such a drastic image as far as the acquittal of man before God is concerned. He indicates that escape from this court is ultimately achieved only via 'deception' (Friedmann, 45:185b):

> You will find that on Yom Kippur, Satan comes to accuse Israel and to report her sins. He calls: "Lord of the World, there are adulterers among the peoples, and also in Israel! There are thieves among the peoples, and also in Israel!"
>
> And the Holy One, blessed be He, brings forth Israel's good works. He takes the scale and weighs their sins against their virtues, and they are equal.
>
> Satan runs off to gather yet more sins so that the balance will fall to transgression. What does the Holy One, blessed be He, do? As long as Satan is out gathering more sins, He takes the old ones and hides them beneath His robe. When Satan returns, they are nowhere to be found.

A common interpretation of the Talmud knows another way to escape condemnation illegally, as it were: the blowing of the shofar. This version maintains that the sound of the shofar confuses Satan so that, in his confusion, he forgets to perform his duties as accuser. According to this passage, when Satan hears the sound of the shofar, he believes the tones ringing in the New Year are actually announcing the final deliverance that marks the end of his era.[5]

The Zohar, usually considered the Kabbalists' Bible, bases its understanding of the biblical sin offering in Leviticus 16 upon a reference to an older rabbinical homily (Friedlander, 363). In fact, it views this sin offering as a bribe for the accuser Samael/Satan, in the hopes that he will accept it and leave Israel in peace for a while (Zohar III: 63a): "Whenever Israel wants to be cleansed of her sins, the Holy One, blessed be He, advises the people to bind their accusers and favorably dispose them with the sacrifices that are brought before the Holy One, blessed be He. Then they can do no harm."

The late Zoharic text, *Raja Mehemna* (fourteenth century), makes the following 'comment' on the very same page:

> The commandment that the High Priest must offer a sacrifice on this day [Yom Kippur] is like that other commandment, which says that an offering must be consigned to Azazel. The mystery of this is, that he [Azazel = the accuser] departs hence from the holy people and does not call their debt before the King and does not accuse them. . . . Through this gift he becomes an advocate for them and is thus edged away from the presence of the King. The holy people give him exactly what he wants, a scapegoat!
>
> This gives rise to the saying: Throw a dog a bone and he will lick the dust from your feet!

This passage can be considered an example of unmitigated sarcastic gallows-humor regarding man's ultimate destiny. It is a literary expression that describes a person's prospects with unsparing candor, since the principle of strict justice would have to condemn him. Moreover, it is meant to show as well as convince the person in question that his own justification will never be able to exonerate him. Instead, it is always and only the grace of 'illegality' and 'injustice' in the court that can ultimately save him, just like the procedures in Kafka's judicial world and the methods employed by its advocates. The later Eastern European hasidic folk tales will further expand upon these motifs in an occasionally grotesque way by introducing its new doctrine of human helpers before the celestial court. I shall come back to this point later on.

During the annual New Year's judgment period a person's fate during the upcoming year is decided upon the basis of his behavior in the previous year. It determines his success or failure, his health or sufffering, in fact, whether he will end the year dead or alive. This outlook sees human life as a cycle of annual balancing acts extending from one New Year to the next. This may be the reason why Joseph K.'s 'trial' also lasts exactly one year, from one birthday to the next. If so, Kafka's dissembling strategy would have transposed the Jewish cycle to an annual cycle more familiar to the European mind.

4

THE ECSTATIC ASCENT TO HEAVEN

As mentioned above, Kafka went to the synagogue on October 1, 1911, Yom Kippur, wrote about "pacifying anger" and attended Scharansky's *Kol Nidre* on October 22. On November 29 of that year he noted the following curious story in his diary (*Diaries*, 112; *Critical Edition* 276):

> The get-togethers of the Hasidim, where they happily discuss talmudic questions. If the conversation lags or if someone doesn't participate, they make up for it by singing. They invent melodies, and if one turns out a success, the rest of the family is called in and they repeat it with them until they all learn it. During one such get-together a wonder-rabbi, known for his frequent hallucinations, suddenly rested his head on his arms folded on the table top. He remained in this position for three hours while the rest of the party kept silent. When he woke up, he wept and then struck up an entirely new and cheerful military march. It was the tune the angels of death[1] sang as they escorted to heaven the soul of a wonder-rabbi who had just died in a far-off Russian city.[2]

It is precisely in this type of ecstatic revery that the hasidic rebbes undertake their journeys to the celestial courts; one illustration is the following legend about the Baal Shem Tov, the founder of Hasidism (*H*, 61; *Praise*, 54):[3]

> Once, it was the eve of Yom Kippur, the Besht [acronym for Baal Shem Tov] saw a great charge being made [in heaven] against Israel to the effect that the oral tradition of the Torah was to be taken away from them.[4] This left him very distressed for the entire day before Yom Kippur. That evening, when the whole town came to him for his blessing, he blessed only one or two of them and said: "I can't go on, so great is our adversity." He blessed no one else and went to the prayer hall.
>
> In the synagogue he preached fire and brimstone. Then he fell upon the Holy Ark and cried: "Alas! They want to tear the Torah away from us! If they do, how shall we continue to exist among the peoples for even half a day?"
>
> He was full of fury and accused the rabbinical scholars: "You're to blame, for it is nothing but lies, freely invented lies, that you write in your books!"
>
> He said that all the Tannaim [the great teachers of the *Mishnah*] and the Amoraim [talmudic scholars] had been summoned to appear before the celestial court.
>
> Then he went to the bet midrash [house of study], and again he spoke words of admonishment and repentance. After that they prayed the Kol Nidre.[5] After the Kol Nidre was ended, he announced that the charge was becoming increasingly grave.
>
> [Next morning, the day of Yom Kippur] the Besht urged all the readers to hurry so that he might begin the Neilah while it was still light, since it was his custom to lead this closing prayer.
>
> Before he began the closing prayer, he once again rebuked them in harsh sermons. He wept, leaned his head backward against the Ark, sighed, cried out loud and finally began to pray first the silent eighteen benedictions [the Shemoneh Esreh] and then the spoken ones.
>
> He had the habit of not looking in the holiday prayer book during the Ten Days of Penitence [between Rosh ha-Shanah and Yom Kippur]; instead, Rabbi Yekel of Mesibos read the verses to him from the prayer book, and the Besht repeated them. When they came to the words "Open the gate for us" or

"Open the Gates of Heaven," Rabbi Yekel read them out a second time and noticed that the Besht did not respond. The Rabbi fell silent, but the Besht began to gesticulate in a dreadful manner: he bent over backwards until his head almost touched his knees. This caused the people to fear he might tumble over. They wanted to catch him in order to hold him up, but they were afraid, so they went instead to tell Rabbi Seev Kuzes, blessed be his memory. He came, looked the Besht straight in the face and gave a sign not to touch him. In the meantime, the Besht's eyes had bulged out and he was roaring like a bull lying on the slaughtering block—and this continued for a good two hours.

Then he suddenly came to himself, straightened up and finished the prayer with great haste.

As was the custom at the end of Yom Kippur, the whole congregation came to greet him. This time they asked the Besht how things stood with the charge against them. He reported the following:

"When it came time for the Neilah, I was able to recite all eighteen of the silent benedictions and passed through one world after another without any hindrance,[6] and even during the eighteen spoken benedictions I continued on until I came to one hall where I had but one more gate to pass through before I would appear before God, blessed be He. It was in this hall that I found fifty years of prayers that had been unable to ascend any higher. And now, since we have prayed with such intense devotion[7] on this Yom Kippur, all of these prayers were able to ascend, and each one of them was as bright as the dawn. I asked the prayers: 'Why didn't you ascend sooner?' And they answered: 'We were commanded to wait for you, Your Reverence, that you might lead us.' So I said: 'Come with me!'

"And indeed, the gate opened."

Then he told his followers that the gate was as wide as the whole world!

"As I set out to lead the prayers onward, all of a sudden an angel appeared and barred the gate and hung a lock on it."

The lock, he explained, was as big as all of Mesibos [his home town].

"I began to fumble with the lock, but couldn't open it. So I ran to my rabbi, the one mentioned in the book *Toledot Yaakov Yosef*,[8] and asked for his help, saying: 'Israel is in such great distress, and now they won't let me enter. If it were any other time I wouldn't be so insistent, but now!' And my rav said: 'I'll go with you, and if it's possible to open the gate for you, I'll do it.' He came to the lock, and although he turned it over and around, he couldn't open it, either. Then he said to me: 'How can I help you?'

"I complained bitterly to my master: 'Why have you abandoned me in a time of such distress?' He replied: 'I don't know what else I can do for you. But come, let's both go to the palace of the Messiah, perhaps we'll find help there.' And thus, with a great outcry I hastened to the palace of the Messiah. As our righteous Messiah saw me approaching from a distance, he called out: 'Don't shout!', and he gave me two letters of the alphabet. I returned to the gate, and thank God, was able to unlock it. I opened the gate and led all the prayers inside.

"There was great rejoicing over the ascent of the prayers, and because of it all charges were dropped and there was no longer any need to plead. The fateful judgment was cancelled, and nothing remained of it except a faint glimmer."

An hasidic rebbe could undertake such ascents to the celestial court at any time, but, as the above example indicates, it was usually during the autumnal High Holy Days when this became urgent, when the whole world and all of Israel was being tested before the divine Seat of Judgment. In his famous letter of 1750 to his brother-in-law Gershon Kutover, then living in the land of Israel, the Baal Shem Tov reported about two such celestial ascents at New Year's, the first in 1746 and the second in 1749. Of the latter he wrote:[9]

As you know, on Rosh ha-Shanah 5510 [= fall of 1749], I made a heavenly ascent and saw there a mighty accusation, [so great] that Samael [Satan] came close to being allowed to destroy whole cities and communities. I fell into deep inner concentration and prayed: 'May we but fall into the hand of God and not into the hand of man!' I was granted that, instead of this fate, a great sickness and plague might come such as had never before raged in any city in Poland or in the neighboring lands. And so it happened. The disease spread far and wide, it was beyond estimation. As far as the plague in the other cities and countries was concerned, I and my companions had agreed to recite prayers upon arising in the morning in order to lift this sentence. A voice from heaven said to me: 'Didn't you yourself choose and say: 'Let us fall into the hand of God?' Why do you now want to lift [the sentence]? There are no accusers, etc.'

From that moment on I said no more prayers to lift the plague—except on Hoshanah Rabbah [the conclusion of the autumnal judgment period at the end of the Feast of the Tabernacles] I and the whole community went to the synagogue, and with the help of several conjurations—in light of the great horror—I again recited a prayer with deep devotion to the effect that the plague should be contained and not spread any farther. And, with God's help, we prevailed.

The penitential period between Rosh ha-Shanah and Yom Kippur is evidently a time when the Gates of Heaven are besieged. Even today the climax of the Yom Kippur service features the recitation of the two Hebrew poems that served the Baal Shem Tov as impetus for his heavenly journey described above:

Open the gates of the heavenly palace quickly
to those who truly keep the faith.
Open the mysterious gates quickly to those who
cling fast to faith in You.
Open the gates of the beautiful halls . . .,
the gates inhabited by the [angels'] camp . . .
the gates of the Crown . . .

The call to open the gates is repeated several times at the end of the service that closes the Day of Atonement: "Open the gate to us!," "Open the Gates of Heaven!"[10]

The judgment of the individual and his passing through the heavenly gates is thus the predominant theme of a mystically influenced Jewish New Year's theology, and one comes across it at every turn in the relevant texts. It can also be seen in a sermon composed specifically for these days by another renowned preacher in Prague, Ezekiel Landau (1713–1793), who was the Chief Rabbi of Prague and Bohemia from 1754 on. Landau was highly renowned as a halakhist and preacher far beyond the reaches of Prague, and the printed anthology of his homilies surely served many a Prague preacher as a guide even in Kafka's day. This is more than likely because Jewish homiletics specialized precisely in the reworking of the older homiletic tradition. Meant to be delivered during the Ten Days of Penitence between Rosh ha-Shanah and Yom Kippur, this sermon is described as a judicial sermon. Here, too, judgment is connected with the soul's ascent to heaven. Once again it concludes with a discussion of the 'slaughter' of man at the end of his earthly existence. The homily begins with a sentence that strongly resembles the one in Kafka's Yom Kippur notation of September 16, 1915 (*Diaries*, 298) where he says: "Suicidal, not to go to the temple!" Ezekiel Landau's homily says:[11]

> Whoever doesn't pray in the synagogue, loses, also in the hour of his death . . . , for
>
> [when the angel] Michael, the heavenly high priest, brings the souls of the righteous above as an offering. . . .
>
> and Israel's offering is intimately connected to prayer—then, if their prayer is accepted, that is, when they pray in the synagogue, then their offering [of souls] is also accepted.
>
> But if a person doesn't pray in the synagogue, his offering is not accepted, nor does his soul ascend before the Lord as an offering after his death.
>
> And the reason for this is because all the foreign countries [i.e., the lands of Jewish exile] are full of shells [evil spirits]. How is a soul there supposed to ascend to heaven when there are many who lie in wait for it along the way, except that this soul should be in the habit of going to the synagogue every day and that its whole life has hallowed its path by obeying this commandment. This path leads through the synagogue after death, and that is where it finds the gate to heaven that leads to the upward ascent. And then the soul is accepted as an offering before the Lord. . . .

> Then its slaughter [i.e., its death] is not executed by Samael [the Angel of Death], whose jagged knife makes the offering unacceptable. But if a person never goes to synagogue, these holy paths will be blocked to him after death as well and the shells will carry him off, and his slaughter is performed by Samael with the jagged knife, and his soul is tossed to the dogs. If the Angel of Death slaughters his soul with the sword, i.e. with the jagged knife, it is unacceptable as an offering for the Lord and is tossed to the dogs.

Once again the same image that appears in the hasidic tales turns up in the sermon for the High Holy Days. The theme of divine judgment is closely connected with ascent to the heavenly halls, be it in ecstacy or the soul's ascent after death. The journey to these celestial halls, or as the Kabbalists say, to the Law, serves a double purpose: on the one hand it enables the person to intervene in the proceedings of the constantly convening court, and it facilitates the return of man to the Light of God on the other. It is surely this tradition of an ascent into the upper halls that finds its echo in Joseph K.'s climb to the attic of the courthouse, as well as in the surveyor's route to the castle in the novel of the same name.

5
"NO ONE ELSE COULD ENTER HERE, FOR THIS DOOR WAS MEANT FOR YOU ALONE"

These words conclude the legend of the gatekeeper in Kafka's novel *The Trial*. They obviously express a legitimate or even inevitable individualization of an understanding of the meaning of the Law. In his discussion of this piece, Gerhard Kurz[1] quite rightly refers to one of Scholem's remarks about the Jewish and especially the Kabbalists'[2] understanding of revelation and tradition. Scholem says: "A widely accepted belief of the later Kabbalah states that the Torah reveals to each individual Jew a particular aspect meant for him and understood by him alone. Thus, each Jew actually realizes his own destiny only by perceiving the aspect meant specifically for him and integrating it into tradition" (*Grundbegriffe*, 112). Equally pertinent, perhaps, is another of Scholem's observations in this context, namely: "The last and most radical step in the development of this principle of the infinite meaning of the Torah was taken by the Palestinian school of Kabbalists which flourished in Safed in the sixteenth century. They started from the ancient idea that the souls of Israel who went out of Egypt and received the Torah at Mount Sinai numbered 600,000. According to the laws of transmigration and the distribution of the sparks into which the soul disintegrates, these 600,000 primordial souls are present in every generation of Israel. 'Consequently, there are 600,000 aspects and meanings in the Torah. The root of every single soul in Israel has been fashioned in keeping with each one of these ways of explaining the Torah. In the Messianic age, every single man in Israel will read the Torah in keeping with the meaning peculiar to his root. This is also the way the Torah is understood in Paradise.' This mystical idea that each individual soul has its own peculiar way of understanding the Torah was stressed by Moses Cordovero of Safed. He said that each of these 600,000 holy souls has its own special portion of the Torah, 'and to none other than he, whose soul springs from thence, will it be given to understand it in this special and individual way that is reserved to him'" (*Symbolism*, 64f).

This individual understanding of the Torah, by the way, is not solely restricted to the goal in Paradise, i.e., in the mystical garden of the divine world; as with Kafka's man from the country, it is every individual's lifelong task. The kabbalistic texts quoted by Scholem also indicate that the mortal life of an individual is ultimately nothing more than a constant penetration into this individual interpretation of the Torah, which in its turn is nothing other than a lifelong concrete entering into and returning from the heavenly halls of the Torah. The number as well as the height of the heavenly halls of the Torah attained by any one individual increase with his growing recognition of his own particular route to the Torah. Naturally, only the one who makes the effort and dares to enter the offered opening will be granted access. In the following Lurianic tractate, the concrete progressive enterings into the 'Law' are equated with the nocturnal heavenly ascents of the human soul mentioned below. In order to present this idea as clearly as possible, I shall quote the entire section of the Lurianic *Book on the Transmigration of the Soul* that deals with this topic:[3]

> A man must concern himself with the four levels[4] of the Torah, which is to say with the literal meaning, the allegorical meaning, the moral meaning and the mystical meaning. And he must bear the burden of the transmigration of the soul (*gilgul*) for as long as it takes to complete all four.
>
> And that is what this is all about.
>
> Know that the total number of souls is 600,000 and no more. And realize that the Torah is the root of the souls of Israel; they were chiseled out of it and are rooted in it. And this is why there are 600,000 interpretations of the Torah; specifically, 600,000

in keeping with the literal meaning and 600,000 in keeping with the allegorical meaning and 600,000 in keeping with the moral meaning and 600,000 in keeping with the mystical meaning.

Thus we find that one soul of Israel has emerged out of each of these 600,000 interpretations. And in the world to come every member of Israel will comprehend and understand the Torah in keeping with the interpretation that corresponds to the root of his soul, for it was created out of this interpretation and emerged from it. And so, after his death and in the Garden of Eden he will also understand in a like manner.

The same holds true every night, when a man sleeps and consigns his soul [to heaven]; it leaves his body and ascends on high. And if a man is found worthy of ascending on high, once there they teach him that interpretation to which the root of his soul adheres. However, it all depends on what he did that day; his deeds during the day determine which verse or which chapter they teach him during the night; thereafter that additional verse blazes within him, one more than the day before. And after another night another verse lights up in his soul, again according to his actions on that day. And they are all in keeping with the interpretation inherent to the root of his soul.

My teacher [Isaac Luria], blessed be his memory, used to look at his students standing before him every evening, and he could read each additional verse from their foreheads, next to the traces of their souls which were also visible there. And he told each one of them a portion of the interpretation of this verse in keeping with the interpretation that belonged to his own soul. And before falling asleep, each student meditated upon this interpretation, one portion of which the master had told him, and he recited the verse aloud so that he might be taught the rest of the interpretation when his soul ascended on high for its nocturnal keeping.

In this way the soul is purified and ascends ever higher over endless and great stages, and new things are revealed to him, even though his body is unaware of them when awake. . . .

However, there are some souls that comprehend two and even more than two interpretations. Know that the soul of Moses our master comprehended all 600,000 interpretations of the Torah, so that he actually already knew everything a

> gifted scholar might discover sometime in the future. This is because his soul encompassed all 600,000 souls of Israel, and that is also why the other wise men of Israel comprehend so many interpretations of the Torah, all in keeping with the aspects of the souls dwelling within them.

In this text Isaac Luria describes human life an as ascent to the heavenly halls of the Torah with the ultimate goal of understanding all the interpretations of the Torah belonging to the root of each individual soul. To do this, a person must prepare himself with his routine day-to-day activities, for this is what clears the way to the next step along his unique path to the Torah. Then, during his soul's nocturnal ascent to the heavens, he must enter precisely those chambers of the Torah where the required text is being taught or where, in the words of the parallel text, "he reads the interpretation corresponding to his root." Night after night he climbs ever higher in keeping with his growing understanding, until he finally arrives at the fullness of knowledge that alone can deliver him, at the all-encompassing Light of the Torah which is the very Light of God itself.[5] Kafka's understanding of the individual's path to the Gate of the Law stands in complete harmony with this doctrine of Lurianic Kabbalah. According to Luria, a person must experience gilgul, or reincarnation, as many times as it takes until he comprehends all four levels of the Torah interpretation belonging to the root of his unique soul. The person who fails to achieve this individual perfection is barred entry to the Law, which is to say to personal well-being, and he must make a new start in an additional earthly existence. Such a person not only misses his individual life's goal, he also does harm to the universe, the earthly as well as the divine world:

> Know that the person who does not study the Torah does damage to the sefira tiferet [which is at the same time the level of the Written Torah and of the Tree of Life], and to be sure in all four levels of the world, for via the sefira tiferet the Torah is present in all levels of the world. And there are four levels in it, namely PaRDeS [Peshat (literal meaning), Remez (allegorical meaning), Derash (moral meaning), Sod (mystical meaning)]. And the one who succeeds in penetrating the profundities of all

> four meanings has achieved the end of all stages, and about him is written [in the Bible]: "No ear has ever heard, no eye has ever seen any God besides You, Who works for the one who puts his trust in Him." (*Scha'ar ha-Gilgulim*, c. 17, 50b)

In the dissertation he wrote in the 1930s, Heinz Politzer (*Künstler*, 258ff) already recognized the Jewish *am ha-aretz* (Yiddish: *Amhorez*), in other words, someone unfamiliar with the rudiments of the Torah, in Kafka's "man from the country" who stood before the Gates to the Law. Ever since talmudic times, such a person was labelled a "man from the country." This widely accepted identification, however, only gains real significance when Kafka took up the kabbalistic tradition that saw human life as a lifelong journey through the heavenly halls of the Torah. It is only thanks to the thirteenth century Kabbalah that the unsuccessful human life in a Jewish sense can even be conceived with the image of the *am ha-aretz* standing before the gates of the halls of the Torah, gates that are guarded by watchmen and which ultimately lead to the Light of Life. Such an image does not appear in the ancient Jewish doctrine concerning the Torah, nor does it hold true in the ancient Jewish hekhalot mysticism. Only after the Kabbalah combined these two traditions was it possible to look upon life as a journey through the halls of the Law, from which the *am ha-aretz*, the one ignorant of the Torah, must remain excluded. Kafka's use of the trope of the "man from the country" before the gates of the Law thus must be considered the final conclusive indication of his dependence upon this kabbalistic tradition.

6
THE GATEKEEPER TRADITION AS IT RELATES TO THE DESCRIPTION OF THE COURT

The theme of a journey through the gates to the halls of the Law is an important and pivotal component of the kabbalistic tractate by Eliahu de Vidas discussed above. It describes the goal toward which human existence aspires as well as the instances which grant permission for this journey to the Torah. Gerhard Kurz called the gatekeeper story within Kafka's *Trial* a mirror narrative (*Judentum*, 214).[1] In the text by Rabbi Eliahu de Vidas it is much more, for here it describes the essential but concealed inner workings of the judicial process. It describes the goal as well as the exigency and thus presents the actual heart of the whole matter.[2] Man's journey is a path to the Torah. This is a path to the Light, the Light of the Torah, the Light of God, the Light of Life, which is to say life in its deepest and most profound sense. During his sojourn on earth, man takes only the initial, albeit decisive, steps along this path, but these steps are already under the influence of that higher realm. Conversely, the inhabitant of this earth seeks to create advocates for himself and to exercise some influence of his own on high. Mortal life and the realm of the gatekeeper are thus the two sides of one and the same coin, sides which are always real, but at the same time necessarily two successive steps. The one is not a metaphor for the other; rather, taken together they both represent the path prescribed for man. Moreover, this path from the multiplicity of the world to the unity of the Godhead, from the impure realm of earthly sin to the holiness of God, is a journey of leave-taking and of testing—it is a judgment. The course of human life is the route through the court that combines both peripheries of reality, God and the world, or God and man.

In the dualistically conceived passages of the Zohar and of the literature that followed it—including de Vidas' *Reshit Hokhma*—the celestial court and its messengers are described as a series of interrelated and mutually dependent holy and profane halls and forces. The profane halls can take on an almost hostile attitude toward God, primarily as the powers of seduction, although de Vidas constantly stresses that even this impure side stands in the service of divine judgment.

It is the Jewish doctrine of man's free will above all else that serves the Kabbalists as justification for the existence of this impure, punitive side. Free will makes man what he is, an individual being independent of God. But this very free will, which is withdrawn from the dispositional power of the Godhead, not only makes possible but is the cause of sin; in other words, what makes man man is, at the same time, the cause or occasion of his ability to be sinful. Intrinsic to the human condition is the ability to sin. However, in those instances where the will of an individual voluntarily opposes the will of God, the relation between the two can only be mediated by the court, for it determines the convergence as well as the divergence of the human from the divine will and adjudicates reward or punishment. The whole purpose of the judicial instances, then, is to return a verdict and pronounce sentence. This means that human life before God is conceivable only as a life in judgment. Of course, I must immediately add that, in every discussion of a Jewish court, the principle of impartial justice is always accompanied by the divine principle of *hesed* which affects that judgment. *Hesed*—perhaps best translated with the word that just happens to be the name of Joseph K.'s advocate, namely, "grace" or "mercy" (Huld).

7
THE STATUS OF MAN VIS-À-VIS THE OFFICERS OF THE COURT

Inherent within the already discussed reasons behind the necessity of the court is an additional set of problems which are also addressed in Kafka's gatekeeper legend. These involve the question of man's status vis-à-vis the officers of the celestial court, and primarily its retinue of angels. According to Moses Cordovero, the mentor of Eliahu de Vidas, and in keeping with ancient Jewish tradition, angels have no free will of their own and are thus necessarily compelled to do the will of God. On the other hand, generally accepted Jewish thought has it that God's dominion can not be expressed in the mechanical obedience of a creature lacking a will of its own. God's dominion is visible and effective only where His creatures, and that means man, make the conscious and free decision to subordinate themselves to the will of God despite the temptations from the side of evil. This is why the true dominion of God reveals itself in judgment over the free will of man, as Chief Rabbi Löw said. The result is a contradiction in the assessment of the relative status of God's creatures, according to which the human servants, capable of rebellion, are ultimately more essential for the Kingdom of God than the angels are. This contradiction gives rise to the dilemma that Kafka also addresses, namely: who actually is higher, "the man from the country" or the gatekeeper as a member of the court? The truly Jewish and kabbalistic answer to this question is expressed in Kafka's commentaries on the gatekeeper legend as but one of many opinions: "Most importantly, the free man is superordinate to the bound one" (*Wedding*, 300).

This is the same context in which Cordovero states: when a person approaches the human ideal, that is, when he becomes a tzaddik, one of the righteous ones, on the basis of his own free will, he is superior to the angelic beings who act only out of compulsion, even though the latter are actually mightier because of their position in the heavenly hierarchy. This leads Moses Cordovero to add the following to his discussion of the heavenly halls (*Pardes*, Bl. 51a): "And now, as the tzaddik climbs to ever higher levels, his soul showers him with the light of its own highest level . . . ; then the tzaddik slips through the hands of these judges and they can no longer condemn him . . . , on the contrary, now he is the source of the stream of blessings which flows out over them [the judges] and they all drink from him and he passes the fulness on to the celestial servants and revokes their duties however he would."[1]

The hierarchy has thus reversed itself. Perfect man now stands higher than the powerful officers of the celestial court. One is almost tempted to echo the words of the cleric in the cathedral: "The proper understanding of a thing and the misunderstanding of the same thing are not always mutually exclusive" (*Trial*, 297). There is no such thing as the "one" truth as far as the relation between a man and the court goes. The truth is different in every case, but even then no one side is true by itself. The truth of the relation between man and court lies in this contradiction. Human beings are subordinate to the celestial court and are impotent before it. However, because of his free will, man is actually superior to it and most importantly so when he exercises this free will in deciding in favor of the Torah and of godliness. This is the basic contradiction inherent in the view the neoplatonic Kabbalah holds of the existence of the world as a whole. The power of man lies in his separation from God—for only then is he a being differentiated from God. At the same time, however, this fact also establishes his impotence, for he is separated from God, he is separated from the source of life.

8
THE HUMAN FACE AS A REFLECTION OF DIVINE JUDGMENT

During a conversation with the merchant Block in the house of the advocate Huld, Block says to Joseph K.:

> "You must remember that many things turn up in these proceedings that are beyond the power of comprehension; one is simply too tired and too distracted for many of them and turns toward superstition as a substitute. . . . One such superstition, for example, is that many maintain they can read the result of the trial on the face of the accused, particularly from the appearance of the lips. These people have claimed that, from what they can tell from your lips, you will surely be condemned, and soon. I repeat, it's a ridiculous superstition and in most cases completely disproved by the facts, but when you live in that society, it's hard to avoid such ideas. Just imagine what an influence this superstition can have. You've spoken to someone over there, haven't you? But he could hardly answer you. Naturally there are many reasons for being confused over there, but one of them was the sight of your lips. Later he said he believed he saw the sign of his own condemnation on your lips as well." (*Trial*, 236f)

It was difficult to escape from "such ideas" in Eastern Jewish society, saturated as it was with the Kabbalah. In fact, not very long ago (1966/67) a Hebrew book was published in Jerusalem that contained many old traditions concerning prosopomancy, the art of reading the signs of the human face. This slim volume, collected "by the Kabbalists" and edited by Meir Bakal, bears the title *Sefer Hokhmat ha-Parzuf* [*Book on the Science of the Face*]. One of the texts reproduced in it is called: "Sod Hakkarat Panim", i.e., "The Mystery of Understanding the Face."

This text begins with the programmatic remark (66):

> "The show of their countenance doth witness against them; and they declare their sin as Sodom, they hide it not. Woe unto their soul! For they have wrought evil unto themselves." (Isa. 3:9)
>
> Know that this verse hints at the secret of reading faces, namely: that the wise man can learn everything from a person's face—what has happened to this person up until now, generation after generation [through various reincarnations] and everything that will come upon him in the future. For it is the seal of the Angel of the Lord, the Name of the Lord is engraved in his face, and all his works can be read from his countenance, whether he is an evil-doer or a righteous man or whether he is on the side of the Lord or on the other side!

Especially significant in our context are the words: "whether he is an evil-doer or a righteous man," for this is the basic wording of the declarations of the celestial court as we have already learned from our discussion of the talmudic description of the New Year's judgment. Also important are the words "and everything that will come upon him in the future." The 'superstition' held by the people hanging around the court in Kafka's novel makes the same claim.

Another of the texts included in this anthology traces the writing on the face back to the twenty-two letters of the Hebrew alphabet engraved in it. This gives rise to the following explanation (78): "The twenty-two letters are one aspect of the soul, and they tell of the soul's perfection or deficiency. . . . And whoever asks the wise practitioner of prosopomancy about this already displays his letters on his own face. And this is because, God forbid, his death sentence has already been decided, which is to say, that he will die within the next thirty days. In such a case, what is needed is a great act of atonement (repentance), and would that it might help to lift this verdict."

In Eastern Europe the art of physiognomy or prosopomancy has not remained hidden as an occult science within narrow kabbalistic circles. On the contrary, as Eastern Jewish folk tales of the last two centuries attest, it has penetrated deeply into the common knowledge of the broad masses. There is an extensive and comprehensive series of legends in which a 'prophet of sin' appears and exposes that which is sinful and impure by means of his intuitive observation of things and people.[1] One of the intuitive techniques of recognizing sinful people, and with it their backsliding before the celestial court, is physiognomy. The prophet, after discovering and exposing these sins, then makes an effort to rescue the transgressor from judgment by prescribing acts of atonement or by directly intervening before the instances of divine justice.

The legends of the Baal Shem Tov tell of three versions of one such judicially relevant physiognomy (*H*, 77; *Praise*, 71):[2]

> I heard the following tale from the rav of our community:
>
> One day the Besht happened to notice a sign of adultery on Rabbi Gershon, his brother-in-law. He was deeply troubled by this and was ashamed to mention it to him, even though he was greatly puzzled by it. When he finally did confront his brother-in-law, the latter accused the Besht of lying, and struck him. The Besht said: "Wait until morning! I still see a sign of adultery on you." During the night he saw it again in his mystical meditations. The next day he said to him: "You have made a vow of abstinence from your wife. But while I was in heaven I heard that the Rambam[3] has decreed that such a man is like him who says to his wife: 'She should be as my mother to me'. And although this is not a binding vow, the traces of an ejaculation did betray you, which is why you fasted from one sabbath to the next. Because you violated the vow of abstinence this way, the sign became stronger, and that's why it's showing up as adultery now." Then Rabbi Gershon confessed the truth: he broke his vow because he wanted to go to the Holy Land but

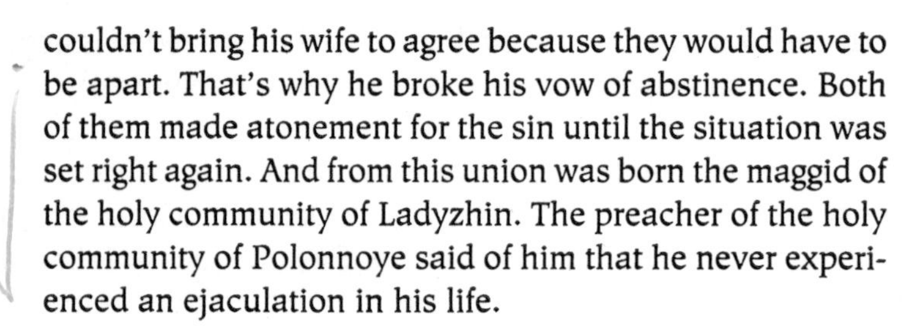

> couldn't bring his wife to agree because they would have to be apart. That's why he broke his vow of abstinence. Both of them made atonement for the sin until the situation was set right again. And from this union was born the maggid of the holy community of Ladyzhin. The preacher of the holy community of Polonnoye said of him that he never experienced an ejaculation in his life.

The second version has it this way (*H*, 141; *Praise*, 140):

> The rav mentioned above [Nahum of Chernobyl] once saw that a man, whom the whole world knew as an adulterer, came to visit the Besht and that the Besht seemed to be on very friendly terms with him. The rav asked him: "Why were you so friendly with that man, especially since he is so well-known as an adulterer?" "Are you any better?" asked the Besht.
>
> The rav began to search his soul and examined all his deeds, but he found nothing. "I swear that's not true," he said to the Besht. But the Besht said: "I see an adulterous act on you! Tomorrow morning I'll give you all the details."
>
> The next day the Besht told the rav: "You made a vow of abstinence and then broke your own promise. Last night I heard that Rambam [in heaven][4] decreed that the vow of abstinence is such as if a man had denied himself his wife and had said: 'You should be as a mother to me.' Look in your book, maybe you'll find it." Thereupon the rav confessed his sin and even found the reference in Rambam.
>
> The Besht experienced three more instances of this same sort.

The dialogue between Block and Joseph K. cited at the beginning of this chapter deals with the fact that many of the individuals involved in a trial believe it possible to read the status of the proceedings against them from a person's face. With this Kafka has taken up an Eastern Jewish as well as kabbalistic topos related to the theme of the divine judgment over mankind.

It is true that Kafka has Block dismiss the art of reading faces as mere superstition and thus lets him distance himself from the ideas supporting this art that were circulating in the Eastern Jewish texts. On the other hand, Block's or Kafka's attitude can not be described as a total rejection of this idea, either. After all, Block does admit that an integral part of the almost incomprehensible routine of court procedure is the fact that people resort again and again to such 'senseless' measures. "You must remember," Block says, "that many things turn up in these proceedings that are beyond the power of comprehension; one is simply too tired and too distracted for many of them and turns toward superstition as a substitute" (*Trial*, 236). All the same, these words do express an understanding attitude toward superstition as one attempt on the part of man, and be it ever so fruitless, to deal with the incomprehensibility of the whole affair and not to let oneself be abandoned in a completely passive way to the apparent opacity of it all.

Kafka says something similar about the meaning and the use of Josephine's musical talents, the objective ineffectiveness of which the narrator himself emphasizes, but whose subjective usefulness in times of distress he nevertheless recognizes. In direct opposition with her assurances to the contrary, Josephine's songs in fact do not do away with the adversity, but they apparently do help the people survive these troubles (Stories, 192). Finally, in his aphorisms, Kafka mentions another 'useless' tool people employ and which they hope will help them master their hopeless situation, namely: the belief in a personal God. Once again he acknowledges a human tool, probably useless in an objective sense, an obvious self-deception, as a helpful support in light of the hiddenness of real help.

This surely explains Joseph K.'s cry that the words of the cleric represented nothing less than turning lies into world order (*Trial*, 303). The cleric had stated previously: "You can't take everything as the truth, but you have to take it as necessary." Evidently the pious self-deception that Kafka had to have seen in many of the Eastern Jewish/kabbalistic remedies that were no longer accessible to him as a western Jew still seems not quite so senseless to him, for it does help a person survive, or at least it represents an attempt to do so. This is the case with the reading of faces in the court, with the mouse people that crowd around Josephine in times of adversity (*Stories*, 193), or with a person who flees from the hiddenness of the Indestructible and from his sustaining faith in it and escapes into a belief in a personal God.

9
THE KABBALISTIC DEPICTION OF THE CELESTIAL COURTS—HISTORY AS JUDGMENT

In the wake of the Zohar, which is to say ever since the thirteenth century, the ancient Jewish conception of judgment took a decisively new turn in the Kabbalah. The celestial court of ancient Jewish classical literature that only convened at certain definite times now became one element of the new mystical cosmology and theosophy, i.e., one element of the speculation concerning the divine manifestations or sefirot. What was formerly the one central celestial court was now broken down into a number of supernatural and inner-deitic, which is to say, inner-sefirotic, judicial chambers hierarchically organized one above the other in the various heavenly halls. Also new is the fact that these celestial courts are now in constant session, day and night, and their pronouncements direct the course of history. In the kabbalistic world view, this court no longer marks the endpoint and the balance of history as did the ancient Jewish divine judgment at the end of an individual's life or as did the eschatological judgment at the end of time. Rather, the court has now become the motor force behind history. The courts make their pronouncements constantly and incessantly, and in this way they determine the course of history of each individual as well as of the world at every moment. To this way of thinking, history is synonymous with judgment. Without judgment there is no history; history *is* judgment. From its very beginning every human life is nothing other than one continuous trial. It begins with the person's life, intervenes perceptibly at some time into this life and finds its climax and conclusion in the death of the person after many "postponements" and "apparent acquittals", as the painter Titorelli tells Joseph K.[1] Death is now only the final verdict of this lifelong trial, a view that finds impressive formulation in the warning, quoted above, that Zevi Hirsch Kaidanover published in his morality book *Ka ha-Yashar*.

The Kabbalah sees judgment, this most profound nature of history as well as the very essence of the universe, as an ontological building block of being. The structure of the world is a judicial structure. The judicial chambers, integrated into the structure of the universe—of the celestial as well as the divine and thus also the terrestial worlds—are fundamental elements of being upon whose pronouncements the weal and the woe not only of the human race, but also of the Deity itself, depend. History and time as determined by judgment, therefore, know only two poles between which they move: acquittal and condemnation. The latter, as far as man is concerned, takes the form of death, which is always the verdict in the end. Of course, this judgment also creates atonement and expiation and leads a person ultimately out of temporal history into the halls of eternal salvation in Divine Light.

The Zohar describes this celestial world of judgment in two baroque, very wide-ranging, at times rather tortuous tractates[2] that were combined into a somewhat more manageable form by the later codifier of Zoharic Kabbalah, Moses Cordovero. His monumental work bears the title *Pardes Rimmonim* (*Garden of Pomegranates*). Since this work is inaccessible to Western readers, Cordovero's depiction appears in translation in the Appendix. The number of different judicial instances is even greater in the text of the Zohar than here, but the "Kafkaesque" aspect of this kabbalistic judgment world is also visible in Cordovero's abstract. In keeping with the dualistic world view of Zoharic Kabbalah, Cordovero presents the co-existence as well as the interrelatedness of two series of seven heavenly halls, the "Holy Side" and the "Other Side," the "Impure Side." In these halls reside the courts. Both sides are equally part of the world of divine judgment and both stand in the service of the celestial court. The remarkable ways of describing the court and its procedures already noted above are depicted here in their bizarre and dualistic extreme.

Cordovero paints a colorful picture of twice seven layered halls superimposed upon each other, those of the pure and those of the impure side, that overarch the terrestial world and penetrate into it. Everything that motivates and determines human life is housed in them in the shape of angels and angelic beings. All of this is portrayed as a complicated and intricate world of judicial chambers and the officers that staff them, mechanically and almost blindly following its incessant and unalterable rhythm; it functions like a huge bureaucracy. In fact, these judicial instances are reminiscent of Kafka's attic courts, of their angular inaccessibility and simultaneously constant presence in the daily routine of human life.

These courts represent an attempt to use the language of myth to depict the confusion and disorder of human existence, the forces and the judgment by which mankind is directed and upon whose mercy it is dependent. Nevertheless, all of this stands under the rule of the Highest One, and the whole apparatus serves but one purpose, which is to mediate between God and man, between the One in His Unity and the confusing and contradictory multiplicity of mortal life. Everything that happens in the world, from the growth of plants to the vagaries of human history, is directed by the decisions and the actions of the beings making up these judicial hierarchies.

These include angels who receive the pleas of man, others who are charged with granting mercy and directing life. The whole scene is alive with advocates and accusers, avengers and rewarders, full of angelic-like eyes that follow the doings of man on earth; with heralds who deliver the pronouncements of the courts from one level to another until they ultimately reach the earth. The duration as well as the support of human life are governed and decided by yet another group, and so on. All of this is part of an almost confoundingly tangled judicial hierarchy housed in various chambers and halls.

The most extraordinary aspect of this system is the fact that the forces of temptation are also integral to these courts—a topos known to Judaism since the days of Job.

These seducers belong to the same twin hierarchies of the twice seven halls. They are carnal desires that have assumed concrete shapes—adultery and prostitution, whose leader, Lilith, is the queen of the demons. "Here are gathered all the kisses and temptations and carnal desires of fornication and adultery, for whose sake man is driven out of this as well as out of the other world."[3] They all represent a type of hypostatized human desire. Even the Torah scholars are mentioned here; the "foreign thoughts" they harbor during study, their striving for pleasure and arrogance all have their origin in the halls of these courts.

Judges and enforcers reign on both sides of this double hierarchy, and next to them the seducers. The co-existence of these two judicial hierarchies is an interplay of advocacy and accusation, of help and hindrance, supervision and temptation, reward and punishment. And yet, as mentioned above, all of these celestial helpers and pursuers, accusers and defenders are nothing other than mythologically hypostatized machinations of man, in keeping with the ancient talmudic saying: With every good deed a man gains a defender at court, and with every misdeed an accuser (*Mishna Avot* 4:11). One could actually go so far as to say that the entire celestial judicial hierarchy is nothing other than a mythological mirror of human behavior and of the human psyche, in its greatness as well as its depravity. In fact, Moses Cordovero said just that at the end of this depiction of the seven impure heavenly halls (*Hekhalot ha-Klippot*, Bl. 58c):

> Clearly the sefirot are encompassed by the halls, and the halls and the shells are one and the same. Corresponding to these seven are seven kinds of evil drives [in man], and these drives get their strength from these seven. The evil drive, therefore, has seven names: Evil, Impure, Abomination, Hater, Stone, Stumbling Stone, Northerner. Corresponding to these are seven chambers in gehinnom, where the sinner is punished in seven ways. And these chambers are: Pit, Den of Iniquity, Duma (the One Suspected of Adultery), Terrestrial Mire, Sheol, The Shadow of Death, Lowest Earth.
>
> The one corresponds to the other. Opposite purity is impurity, opposite fitness is that which is unfit, opposite the permitted is the forbidden, opposite justice is sin. "For God hath made the one over against the other." (Eccles. 7:14)

In addition to Ecclesiastes 7:14, the Kabbalists were particularly fond of quoting Job 19:26 ("Yet in my flesh I shall see God") as biblical support for their all-encompassing doctrine of parallels. According to this doctrine, the world, including the divine world, is a reflection of man. Ultimately, then, even this entire judicial world is nothing other than a mirror image of the human psyche and human society. Within them are engendered reward and punishment, condemnation and acquittal, which the Kabbalist paints in his mythological images. Man journeys through these judicial halls and into the essence of the Torah, which forms the center of the divine world of the sefirot. This journey is simultaneously also a journey through human existence. Just *how* one traverses this path to divine Unity, which leads to the absorption of the human ego into the fulness of Divine Life, is appraised via a continuous judgment of the ego-addiction of mankind. This conflict, as another author of kabbalistic morality teaches us, becomes more acute the higher a man ascends (Horowitz, II: Bl. 42a), and the judgment aspect begins to be of interest only after the person reaches a certain stage in life: "Whoever attains greatness and a certain high level begins to provoke Satan, who ascends and makes accusations against him" (Horowitz, Bl. 85b). Could that have been the case with Joseph K., who even flattered himself about his high position and was constantly jockeying with the temporary director for attention and promotion?

A comparison of Kafka's shabby and dirty judicial chambers—"How dirty everything here is!" (*Trial*, 76)—with those of the Kabbalah, one aspect of which is expressly called the "impure side", is surely not too far-fetched. Moreover, in the kabbalistic texts we frequently meet temptation, especially of the sexual variety, as an integral part of the judicial hierarchies, and the same holds true in Kafka's courts, as well. Finally, if we consider the fact that the law books of these courts are not much better than pornographic texts (*Trial*, 76f), we are reminded of the mythological dark side of human depravity and carnal desires. According to Cordovero, these play a decisive role in the proceedings of the celestial courts.

In 1934, Gershom Scholem sent Walter Benjamin a copy of Kafka's *Trial* together with a rather long poem (fourteen stanzas), in which he explained his interpretation of the novel in terms of the Kabbalah. In the seventh stanza Scholem reaches a conclusion very similar to the kabbalistic understanding of the judicial hierarchies:

> What we are
> is reflected in endless instances.
> No one knows the whole route,
> for we are blinded by each portion of it.[4]

If one can say that the celestial courts of the Kabbalists are ultimately a reflection of the inner depths of the human psyche, which is precisely why they are so dirty and so chaotic, then this contains a not inconsiderable threat for the portrayal of the world as well as the Godhead, for they are both inextricably tangled up with the whole human mess. Moses Cordovero saw this danger and tried to skirt around it with an idea he gleaned from the neoplatonists. According to this medieval system, which left deep traces of its own on the Kabbalah, the ideal worlds anchored in the Godhead are reproduced on every level, but with the quality of that respective level, be it higher or lower. In other words, that which is pure and spiritual in the Godhead becomes more and more reified the greater its distance from the source of the emanation, and it becomes darker and progressively cruder. This means that the higher one ascends through the judicial hierarchies the less coarse are the things one meets along the way. On the other hand, the lower one descends, the more the levels of the court resemble terrestrial reality.

The kabbalistic world view consists of four levels; standing at its apex ever since the late phases of Zoharic texts is the world of atsiluth, which is the world of the sefirot, of the revealed Godhead. This is followed by the beriah world, which is the world of the Throne of God, followed by the world of yetsirah, of angels. The last is the world of action, asiyah, which represents the lower spheres of our everyday life. Of these four worlds Cordovero says the following (Pardes, "Scha'ar ha-Hechalot," (24), c. 11, Bl. 51a):

> Because the sefirot stand close to the source, they cannot change. But this atsiluth world expresses itself in the beriah

> world. And as the Emanator is related to the atsiluth world, so is the atsiluth world related to the beriah world. And although the differences and distinctions between things are reproduced unendingly, the beriah is still close to the atsiluth and does not yet receive any differences—but it expresses itself in the yetsirah world. And the beriah world is related to the yetsirah world the way the atsiluth is related to beriah, and the yetsirah expresses itself in the asiyah world as far as the types of punishment and the impurities of the soul, the purification and perfection of the soul, and the defects of man, as far as their blows and their punishments are concerned, all of which are supposed to bring them closer to divine service. This is the purpose of the asiyah world, which is called the Whip and the Rod. This is why the things of yetsirah [that is, the judicial halls] in their diversity resemble the actions of man. One weighs, the other counts, he is the witness and the former the advocate; some are criminal judges and others are judges for thieves and these are judges for damages and those are judges in money matters and those other ones are judges over life and death. They are as close as can possibly be to the differences [among human beings]. And the asiyah servants [that is, the avenging angels who descend to earth] are there to punish in cases of property disputes, to expunge, to kill, to prohibit, to injure: as the judges order so do these judges' minions execute those orders.

The lower one descends through the judicial hierarchies, the more they come to resemble the terrestrial world, so that the lowest courts are ultimately indistinguishable from the mundane, a concept that was clearly expressed in the passages from the book *Reshit Hokhma* cited above. Every aspect of daily life is part of this judgment; they represent the lowest levels of the judicial hierarchy.

The same state of affairs holds true for Kafka's courts in *The Trial*, or, *mutatis mutandis*, for the lower agencies of the castle in the novel of the same name. Daily life in all its aspects is an integral part of the judicial instances; their meeting places, their offices and their personnel are identical to the mundane activities of life. Thus Kafka's hero Joseph K., just like the person in the kabbalistic texts, occasionally ascends from the lower judicial realm into higher instances, but never so high that they are fundamentally different from the already familiar lower regions. The person climbs stairs and passes through one door after another only to find himself in miserable attics where he is stopped and occasionally interrogated. This all corresponds to the judicial halls of the Kabbalah and man's attempts to enter into them. It is only in his parable of the gatekeeper that Kafka allows a glimpse into the higher regions, and these in turn are reminiscent of the higher halls of the Kabbalists which harbor the splendor of the Divinity.

Kafka, however, is no Kabbalist in the traditional sense of the word. His vision of the radiant transcendental realms of kabbalistic tradition is obscured, and this is why he pulls the whole hierarchical structure lower yet, until it coincides with terrestrial reality. For Kafka, the celestial courts become a second-rate version of the same old petty and dirty story that comprises daily, mundane life. When viewed in the proper perspective, however, this reduction brings him very close to the imagery of the Kabbalists. When compared to the abstract and rational concepts of transcendence so characteristic of medieval Jewish philosophers, even the kabbalistic celestial halls seem like a shined-up version of a plebeian paradise.

To summarize then: the courts in Kafka's *Trial* and the agencies in the *Castle* represent a demythologized, at times cynically sarcastic transformation of the ancient celestial hierarchies. Kafka transplanted the lost paradise of the Kabbalists into a European, petit-bourgeois milieu. Only once does he dare glance upward, much like the passengers in a train accident who can dimly see the light at the end of the tunnel but repeatedly lose sight of it because it is so weak (*Stories*, 297). Kafka situates this light in the one place on the European scene that is still capable of evoking a hint of the sacred and the transcendental, namely, in a cathedral.

10
THE INCURSION OF JUDGMENT INTO HUMAN LIFE: DISEASE AND DREAMS

The celestial courts direct the course of an individual's life, but, as indicated above, man is initially and for the most part oblivious to this fact. And yet, at some time the celestial judicial proceedings can interfere in human life in such a way that the person affected can no longer repress it from his consciousness. The Kabbalists believe that this occurs when the accusation on high reaches a certain intensity—and the indications of such intensity are always the same: disease and every conceivable affliction. "When a person is sick, they look into his files; some lean toward acquittal . . . and others lean toward condemnation" (Zohar III:309a).

The incursion of judgment into temporal life does not always have to lead immediately to the ultimate sentence of death. This eventuality can frequently be fended off a number of times—whenever one recovers from an illness, for example. Nevertheless, as the painter Titorelli says, such an acquittal is only an apparent one or a postponement (*Trial*, 205),[1] for the court can intervene again at any time, and experience shows there is no escape from the death sentence in the end.

Another feature of this continuous and latent judicial procedure hanging over the individual is the daily, or more accurately, the nightly interrogation. A person's soul leaves his body every night during sleep and appears before the celestial court. In the words of the morality book *Kav ha-Yashar* (c. 73):

> While the body lies sleeping in bed, the person's soul leaves and bears witness to everything he did on that day. And the soul is judged, be it for good or for evil, for the celestial courts convene in the night and pass judgment. . . .
>
> In the beginning of the night people slumber on their cots, and their soul bears witness as to their deeds of the day, and they stand in judgment . . . ; at midnight a mighty northwind blows and a sentinel rises up and strikes with the wind as with a whip.[2]

The soul's ascent to the nightly court is simultaneously a journey through the world and the universe, a journey the sleeping body perceives as a dream. This nightly journey to the celestial court is thus associated with dreams, so that the ascent to the courts can seem to the sleeper as a dreamlike passage through the mundane realities and activities of everyday life. However, since the subject of the dream experience, namely the soul, is at the same time the dreamer's actual self, this view places dreams on a continuum that only gradually differentiates between the reality of the waking state and that of the dream world. In other words, the dream world and the waking world communicate so directly that, as the folk tales that follow will demonstrate, the dream events can be simply continued in the waking state, and vice versa. The welts one received in one's dreams as a result of a whipping at the hands of the celestial chastisers can still be seen on the person's body after waking. This was the case, for example, in the story about the tax collector who dreamt he had appeared before the celestial court and who still bore the bruises from the blows of the avenging angels after he awoke. The small anthology *Nifleot ha-Shem* that appeared in Lemberg in 1912 tells of a pious and wealthy but very selfish village farmer who never opened his door and never gave alms to any of the many Jews passing through his village, regardless of how desperate they may have been (41–52). One night he dreamt he fell sick and died soon afterward. The family was so niggardly that they provided only cheap linen for the dead man's shroud. As they bore him into the city on a cart, the burial brotherhood (*Hevra Kaddisha*) refused to bury the notorious cheapskate for the paltry sum it was offered, with the result that the body was forced to endure a shameful delay. Once the requisite burial expenses were paid, the body was buried, but not before the brotherhood of the funeral society had thoroughly beaten and abused the corpse. The dreamer continued:

> After that, I spent the whole day lying in the grave, and to my great astonishment no one asked after me, even though Iknew that you have to answer for what you've done after death. . . . So I lay there three days . . . , when an angel appeared and woke me up and said: "Get up from your [death]bed and come with me!" . . . I followed him past horrible places until we came to the celestial courtroom, where they judge men according to their deeds. The angel stood me by the door in front of the judges, and my knees trembled for fright.
>
> The warden said to me: "Come forward!" I went forward, and he said: "You know that you have died and were brought here to give an account of all your deeds during your whole life?" "I know," I replied. And he asked: "Did you study the Torah?" "Yes!" "And who can vouch for that?" he wanted to know. Thereupon all the tractates of the Babylonian and the Palestinian Talmud passed by, and each one vouched for the fact that I had studied it. And the other books as well, those of Maimonides and the Turim [of Alfasi], each one spoke up for me, and I was full of joy.
>
> Then he asked me: "Were you honest . . . , did you give alms and have you done good deeds?" I was nonplussed . . . and said nothing.
>
> The warden cried: "Let the witnesses come forward." And there came all sorts of people, poor people, miserable people, without number and from all over, and they all attested to the fact that I had denied their requests for alms, food and drink and had turned them away from my door. . . .
>
> I was sentenced to choose between one month in gehinnom [purgatory] or another life in gilgul [reincarnation]. . . . I chose gehinnom, and an avenging angel appeared immediately and led me to gehinnom [along . . . a horrible route that lasted] three weeks. I could hardly bear it any longer and wondered when I would ever arrive in gehinnom. Whenever I tried to rest a while from the hardships of the journey, the angel shouted at me and beat me. In this manner I had to march on, day and

> night, for four weeks . . . , and it got hotter and hotter. Finally [after I had thrown off all my clothes because of the heat] I told the angel he should bring me back to the judges, because I really preferred the second punishment, reincarnation, because I couldn't bear the heat any longer. But he only struck me and screamed: "Keep going, I have to do my duty or else I'll be punished myself!" [This happened three times and the man finally said to the angel, out of pure agony]: "I'll take your punishment, too!" The angel agreed to this and said: "If you take my punishment upon yourself as well, I'll bring you back to the judges." [After another four-week journey] I was once again standing by the door. The warden looked at me and cried: "What are you doing here?" I replied: "Listen, Lord, I can't bear the gehinnom punishment; I beg of you, let me choose the other alternative . . ."
>
> The warden turned to the angel in anger: "Why haven't you done your duty?" The angel told the judge: "The man is willing to bear my punishment as well, so I agreed!" . . . The judge said: "Let it be so . . . , but the angel's punishment, which you have taken upon yourself, has to be meted out at once." That same instant an angel with an iron whip appeared and beat me on the bottom. I screamed pitifully and bitterly.
>
> My screaming woke me and all the members of my household. . . . When I was fully awake, I felt an enormous pain, my whole backside was swollen from stinging lashes. And one welt from the whip has remained on my backside to this very day.

From that moment on the man abandoned his mean ways and became an advocate for all poor people!—The whole episode was a dream, but the welts remained even after it was over. Dreams, then, are part of the reality determined by the court, a reality that encompasses day and night, waking and dreaming.

I shall cite two more tales that tell of experiences in the realm of the celestial court or of the execution site; both show how interconnected and interwoven waking reality, dreams and celestial judgment were in the thought of Eastern Jewish bards and their audiences.

Judgment in Paradise

Rabbi Shneur, the son of the tzaddik, Moses, our teacher and former maggid in the holy community of Rashkov, told us that he, Rabbi Shneur, had seen a manuscript of a certain rav who was known as the author of the book *Toledot Yaakov Yoseph* [Rabbi Jacob Joseph of Polonnoye]. He saw this manuscript in the holy community of Lodmir, and read in it the following tale:

The author dreamt that he had entered a palace in Paradise so splendid he could not get his fill of looking at it. He lingered in that palace for a long time and marvelled at its beauty. Meanwhile he saw Satan enter the palace in the form of a dog and watched him as he appeared before the court that was then in session. Before this court Satan maligned a Jew who lived in a certain village: "It is true," he began, "that he studies constantly, nor does he fail to give alms, but I still have a charge against him. He has been living in this village for years now, and every year he steals from his gentile neighbors." Thereupon Satan drew up a tally before the court amounting to a considerable sum.

Even so, the court snapped at him the way people talk to a dog, so that he ran away.

It pained the rav very much to hear this calumny. And yet, he wouldn't budge until he found out how the story ended.

Half an hour later Satan appeared once again to make his accusation, and once again he was chased away. Finally, when he returned a third time, he posted himself before the court and cried: "Lord of the World, I come before this court with an accusation, and no one pays attention to my words." The voice of a herald from on high proclaimed that they should reach a verdict, and they wrote their decision: either the lord of the village was to confiscate all his possessions and imprison the man together with all his family, or one of his children was to convert to Christianity. The choice was left up to the accused tenant.

In the guise of a dog, Satan snatched the verdict in his teeth and ran off with it.

Then the rav woke up from his sleep. He felt sorry for the man, for he liked him very much; indeed, even Satan was forced

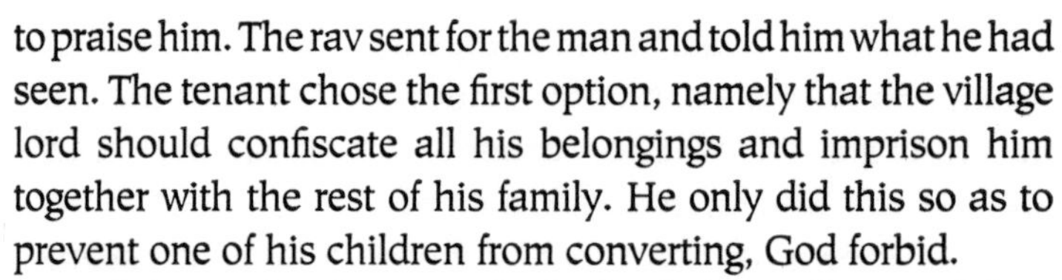

to praise him. The rav sent for the man and told him what he had seen. The tenant chose the first option, namely that the village lord should confiscate all his belongings and imprison him together with the rest of his family. He only did this so as to prevent one of his children from converting, God forbid.

And that's what happened. The lord of the village took him and his possessions and cast the man with his family into prison.

But the rav felt obliged to travel around and collect money for his release, and he did so until he had finally freed the man and his family.

Learn from this that you should not steal from the goyim, as is written in all the books. For if you do, Satan will demand retribution before the celestial court. (*H*, 112; *Praise*, 114)

A Visit to Hell

There once was a young man, a relative of Rabbi Selig, who dreamt that he went for a walk in the fields with two Hasidim. As they were walking along, one of them said to the other: "Let's visit gehinnom [i.e., hell or purgatory] and see what's going on there." They walked on until they arrived at gehinnom where they saw a great gate. They opened it and realized that they probably weren't in gehinnom yet. Meanwhile, they noticed that one of them had disappeared. They opened a second gate and saw that this, too, was only a corridor—and that the second man had disappeared. The young man was all alone and considered whether he should go on or not. He said to himself: "Since I've come this far, I'll continue."

He went in and saw that this was gehinnom! Standing by the gate was a man wearing the talis [prayer shawl] and tefillin [phylacteries]. He asked the young man: "What are you doing here? Where do you come from?" Of course, he came from Mesibos, but the people of Mesibos were accustomed to saying that they came from the holy community of Bar that was close by. Thus the young man said: "I'm from the holy community of Bar and have come to see gehinnom."

Then he saw bodies that had been consumed by fire, like a brand plucked from the fire (Zech. 3:2), heap upon heap, just like sheaves on the thrashing floor.

The man at the gate cried: "If you're from the holy community of Bar, go to the other side of this heap. You'll find another young man from your community lying there." The visitor was ashamed to be seen by him, however, for he was considered an upright man, and so he turned back toward the gate and noticed that the bodies were lying peacefully and not being punished. He asked the man at the gate: "Why are these sinners not being punished today?" The man answered: "I see by your question that you neglected the '*Yaaleh ve-yavo*'[3] during your evening prayers because you've forgotten that this is the night of the new moon." And this was the case.

Then the young man asked the man at the gate to let him leave. "By no means will I let you pass!" The young man continued to implore him: "Let me go, I'm an upright man!" "Where was your righteousness" the man at the gate wanted to know, "when you went to collect the donations and entertained yourself with evil thoughts while doing so?" And he repeated all his thoughts to him. "I have to pay for my schooling," the young man replied. The man at the gate began to lick his lips and hissed: "Fine, very good. But I still can't let you leave."

Now the young man began to beg and to beseech the man at the gate, who finally gave him this advice: "Here, hide beneath my talis. The Prince of Gehinnom will come along any second now in the midst of a great storm. When the gate opens, sneak out behind him and go!"

As soon as the raging of the Prince of Gehinnom was heard in the distance, all the bodies began to tremble and quake, and the young man hid himself hastily beneath the man's prayer shawl. When the Prince of Gehinnom threw the gate open, the young man stole his way out and emerged from hell.

Unfortunately, a little bit of the storm wind penetrated into him, which caused him to cough, and this woke him up. The young man was unable to lose this cough from then on, and it lasted a full year. This was the illness that finally killed him.

As for the other man from Bar, the one he met in gehinnom, he lived on for only two more years after this event. (*H*, 111; *Praise*,113)

In these stories, the celestial instances employ disease or dreams to intervene in the life of an individual for purposes of chastisement, or else they use them to herald the beginning of the end, the imminent death of the person. Kafka himself surely stands within this tradition that attributes such realistic actuality to dreams and sees in them life-determining and therefore relevant events; after all, he took his own dreams so seriously that they not only motivated and characterized his stories, but even became the focus of his life: "As far as literature is concerned, my fate is very simple. My sense of depicting my dreamlike inner life has relegated everything else to the background, which has become terribly stunted and continues to fade away. Nothing else can ever satisfy me." (August 6, 1914; *Diaries*, 262)

11
"WOMEN HAVE A GREAT POWER"—THE FEMININE ELEMENT IN THE HIERARCHIES OF THE COURT

The women in Kafka's novels wield a dark power that even Joseph K. believed ought not be overlooked (*Trial*, 290). In his *Kafka Kommentar*, H. Binder claims that Kafka's female characters labor under the same ambiguity regarding their power as burdens Jewish society as a whole: women "are for the K.'s a means to an end, helpers and weapons in the confrontation with the outside world; in *The Man Who Was Lost Sight Of* (later: *Amerika*), on the other hand, they are temptresses diametrically juxtaposed to Karl's sexual innocence" (43). In traditional Jewish society, the woman is the mainstay of the home, the focal point of the family; she is the person whose modesty and diligence support the family and who cannot be praised enough for doing so. A parallel theme, however, and one particularly current in the ascetic literature of the Lurianic school, sees the woman in the role of temptress, the one who distracts the pious Kabbalist from his saintly thoughts and turns his attention to those of lust; she even pursues him in his dreams, thereby causing involuntary and sullying ejaculations. This role can hardly be overrated. The problem of sexual lust and of the wasteful spilling of one's seed gave rise to an entire literary genre, but the kabbalistic ascetic who sought to eliminate his carnal desires by means of extreme asceticism, cold baths, rolling oneself in the snow and fasting or who tried to repress them by constantly contemplating the Name of

God—such an ascetic had to perceive this inescapable power of sexuality as being the final and almost unsealable trap door belonging to the Other Side and its temptations. Rather in keeping with Moses Cordovero and his ideas, such a person was obviously unable to imagine the role of woman in any terms other than those that saw her as being a genuine part of that judicial apparatus whose sole purpose was to question man's conduct and bring his transgressions to light. According to Cordovero, the temptations of sex overtake a man from their origins in the sixth hall of impurity. Not only the sexual, but all forms of overt and subtle temptation are part of the judicial apparatus in the service of justice; its purpose is to test a person under judgment. Lilith, the mother of demons, embodies and incorporates all the powers of female seduction and is looked upon as the highest feminine element of the impure anti-sefirot. Like their divine counterparts, these anti-sefirot possess feminine powers as well. What Cordovero only hints at in his systematized excerpt from the Zohar is described in the Zohar itself with the following words (Zohar I:148a):

> Out of the mighty midday flame [of divine judgment] . . . sprouted forth a shameful plant that encompassed both the masculine and the feminine, red as the lily, and it spread along every path and wayside. The man is called Samael, his wife is always encompassed within him. Just as there are man and woman on the side of holiness, so also are there man and woman on the 'other side'[1], the one encompassed within the other. The wife of Samael is called the Snake, the Whore, the End of All Flesh, the End of Time. Two evil spirts sticking together, the spirit of the man is pointed, the spirit of the woman flows out upon all paths and all byways, looking to seduce mankind. Fool, he who draws close to her. She seizes him to kiss him, and pours him aged wine diluted with snake venom. As soon as he drinks, he follows after her. When she sees that his following has led him off the path of truth, she divests herself of all the jewels she put on for this fool. And this is the way she adorns herself to seduce mankind: her hair is as red as a rose, her face pink and white; six rings hang from her ears, and around her neck she wears Egyptian cords fashioned from the glorious materials of yore. Her mouth is slightly and

> sweetly open, her tongue as pointed as a sword; smooth as oil are her words, her lips as charmingly red as roses, sweeter than all the honey in the world, and purple is the color of her dress in ninety-nine patterns. The fool follows after her, drinks from his glass of wine and fornicates with her, seduced by her charms. And what does she do? She lets him sleep in bed while she climbs on high and accuses him with a false tongue and then gains permission to go back down again. If he wakes up, the fool, and thinks only to play around with her as before, she casts off her trinkets and turns into a mighty warrior who stands before the man in a firey garment. The man's body and soul tremble with terror; her nakedness is full of horrible eyes, the jagged sword in her hand drips with bitter drops. This warrior kills the fool and hurls him down to hell.

This bizarre description has its own peculiar echo in Kafka's personal life. "This afternoon," Kafka noted in his diary on November 16, 1911, "before falling asleep—and I never did fall asleep—the upper body of a woman made of wax lay down on top of me. Her face was bent back over mine, her left arm pressed against my chest."[2] A Kabbalist would surely have interpreted this as the visit of Lilith or one of her demons.

In Eastern European Judaism, on the other hand, there actually were those who saw something very good and very important in this kind of seduction. The talmudic saying: "At the place reserved for penitents, no righteous man may stand" (Babylonian Talmud Ber 34b; Sanhedrin, 99a) led many a pious Eastern European Jew to the conclusion that he who wants to reach this higher level of the penitent must first succumb to the realm of sin in order to have something to atone for. In this view, sexual temptation and relations with women have an almost beneficial power. Thanks to this involvement with sin, one can attain a higher level of sanctity. Such ideas were propagated not only by the heretical followers of Sabbatai Tzevi[3] but also by pious men still considered "orthodox." One such man was the Rabbi Aaron Samuel Kaidanover (died 1676/77) of Frankfurt, who went so far as to say that, if a man wanted to obey the biblical commandment of atonement, he must first have truly wallowed in sin.[4] The discussion of this question evidently drew wide circles. In his book *Olelot Efraim*, the famous

Prague preacher, Rabbi Ephraim Lunchitz (1550–1619) polemicized against the widespread interpretation of the above-mentioned talmudic passage that held that the penitent must first have gone to a secluded spot with a woman. Obviously, any righteous man was forbidden to do such a thing. The fact that Rabbi Ephraim was not just airing a private peeve with his objection is demonstrated by a letter written by a scholar who had made this particular cause his own. Rabbi Perez Ben Mosche wrote: "Why is the penitent greater than the righteous man? It seems to me because a totally righteous man is forbidden to be alone with a woman; he is not permitted to be alone in a room with her. As for the penitent, on the other hand, he is allowed to be there, he is allowed to be alone in a room with a woman, so that he may then make an act of atonement!" (Piekarz, 187) Significantly, this treatment equates the matter of sin and atonement with that of erotic temptation.

These arguments show that there were Jews within the Eastern European tradition who viewed the power of sex not only as a snare in the service of the celestial hierarchies of the court, but also and quite paradoxically, they also perceived it as being a stirrup toward a higher level on the path toward salvation. Joseph K., the land surveyor and Karl Rossmann in *The Man Who Was Lost Sight Of* also frequently turn to women on their way through the courts, through the castle and through alien America, and they expect to get some help from them along the way. Joseph K. was even forced to listen while the cleric reproached him during their conversation in the cathedral: "'You look for too much outside help,' said the cleric disapprovingly, 'and particularly from women. Don't you know that that is not true help?' 'Sometimes and even often I might say you were right,' said K., 'but not always. Women have a great power. If I could persuade a few women whom I know to work together on my behalf, I would have to get through.'" (*Trial*, 289f)

In Eastern European Judaism attitudes toward the helpful role of the feminine or even of the sexual were couched in even more positive terms at times, especially in those instances where the feminine element of the holy side was seen in the light of the sexual-erotic. In this view, the almost conjugal union with this feminine element of the divine world became the path of redemption, even if in a somewhat sublimated form. This is the burden of the following promise the Zohar makes to the pious worshipper who is the first to enter the synagogue in the morning (II: Bl. 131a):

> Hallowed be the holy people whose Lord bids them enter and calls them together to bind them close to Himself, when the holy people want to gather and enter the house of prayer. And the one who is the first to arrive will be joined in a union with the shekinah [the tenth and feminine power of the sefirotic system]. Come and see! The first one in the house of prayer, hallowed be he, for he stands on the level of the tzaddik [Sefira 9. He is the symbol of the phallus, by means of which the King, Sefira 6, unites with the shekinah] next to the shekinah. And that is the secret of the scripture: "Those that seek me earnestly will find me" (Prov. 8:17); he has ascended to the highest level.
>
> But if you say: The sages taught: the very hour that the Holy One, blessed be He, comes into the assembly house and fails to find ten men there, He becomes angry. And then you say that the shekinah unites with the one who is the first to come and that he stands on the level of the tzaddik? . . . [The objection is cleared away. Then: For it is so that] when someone enters the synagogue early and the shekinah comes and meets him there, then that counts as much as if all were there . . . . The shekinah unites with him immediately. And they sit in the [conjugal] union (*sivvuga*) and she converses with him and puts him in the place of the tzaddik.

Yeshivah students, scholars in the talmudic academy and other pious men were all assured that the shekinah steps into the place of their wives when they are separated from them (Zohar I: Bl. 49b). "Once he has said his prayers and his parting song of praise, the shekinah rests upon him; then, if he goes out, she unites with him (*isdavvagat*) so that male and female remain together."

To this holy feminine form of the pure side of the ten divine sefirot is now attributed judicial functions in its own right, as, for example, when it says: "If there is any defender in the world, it is the *Matronita* [mistress = shekinah]; if there is an accuser in the world, it is the Matronita" (Zohar III: Bl. 74a). The shekinah is like a mother who protects Israel, her son, against her husband (the

King and Lord of the sefirotic system); at the same time, she is also the one who chastises the son in order to move him to repentence.

Naturally there are also opposite attitudes toward the feminine which stem from the mystical concentration on the other world and thus reject everything of this world. I mention this here because there is a text in the hasidic literature that comes very close to a reflection Kafka noted in his diary. On August 14, 1913, Kafka wrote (*Diaries*, 198): "Coitus as punishment for the joy of being together. To live as ascetically as possible, more ascetically than a bachelor—that is the only possible way I could bear being married. But she?"

Compare that to the hasidic legend of Avraham the Angel, the son of Dov Ber, the great Maggid of Mezhirich:[5]

> The son of the Maggid, the saintly one, our teacher Rabbi Avraham, the Angel . . . , his piety and chastity and holiness were so wondrous and so astounding that they called him the Angel. . . .
>
> This is one of the tales they tell about him: After the wedding, as he was being led for the first time to the conjugal union with his pious wife, he raised his voice in horrible lamentations and sighs, because it was exceedingly difficult for him to lower himself so and become one with the material [the flesh]. Because of these lamentations, his wife fell into a swoon and they had a hard time reviving her; she remained ill for a long time. After a while, as he again went to the conjugal bed, he sighed and lamented as usual. However, this time his wife took heart and gathered all her strength until after the act, with the result that he fathered two god-fearing sons. . . . And from that moment on the Rav, the Angel, never 'knew' his wife again and remained abstinent all the days of his life.

12
THE JUDGMENT THEME IN EASTERN JEWISH FOLK TALES—KABBALAH AS NARRATIVE

"The final decisions of the court are not published, they are not even available to the judges, and as a result all that is left are legends about ancient court cases. Actually, though, the majority of them contain real acquittals; you can believe them, but they can't be proven" (*Trial*, 208). These words of the painter Titorelli might well serve as introductory motto for the Eastern Jewish legends whose themes of celestial courts and human life under the ban of judgment found widespread response. These are the stories generally known as hasidic tales.

In comparison with the kabbalistic tractates on the subject, an examination of the Eastern Jewish folk tales that treat this judgment theme shows that this different literary form, the short folk tale, produced a number of significant new aspects that lead one step closer to Kafka, especially as far as literary narrative is concerned. In stories, events are narrated, not described; the message is transposed into action. In the narrative tale, living persons of flesh and blood appear as accuser, accused and defender. They travel back and forth between the different levels of the celestial world of judgment and everyday reality without overstepping fundamental boundaries. As we have already seen, the dream is merely a functional and hardly extraordinary means of crossing the boundaries of one world to the other.

The heroes of these tales stride through the celestial halls of justice even in broad daylight while still remaining on earth. In other words, the Eastern Jewish tales, so very like Kafka's later *Trial*, depict the passage between different worlds which, in their view, are really one: this "one" is the astonishing coexistence of everyday life with the strange courtrooms. It is exactly the way Mendele the Bookseller once described the "Jewish" heaven: "Heaven is a big fair for the Jew," for "Jews are convinced not only in this world but in the next as well that one only needs set one's foot on the other side to be immediately greeted by the Angel of Death asking 'What's your name, neighbor?'" (Sfurim, 5).

Kafka himself recognized and deeply sensed his attraction to Eastern Jewish "hasidic" folk literature. In a letter dated the end of September 1917, he wrote to Max Brod: "The hasidic stories in the *Jüdisches Echo* are perhaps not the best, but, and I don't know why, all of these stories are the only thing Jewish in which I feel immediately and always at home, regardless of the mood I'm in" (*Letters*, 172)[1].

Kafka cultivated this feeling of being at home and actively pursued it by frequently joining[2] the followers of the Rabbi of Belz in Marienbad (1916) or by going to the house of the wonder-rabbi then living in Zizkov (September 14, 1915; *Diaries*, 297). Kafka obviously made the most of such opportunities to hear genuine hasidic tales that had not gone through the Western literary laundering of a transposition into German. The three diary renditions of such stories are one indication of this, though only a modest one.[3]

Kafka's reference to a feeling of kinship with this Jewish literary tradition can be verified objectively as well. This genre is composed of short stories employing narrative techniques, dramatic gestures and an understanding of the real world that in fact overlap with much in Kafka's stories. Kafka's sense of closeness to the tales of the Hasidim, however, probably had an even deeper source. The so-called hasidic tales were quite widespread throughout hasidic circles, and many of them do indeed express specific hasidic views. The majority of them, however, in their nature as well as in their themes, are sooner to be ascribed to the general genre of the Jewish folk tale, whose narrative tradition goes back beyond the Middle Ages and reaches deep into the talmudic and pre-talmudic period.

I think this is significant, because the tales of the Hasidim formulated ideas and views that had been part of the subsoil of Jewish folk piety for centuries.[4] These are the attitudes passed down from parents and grandparents—Jewish thought, in other words, that one could absorb even as a "peripheral ghetto inhabitant" or as a recently assimilated Jew lacking any substantial traditional upbringing. These attitudes and beliefs left their mark on the outwardly visible customs, the behavior and the actions of the simple Jew. It also explains why Kafka felt particularly attracted by and to this literature.

The strictures of the narrative form require these traditional tales of judgment to always start with the precise moment when the celestial "accusation becomes so strong" that it breaks into the everyday reality of the temporal world. As we have already seen from the Kabbalists' homilies and tractates, it is usually a disease or at least some type of adversity that marks the moment the individual is forced to take cognizance of his trial. In the hasidic tales it is more frequently an announcement by the rebbe who then knows how to turn the misfortune to good avail via his role as successful advocate, or else it is an unexpected or unknown messenger who informs the accused of his impending trial. Something like this happens in the following tale, where two dead women appear to a pious man in his dream. As it turns out, these two women are none other than his own mother and grandmother:

> A famous pious Hasid . . . was sitting on the night that marked the first year of his mother's passing, and he was reading mishnah for her soul. In the midst of his learning he feel asleep. [During his sleep] he heard a voice from outside calling his name. He jumped up at once and went out. He found two departed people standing there, dressed in white garments. He recognized one of the deceased as his mother, but he did not know the other. His mother said: "I am your mother and this is your grandmother. My son, we've come to tell you that there are mighty accusations against you in the celestial court, and the death sentence has been announced. Every member of our family has spoken up in your favor, but it hasn't accomplished a thing. Therefore, my son, see what you can do on your own behalf. . ."[5]

This trial intrudes completely unexpectedly into the life of the hero and, despite the strange, unworldly message, the proceedings have concrete effects on the everyday life of the accused. He immediately pushes his daily routines aside in order to attend to the matter of his trial, which, in this case, means looking for an appropriate attorney or advocate—but more about that later.

A second tale, also very reminiscent of Joseph K.'s arrest, deserves mention here as well. The accused in this story is an obviously pious man who experienced the following events while studying the Torah:

> He sat down to do his customary daily studies. Suddenly a messenger appeared, but he didn't know who it was who was calling him. He got up from his book and went outside. A storm wind swept by, carrying him many miles into the desert, where it left him standing in terror. He had no idea what sin he was being punished for . . . And lo, in the distance he spied a brightly lit house. He thought to himself: surely this is a robbers' den. Nevertheless, he wanted to get closer—but his limbs were leaden. He finally crept his way wearily on all fours and, as he was sitting before the house, he suddenly heard a voice from within saying: "Clear the path for David, the King of Israel! . . . and after that: "Clear the path for Rabbi Israel Baal Shem Tov!"[6]

While waiting outside the house, the man listens as the people inside sit in judgment over him. The sentence is death! Nevertheless, the crafty Baal Shem Tov succeds in playing upon the honor of the accuser David to achieve an alternative verdict, which is then presented to him as he waits outside; he is to choose between the two alternatives. He accepts, is wafted back into his own house and immediately transforms the stipulations of the celestial Davidian judgment into concrete aspects of his daily routine.

Something very similar happens to Joseph K. An unfamiliar messenger leads the man, with no explanations, to a strange place; in a house that seems to him to be a robbers' den, he finds a court sitting in judgment over him. He himself remains excluded outside the door and eventually returns to his daily routine which from that moment on is essentially determined by the stipulations imposed by this strange court. The advocate, like the accused man himself, hails from the same temporal and material world of this side, and, like him, has access to the celestial Davidian court in the "robbers' den."

In other variants of these same tales, it is a dream or feverish delirium that provides direct access to the celestial court, whereas the hasidic rebbes have unrestricted access to these heavenly chancelleries at any time, day or night.

The actual location of the court in the hasidic tales is naturally first and foremost heaven with its various halls; occasionally such judicial halls are unexpectedly located in the Garden of Eden or even in something resembling a robbers' den in the middle of the desert, as the last example had it. At times the celestial chancelleries are reminiscent of the proverbial Jewish *shul* where great convocations and often deafening tumult reigned. Also striking is the number of chambers. Trial participants have to scurry from hall to hall to find where the court holding jurisdiction over their case is to convene. When Michel of Zolochev stormed before a celestial court "with a great cry" to present his case about the burning of hasidic books, the court let him know that "this does not belong before our court, but higher and higher still (stands a watchman and over them still higher ones)" (cf. Eccles. 5:7; also *Praise*, 260f), whereupon he charged ahead. In the midst of this noisy rushing through the judicial halls, it can sometimes happen that the doors are abruptly bolted right in front of one's nose. This was the fate, for example, of the advocates' prayers, which, like Kafka's accused, hang around in the passage ways of the court until they finally gain admittance. The Baal Shem Tov related such an instance in one of the tales discussed above: "and [I] passed through one world after another . . . until I came to one hall . . . in this hall I found fifty years of prayers that had been unable to ascend any farther" (Mintz, 64; *Praise*, 56). Another told how they had just loaded the prayers of a lifetime onto the scales of justice when an angel appeared and blew them all away with one mighty snort:[7]

> A story of the saintly son of the divine Rav, our teacher Michel of Zolochev, Rabbi Joseph of Hannipoli. . .
>
> One day he was very sick, close to death . . . , and as he was lying there, sick as he was, he saw that all his good deeds were

> being weighed. They produced all the prayers he had ever recited from his childhood to that very hour, and not one single one was missing. Suddenly he saw a fearful angel coming toward them and saying: "What are these prayers supposed to mean?" He blew on them and scattered them with a single puff—and only one prayer was left behind. . . .

The bailiffs of these celestial courts are just as unpredictable as Kafka's—they peremptorially bolt the doors of the court whenever a potential advocate turns up (Mintz, 72; *Praise*, 75).

Another man, having lost his way in the vestibules of hell and who was being interrogated by a watchman, began to flatter him, whereupon the watchman "began to lick his chops and hissed: 'very good, very good.'" The watchman ultimately hid the transgresssor under his prayer shawl and let him escape at an appropriate moment (*H*, 111; *Praise*, 113).

Walter Benjamin expressed a very perceptive insight when he wrote to Scholem: "I think the key to understanding Kafka would fall to the person who appreciates the humorous side of Jewish theology" (*Briefwechsel*, 293); for look and listen as one may, in these celestial courts everything seems to depend more upon personal contacts and less upon an objective and well-founded argument or even upon proof of innocence. Take, for example, little Joseph of Hannipoli in the previous tale, the youth who was standing helplessly before his judges in one of the celestial halls without knowing why, when his father and another rebbe happened to pass by while attending to another matter. Begged by the boy for their assistance, they both promise to help him, each one adding the caveat: "if I don't forget." Their own case is more important to both of them, and they do in fact forget the poor boy (Mintz, 163; *Praise*, 260).

What one needs before such a court is a reliable helper, someone who knows his way around the court and has influence on high—a man like the Baal Shem Tov, for example, who enjoys high regard in the upper world and constantly storms through the celestial halls with a great deal of noise and commotion, "roaring like a bull." All he has to do is say the word (Mintz, 163; *Praise*, 261) for the court to let the accused person go. One such man, whose trial was still pending long after his death and who was therefore being detained in a chamber somewhere between gehinnom and the Garden of Eden, said bluntly to the angel who was guarding him: "Get up, run to the court and tell them I was a friend of Rabbi Elimelech, and that I don't want to stay in this room."[8] The delinquent came to this bold decision after he learned how great was the respect the former friend of his youth, Elimelech of Lisensk (1717–87) enjoyed in heaven: "When I heard that, I remembered that I had been a friend, indeed like a brother, to Rabbi Elimelech. So I thought: if Rabbi Elimelech is so highly esteemed in heaven and I was his friend and I served him, then they'll let me in the Garden of Eden for his sake" (26).

In the previous story about the two women messengers of court, the dead grandmother says to her accused grandson:

> You have only one chance, and that is the Rav Dov Ber of Lubavitch,[9] he is highly regarded up there. All they have to do is hear his name mentioned up there and the celestial court trembles—so take my advice, go to his holy reverence, surely he will do something.[10]

In other words, what is needed here is not a knowledge of the legal halakhic codes, but rather connections and infuence—even ignorance on the part of the advocate can occasionally prove beneficial. For example, when the Jews once beseeched Rabbi Elimelech to do what he could to lift a verdict Heaven had imposed on them, he said he couldn't help because he knew all the details of the situation. He then told them they "must go to a tzaddik who does not know the reason for the sentence and has no knowledge of the verdict either; such a man can then pray that the verdict be lifted; perhaps he can do something."[11]

There is an additional point to be made here, one that I consider particularly important for an understanding of these courts and one which can contribute directly to a deeper understanding of the trial procedures in Kafka's works. It has been mentioned before in various kabbalistic tractates, namely: the interrelatedness of the apparently separated spheres of the celestial court and the temporal habitation of man. Both levels must properly be looked upon as two sides of the same coin, as one single reality. A particularly instructive example taken from one judgment tale is cited below as an illustration of this unity. It contains many of the motifs just discussed: the life-long trial, the sudden intrusion of judgment into everyday life, and the cunning of the helpers before the court. In addition, this story also introduces a type of execution that lacks nothing of the horror of Kafka's scene with the knife in the quarry, which depicts the conclusion of Joseph K.'s trial. This story is found in the collection of legends about the Baal Shem Tov:

> One day the Besht suffered such an attack of weakness that he was unable even to speak. As he lay there, he motioned to the people standing around that they should bind the phylacteries on him as quickly as possible. And then, wearing the tefillin, he lay there for a few hours, and only gradually regained his speech.
>
> When they asked him what had happened, he said: "An old sin of my youth arose again over me and brought a strong accusation against me in heaven. But my heavenly rabbi [Ahijah the Shilonite] ran up to me and said: "Hurry! Put on the tefillin!"
>
> Then the divine accuser came, dressed in the garb of a mighty warrior with a large sword and a long spear, and he wanted to cut my head off. But because of the tefillin, he couldn't harm me. He raged at me furiously in Russian: "Take these strips of leather off or else I'll skewer you!" But I didn't pay any attention to him. He roared and roared until he vaporized away.[12]

Once again it is the clever advocate who cunningly thwarts the obviously justified accusation. However, I am more interested in the other aspect. Putting on the tefillin here on earth can directly affect the outcome of the trial taking place in heaven, and what's more: what happens here below is itself a part of those judicial proceedings—routine daily activities are legally relevant.

According to a report in the *Book of the Godfearing* by Elasar Askari (Asikri) (1533–1600), the Kabbalist Joseph Gikatilla had already resorted to the same means in the thirteenth century:

> One day it happend that the Rav, our master Joseph Gikatilla, fell sick and was close to death. He was sleeping and yet wasn't sleeping, kept watch and was still not awake,[13] when he

> saw that two men were weighing his sins and his merits on the scale, and they held the balance.
>
> Then he awoke, gathered all his strength together, took the tefillin and put them on. He began to feel better immediately and climbed out of death back into life, for he tipped the scale in favor of his merits.[14]

In another instance, it is an argument between the Besht and a woman in an inn that unexpectedly turns out to be part of a celestial trial. In the argument, the woman took the part of a notorious adulterer, maintaining that he was basically innocent since he did not know the Torah very well and therefore was not aware of how serious his offense was. These very words of this woman, who cleverly introduces the legal principle of ignorance of the law, served as an acceptable defense before the celestial court that was at that very moment in session (Mintz, 94; *Praise*, 121):

> Toward evening [the pious Rebekkele] came . . . to the Baal Shem Tov and said: "There's a dying physician over there; pray for him that he might live, for the situation is grave." The Besht responded: "There'll soon be one less adulterer on earth!"
>
> "Who says that's so?" she snapped back at him. He asked the people standing around him: "Is it the truth I say?" "Yes, the truth," they assure him. She didn't give up and protested as follows: "First of all, they didn't see how the makeup-stick went into its case[15]. And what's more, he doesn't know the law and therefore doesn't know how serious this offense is. Had he known, he wouldn't have sinned."[16]
>
> Actually, the Besht had already heard the accusation against the sick man in heaven above, and he repeated it before the woman so that she might defend him. And lo, her speech in his defense was accepted above, and the physician was cured of his disease.

An especially fine example of the thoroughly amusing legal relevance of everyday life is the incident that tells of the Besht interrupting his prayer and suddenly leaving the synagogue to go chat with a Catholic priest in the marketplace. During the course of their conversation, which included a discussion of celibacy, the

Besht succeeds in arousing such lascivious desires in the saintly priest that he sullies himself with an ejaculation. By means of this staining of the pious Christian man a celestial charge against the obviously less holy Israel is aborted (*H*, 263; *Praise*, 248):

> On the eve of Yom Kippur, shortly before the *Kol Nidre*, when the whole congregation had already assembled in the bet midrash, the Besht stood before the Ark but did not start the prayer. He was very disconcerted and everyone noticed it. The congregation waited until they felt they could wait no longer, and they finally began to weep because each one understood perfectly well that this was not an insignificant event.
>
> The rav stood there for a long time. As he happened to look out the window, he saw an old priest walking by. The rav hastened outside to meet him, caught up with him and began a conversation. He asked the priest how he was doing and so lost himself in the conversation that he accompanied the man all the way home.
>
> The rav asked the priest why he had never taken a wife, particularly since God hadn't created the world to leave it empty, ("but rather that it should be inhabited", Isa. 45:18).
>
> "And even if what you say is true," the priest responded, "our laws prohibit a priest from taking a wife." The rabbi debated this topic for a long time, stressing that in his old age he should definitely fulfill the commandment to be fruitful and multiply (Gen. 1:28); the priest should renounce his post. The priest, however, felt that marriage to a woman of a lower social standing would be below his dignity and that no woman from an appropriate family would ever consent to marry him.
>
> The rav went on to say that a nobleman with a very pretty daughter lived in the neighborhood; he was certain this prince would agree to give his daughter in marriage to the priest. He talked on and on in this vein until the priest's mind was diverted and the princess' beauty struck a chord in the cleric's heart. He was overcome by a deep desire and experienced an orgasm.
>
> At this moment the rav hastened back to the bet midrash and began to pray the *Kol Nidre*.
>
> After the prayer, the members of his congregation gathered around the rav while he explained what had happened. "An

accusation [against Israel] had just been raised [in heaven], a charge so great that our prayers were unable to ascend precisely because this particular priest had managed to live as long as he had without every having experienced an ejaculation. That's why I had to engage him in such a conversation until he had an orgasm."

In response to their question as to how he knew the priest had had an ejaculation, he said that from that moment on it was impossible for him to stand anywhere near the man.

"And with God's help all the accusers were silenced."

A similar tale from the same book (*H*, 260; *Praise*, 242):

One day, as the rav was leading the prayer before the Ark, he interrupted his devotions and went out to the street in front of the synagogue. There he found a goy selling wood. He bought the whole load, whereupon the goy followed the rabbi to the bet midrash to deliver the wood. In response, the Besht offered to pay the peddlar not only for the wood, but for the delivery of it as well. To top it all, he also gave the man a brandy. The goy cried: "Praised be the God of the Jews, whose people are so saintly!" Had one of the uncircumcised bought his wood, he surely would not have been offered anything extra.

When his students wanted to know why the Besht had broken off in mid-prayer, he told them this reason. While praying, he had seen that charges were being made in heaven against the people of Israel who happened to live in their villages. These charges accused the Jews of cheating the goyim in business transactions. The only way to silence the accuser was to have this uncircumcised man praise the Jews to the sky. This silenced the accusations (in the celestial court).

In these and similar stories, the separation of the celestial judicial sphere from everyday terrestrial life dissapears completely, and someone on earth may have the same experience as Joseph K., who was repeatedly surprised to learn that ever new, unexpectedly routine, even uncouth scenes become a part of the court and its regular proceedings.

This rather blunt introduction addresses a thought already mentioned above, namely: the totality of human life with all its apparently insignificant banalities plays a role in that judicial procedure under whose ban it has been placed.

The Eastern Jewish folk tale is kabbalistic Jewish judicial theology turned literature. Although this narrative tradition is aimed at the broad masses of simple people, it treats serious questions concerning the justification of man before the celestial courts that constantly control his every deed in a manner—offensively, bluntly, crudely and embarrassingly—we already know from our familiarity with Kafka's treatment of these same themes. He thus demonstrates his closeness to Eastern Jewish thought not only theologically, but stylistically as well. What connects them both is the freedom to depict serious questions touching upon theology and the meaning of human life in a scandalously droll way, very closely related to the unsavory side of mortal existence while it remains simultaneously aware of nothing short of absurd alienation. The same will be found in other tales originating in the Jewish regions of Eastern Europe.

13
THE ANIMAL STORIES

"Perhaps the butcher's knife would be a deliverance for this animal."

The heir of the strange animal, half-cat, half-lamb, that weeps human tears and possesses human ambition in Kafka's story "A Hybrid" (*Stories*, 295f) poses the compassionate question introducing this chapter, a question that many Eastern Jewish kabbalistic tales would have to have answered in the affirmative. Common to all these stories is the divine judgment over man, the theme Gershom Scholem had already perceived as being central to all of Kafka's works (*Friendship*, 212). In this particular story, the divine judgment over man finds its expression in the punishment of "gilgul"—reincarnation or the transmigration of the soul. This sentence is imposed upon those souls whose sins cannot be expunged in purgatory or those individuals who had failed to achieve the perfection of their soul during their lifetime. Numerous reincarnations via gilgul not only result in bringing the human soul back in the form of a new [human] life, but in the form of an animal, a plant or a mineral as well.

Isaac Luria's Kabbalah lays the foundation for the theological/anthropological background of the gilgul stories. Luria's teachings spread from sixteenth century Palestine via Italy into Eastern and Middle Europe and immediately became the dominant Jewish theology in a variety of popularizing tractates and moralistic texts. According to this doctrine, a catastrophe occurred during the creative process in which the Light emanating from the hidden Godhead, the *En-Sof*, was supposed to take on the shape of a stabile configuration of light encompassing the revealed divine world and the whole universe. The initial structures, or vessels, which were to hold the Infinite and thus make creation possible, were unable to contain the fullness of the Infinite Light, and they broke into pieces. Light streamed back into the concealed Godhead, but a portion of it plunged to the depths along with the shards of the broken vessels where it became the realm of the shells and of evil. In a second attempt, the emanation of the Light did succeed in establishing sturdier light structures, and thus came into being the world of reconstruction or cosmic repair, the world of *tikkun*. The concluding act of this restructuring of the emanation into one whole and undifferentiated world was reserved for the First Man, Adam, who was supposed to complete and perfect this two-pronged structural plan for the universe through an opportune mating with his wife.

In his impatience, however, the First Man did not wait for the proper moment for this act and thus not only left the concluding tikkun undone, but actually caused a new cosmic break in which every cosmic tier sank to a lower level. They were not alone in this fall, for the soul of the First Man (which, in keeping with the number of parts of the human body as well as of the traditional commandments of the Torah, was made up of 613 psychical roots) splintered and dispersed into innumerable psychical sparks as well. It was now up to these sparks to do the work of repair (tikkun) that was assigned to Adam, and it was to be accomplished through an infinite number of individual deeds. These sparks were planted in the bodies of humans, in animals, in plants and in minerals, in ever recurring gilgulim or reincarnations, until each and every spark should reach its individual specific tikkun and once again reunite with and become part of Adam's macro-soul. Only after this macro-soul is restored can man, Adam, accomplish the work of cosmic repair (tikkun) assigned to him. It is at this point that the Messiah will enter the reconstructed world, not as its fulfillment, but as a beneficiary. Kafka expresssed an analagous belief when he said: "The Messiah will only come when He is no longer needed, He will only come one day after His arrival, He will not come on the last day, but on the very last day" (*Wedding*, 67).

The Jewish folk tale took up this theme not long after Isaac Luria's death (1572) and created new and unique narrative forms for dealing with it. The result were stories about the transmigration of souls and of acts of tikkun never before known to the Jewish folk tale. In these stories, souls that had been reincarnated into animals for the most part must bear the punishment of gilgul while remaining ever aware, whether openly or hiddenly, of their previous life with its unique traits as well as its transgressions. These two residuals leave their mark on the present life of these creatures in much the same way as the man-ape in Kafka's "Report to an Academy" observes: "The storm that drove me out of my past has subsided; today it is not much more than a draft that cools my heels" (*Stories*, 155). The mere report of such an existence, which has already left the "hole from which it came" far behind, is calculated to provoke "the judgment of man", which also happens to be the way the man-ape views his own situation. The very report can be taken as a justification of the new life. As such, it also represents the core of the traditional gilgul stories, which is to justify one's current life by reporting about a previous one. The hero's individuality, his existence and his experiences are thus rendered understandable and acceptable as being part of an encroaching "trial." Gilgul stories explain human life and human suffering as but one phase in a judicial process extending over several generations. One must resign oneself to it or try to make one's own contribution to turning it around.

As far as the admonishing Lurianic texts are concerned, life in gilgul is a life in judgment, a life of constant justification:

> Know that a herald goes before every person who finds himself in gilgul and every person who was condemned in the celestial court. This herald announces his punishment and his sin, and does so for all times; such a person will never escape as long as this verdict or this gilgul hangs over him.
>
> [If the person has been condemned to gilgul in water] there is also a guardian angel who throttles him in the water and drives him through this gilgul—and so it goes with all reincarnations. These angels never leave his side until the sentence has been completed. Moreover . . . a court goes before them as well, which judges them continuously and alters their punishments, all in keeping with the sentence they have deserved.[1]

If a person is reincarnated in an animal, he knows that his previous life was that of a human being on this earth.[2] Vice versa, the experienced eye can discover the residual gestures of an animal in a man who had been an animal in a previous life, just like the narrator in Kafka's "The Advocate": "We have a new advocate, Dr. Bucephalus. Little of his outward appearance is reminiscent of the time he spent as the Great Alexander's steed. Even so, any person familiar with the details will notice a few things. Just the other day on the outside terraced staircase I saw a simple, naive court assistant stare at the advocate with the expert look of a regular patron of the races as the latter lifted his leg and climbed up the stairs with a stride that resounded on the marble" (*Stories*, 125).

The Lurianic author of seventeenth century texts on morality quoted above said essentially the same thing, albeit less gracefully and less poetically:

> In the writings of Ari [Isaac Luria] we read: When you see people with a cocky expression, who have no shame before other people, know that they have previously wandered through gilgul as cattle, as wild beasts or unclean birds and, like them, they lack all sense of shame, for these people act according to what they have learned previously.[3]

In the stories that follow we will come across such men whose "trained eye" can recognize a soul in gilgul at every turn, whether in man or in animal.

It is not at all extraordinary for the story of a person's gilgul to reach back as far as did that of Dr. Bucephalus. The Lurianic texts pride themselves on being able to trace the fate of souls as far back as biblical times, even to Cain and Abel. It is said of the Baal Shem Tov, for example, the founder of Hasidism, that he was the reincarnation of Rav Saadyah Gaon, the first Jewish philosopher of the Middle Ages (ninth century) (*H*, 105; *Praise*, 106). According to the legend of the golem, Chief Rabbi Löw of Prague used to claim his soul housed a spark of King David's soul, and his adversary, the cleric Thaddeus, who persecuted the Jews, was supposed to have had a spark of the soul of Goliath the Philistine[4] in him. In fact, all the Jews in Prague who did not obey the Rav supposedly bore the souls of Korah's rebels, who, according to Numbers 16, once made so bold as to challenge Moses.[5] All of this may have been known to Kafka, who actually attempted his own golem legend in April, 1916 (*Diaries*, 310).

In his book on transmigration (*Sha'ar ha-Gilgulim*), Luria's disciple Hayyim Vital (1542–1620) traced the reincarnations of the souls of Cain and Abel. These passed through, among others, Jacob and Esau, Nadab and Abihu, the prophets Samuel, Elijah and Elisha, through the Maccabbean Mattathias, the early talmudic scholars Rabbi Akiba and Jochen ben Sakkai, the late talmudic scholar Rabbi Ahai, the even later gaon Rav Shabha, via Don Vidal of Toulouse, Maimonides (twelfth century) and Nachmanides (thirteenth century) (117), to finally arrive at himself (126b), whereby the relationships work themselves out in repeating behavior patterns or fates of the respective periods, rather like the way things happen in the following brief tale about Isaac Luria and his neighbors:

The Cantankerous Neighbors[6]

Once there were two neighbors of the rav who were constantly quarreling with him. One day he said to them: "You still won't stop? If I wanted to, I could make it so that the earth opens its mouth and swallows you up!"

Whereupon they asked him what he meant by that. He explained that they were the gilgul of Dathan and Abiram[7] and were still squabbling and bickering with him, who was a spark of Moses. That's what his words meant.

Kafka's story that seems to be most closely related to the gilgul theme is the one about the hunter Gracchus.

"Are you dead?" the mayor asks the hunter who had just come ashore. "Yes," said the hunter, "as you can see. Many years ago, it must have been an awfully long time ago, I fell down a cliff in the Black Forest— that's in Germany— while chasing a chamois. Ever since then I've been dead." "But you are still alive," protested the mayor. "To be sure," replied the hunter, "to be sure I am still alive. My funeral barge missed its mark . . . so, after my death, I am still roving . . . through all the lands of the earth" (*Stories*, 272).

Even if the Flying Dutchman and other mythological motifs known to Kafka may have influenced this story, its close relation to the Jewish theme of reincarnation is incontestable, especially when one considers the further dialogue between the mayor and the hunter:

> "And you have no part in the world beyond?" asked the mayor with a frown. "I am," replied the hunter, "always on the great stairway that leads upwards. I hang around on this broad staircase, sometimes up, sometimes down, sometimes higher, sometimes lower, sometimes on the left, sometimes on the right, always on the move. The hunter has turned into a butterfly."[8]

The uneasy existence between life and death of Kafka's hunter Gracchus contains many details reminiscent of the gilgul stories about a certain Rosa Bat Pircha, whose unsteady spirit was interrogated by the Kabbalist Yehudah Ben Moshe Patia (1849–1942). This spirit, which was restlessly tossed from court to court and from verdict to verdict, reported, among other things: "After I spent two years hovering about the place where wild animals live, I was finally condemned to fly over the ocean's edge, year after year for seven years, then two more years over the graves of my native Bagdad. . . ."[9] This Rosa bore the fate that Hayyim Vital briefly summarized in his book about reincarnation (c. 22.58af):

> Know that transgressors come to gehinnom after death and receive their punishment, and they remain there for twelve whole months, to atone for their sins.
>
> However, there are other sinners as well, about whom the Bible says: "And the souls of thine enemies, them shall he sling out as from the hollow of a sling" [I Sam. 25:29]; these are not even worthy of falling into gehinnom after their death so that they might expiate their sin.
>
> Instead, their soul is rejected and falls from one repulsion into the other, the strangest forms of gilgul . . . and no definite time limit is set for them. Sometimes they wander twenty years in gilgul or a hundred or a thousand—it all depends on the severity of the sins they committed in this life. . . .
>
> After a person's death and before he is allowed to enter gehinnom, all his sins are called to account in various forms

> of punishment, all of which are forms of gilgul. That means he is reincarnated either in minerals, in plants, in animals or in human beings. And the majority of people do not escape this reincarnation.

The restlessness of the unreconciled soul along the lines of a Gracchus and the existential correspondences between one's previous and one's current life, as in the case of Kafka's man-ape, Dr. Bucephalus, and the dapple-gray horse called Isabella which will be discussed below, are primarily concerned with the ethical-moral realm in the kabbalistic gilgul stories. One's well-being in the present life is always predetermined by one's behavior in the previous life. The person who sinned with water is punished with water in a subsequent reincarnation, as the story of the Baal Shem and the frog (see Appendix) shows, or as happens in the following story of a ritual slaughterer whose former profession plays a role in his soul's gilgul, or, finally, as demonstrated by the lecherous Jew reincarnated into a dog. Life in the body of an animal or in the form of a plant or mineral is thus always conceived as punishment for sins committed during the previous life. In reversals, such as the case of Dr. Bucephalus, the man-ape, and Isabella, a stigma from the previous chastisement in animal form still clings to the human life.

The Eastern Jewish gilgul stories always look upon human life in animals and in things as a life in judgment, as a life in sin and in atonement yet to be made. According to Lurianic Kabbalah, the people who live with such animals always bear a very personal responsibility for them, because these animals share the same spiritual root as the person who actually comes in contact with them. In other words, the person who encounters an animal participates, as it were, in the animal's sin and is obligated, as a related soul, to demonstrate active solidarity by assisting the soul in the animal achieve its atonement. We should keep this in mind when trying to understand at least a few of Kafka's animal figures.

It is no coincidence, for example, that the half-cat, half-lamb creature in Kafka's story "A Hybrid," is an old family heirloom. "It is an heirloom from my father's estate" (*Stories*, 295). "It sticks to the family that raised it. This is probably not just some kind of unusual loyalty, but rather the proper instinct of an animal that has many in-laws on earth, but perhaps no one single blood relation, and to whom the shelter it has found among us is therefore a sacred thing" (*Stories*, 296). Even as an animal, Gregor Samsa, the protagonist in "The Metamorphosis" (*Stories*, 39ff) remains part of his family. The ties binding animals and things to the human world in Kafka's works are not up-front and natural ones. Rather they are ties that lie hidden behind the outward apearance, ties that can more than likely be explained by the kabbalistic doctrine of reincarnation.

The following brief tale of a person-to-person gilgul shows very clearly how a new, current life is marked by deeds done in the previous one, by the sin committed during that life. It also demonstrates the solidarity among families of human souls that continues for generations and which obligates an apparently innocent man like the hero of our tale, Hayyim Vital, to perform acts of atonement:

The Careless Shohet [*Ritual Slaughterer*][10]

> One day the saintly and pure Rabbi Isaac Luria, blessed be his memory, suddenly called his pupil, our teacher Hayyim Vital, to him and said: "I charge you to oversee [during ritual slaughtering] the removal of the ligaments and fat [which people are forbidden to eat], to make sure that the men are doing it correctly." Rabbi Hayyim Vital asked: "Rabbi, what is so special about today?" He said: "A little while ago the soul of a tzaddik named Joshua Suryano entered into you via gilgul, because he once erroneously ate a tiny piece of forbidden fat. For this reason, his soul has not been accepted on high until such time as this blemish should be rectified. By your watching over the removal of fat and ligaments for a period of time, you will provide rectification for his soul (tikkun) so that it can ascend on high to take its rightful place of honor. This good deed will be done to him through you . . ."

According to Luria's teachings, the same correspondences between the previous and the present life are especially valid for reincarnations into non-human bodies. Occasionally, the texts provide detailed correspondences between the transgression and the respective punishment that tell why a person has to live as a leaf on a tree, as a bird in the air, or as a creature in water. Hayyim Vital even mentions gilgul in dogs, which is certainly not rare in Kafka's works, and classifies it under those forms especially reserved for men who commit adultery with non-Jewish women.[11] In the following tale, such fornication took place between two Jews (Benajahu, 238):

> Once there was a pious man by the name of Rabbi Abraham Ibn Pua, blessed be his memory. He was very rich and generous toward the poor and the suffering. He had a neighbor who had done some business with Rabbi Abraham's wife, for his wife was skilled in business.
>
> One day the neighbor suddenly fell sick and lay a long time in illness until his flesh rotted and his shame disintegrated and fell away from him in bits and pieces. He spent a lot of money on doctors, but found no cure for his ailment. He screamed out in pain so loudly he could be heard everywhere, and he finally died in great agony.
>
> Several years after his death people noticed an ugly black dog prowling around Rabbi Abraham's house. The people who saw it were frightened as if by a demon, God forbid. The dog always found a way to get into the house, and they had to chase it out again with sticks.
>
> The dog was standing at the door whenever Rabbi Abraham left his house in the morning to go to synagogue; it waited until the door opened and then it quickly slipped inside. Rabbi Abraham chased it away every time and ordered the door be bolted behind him. When he returned from synagogue, still early in the morning, he found the dog scratching at the door and jumping against it in an effort to push it open; again Rabbi Abraham chased him away.
>
> One day, however, it happened that Rabbi Abraham left his house early in the morning and forgot to bolt the inner as well as the outer door. The dog immediately sprang into the house, went from the winter room into the chamber whose door was likewise open, and he entered the bedroom where he found Rabbi Abraham's wife sleeping. He jumped up on her, bit her sorely all over her body, and then ran away.
>
> All of this was brought and told to the saintly Ari [Isaac Luria], blessed be his memory. He explained that this woman had slept with that neighbor, and it was his soul that was now

> wandering about in the shape of the dog. The Rabbi's wife had once seduced him and led him to this sinful act, and that's why he was now seeking revenge.
>
> They made the wife take an oath to tell the truth and she confessed that it had been so, that she had slept with that neighbor. That's why his shame had fallen off and his soul was reincarnated into the dog.

An echo of this sexuality theme in reincarnation can perhaps be found in the strange episode in "The Investigations of a Dog" where the scientist, while still a pup, encountered those seven dogs and had to wonder: "But weren't they really dogs, though? How could they not have been dogs . . . didn't I hear their soft calls just now, while I was listening closely. . . ." And then: "They had good reason to be quiet, always supposing that they did so out of a sense of shame. Look how they behaved; I didn't notice it before because of the music, but they really cast off all sense of shame. The miserable creatures did the most ridiculous and the most indecent things all at the same time: they walked upright on their hind legs. Pfooie! They exposed themselves and boldly showed off their nakedness; they were very proud of themselves. Once, when they momentarily followed their better instincts and lowered their front paws, they were literally frightened, as if it were a mistake, as if nature were a mistake. They quickly lifted their legs again and their glance seemed to beg forgiveness for the fact that they had had to hold back a bit in their sinfulness" (*Stories*, 338).

By the way, the expression "good instinct" (*good yezer*) is a popular technical term taken from Jewish anthropology; its opposite, the even more frequently occurring "evil instinct" (*Yezer ha-Ra*) refers to that drive whose essential and almost proverbial activity is encompassed by the term sexuality.[12] All of this at least goes to show that Kafka described this sexual moral lapse on the part of the dogs in terms of specifically Jewish anthropological/theological concepts. A Jewish saying actually ascribes the giving in to one's desires to dogs: "Only dogs follow their instincts."[13]

Hartmut Binder (*Kommentar E.*, 263) makes similar observations with respect to the "bachelors" in the *Castle* who "abandon themselves to dog-like desires" (*Castle*, 345) as well as to passages in letters to Brod such as this one from 1917: "F. has just written a few lines. I can't catch her, or better: I catch her, but I can't hold on to her. I bark and run circles around her like a nervous dog around a statue" (*Letters*, 164). A diary entry of the same period reads: "Live the way we have to, don't run around so like a dog"[14], or:

> My only fear—nothing worse has probably ever been said or heard— my only fear is that I will never be able to possess you. That, in the best of circumstances, like a senseless and loyal dog, I will be limited to kissing the hand you absent-mindedly reach out to me; this won't be a sign of love, but merely a sign of the desperation of an animal condemned to silence and an eternal distance. (*Felice*, 351f)

One may well ask whether there isn't an expression of this type of guilt complex in Kafka's self-representation as a dog-like man, and all the more so since he was himself quite occupied with thoughts about the doctrine of reincarnation so very widespread within Eastern Judaism. In a diary entry of 1922, Kafka noted: "Hesitation before birth. If there really is such a thing as the transmigration of the soul, then I have not yet attained the lowest stage. My life is the hesitation before birth" (January 24, 1922; *Diaries*, 350; *Critical Edition*, 888). And: "Proofs that there really is a former life: I've seen you before, [as well as] the miracles of time immemorial and [those] on the last day" (*Wedding*, 88).

Such re-encounters as Kafka hints at here turn up as a frequently repeated element in the Lurianic tales of gilgul. They serve to explain the otherwise incomprehensible guilt one finds oneself entangled in for no apparent reason, and they do so by attributing it to transgressions stemming from an earlier life. The traditional stories about reincarnation represent folk attempts to understand human fate and one's state of health in terms of a web of sin. Such an outlook enables the individual as well as the broad masses to accept the suffering inherent in human existence. For one thing, these stories explain and make comprehensible the harsh fates some individuals must endure— a horrible death or extraordinary misfortune, for example—by tracing them back to the depths of previous reincarnations. These gilgul stories always end in death, which represents liberation in the sense that Wilhelm Emrich perceives in the case of Gregor Samsa: "His death is not merely a meaningless annihilation, but a liberating realization. Gregor says 'yes' to his own death" (*Critical Study*, 145). Of course, these stories are also meant as an admonishment to lead a pious and moral life; they are meant to sharpen one's awareness that every act a person does has significance and that everything is thrown onto the balance at the final judgment: "The court doesn't forget," Titorelli reminds Joseph K. in *The Trial* (214). This reminder revives an ancient talmudic principle that is also repeated in the Zohar.[15]

There are two fundamentally different types of gilgul tales. At the center of the one stands a man whose life seems to be under the influence of a particularly unfavorable star—adversity, suffering or death. This type of tale seeks to explain contemporary life and its frustrations as the consequence of the transgressions committed by a person in a previous reincarnation, and it does so by recalling the sins that were committed but not atoned for at that time and which are now finding their atonement in the present life via suffering and misfortune. This might be viewed as a type of traditional folk theodicy, and it can be seen in the following tale about Isaac Luria. Alexander Eliasberg included this story in his anthology of *Sagen polnischer Juden*, which appeared in Munich in 1916 and with which Kafka was familiar:[16]

> Rabbi Isaac Luria, the founder of the Kabbalah, was once invited to a wedding. The bridegroom was a renowned young scholar, a very pious man, holy and pure and upright, distinguished by a fear of God and all the virtues. The ceremony was followed by a great feast. As the newly married man ate a piece of chicken, a bone became lodged in his throat so that he choked on it and died.
>
> All the guests lamented and wept, and Rabbi Isaac Luria was the only one who did not weep. He even seemed to be happy. They were all very astonished at this and asked the saintly rabbi why he was so pleased. The holy man gave this answer:
>
> "Know that the soul of the young man was just released from its last reincarnation. The young man had already been a pious, pure and saintly man in a previous existence, distinguished by all the virtues, and during his life he had washed clean all the blemishes that clung to his soul from earlier

gilgulim. The fact that his holy man had yet another gilgul to make was because of this:

"In his previous life this man was a city rabbi and as such had to decide various questions of ritual. At that time, however, an unredeemed soul was wandering around in the world. A decree went out from the celestial court to the effect that this soul should enter into a pure, kosher bird; and that, when the bird finds the grace of being eaten by a holy and pious man on the sabbath or at a feast, it should finally be redeemed. And so it happened: the soul entered a chicken that was purchased by a god-fearing scholar for the sabbath. This was a great blessing for the soul and it believed itself already redeemed. But the scholar's cook had some doubts whether or not the chicken had been slaughtered properly and whether one might eat it. Therefore, as was the custom, she went to the rabbi in the city so that he could decide the question. The city rabbi didn't examine the chicken carefully enough and decided that it might not be eaten, although, upon closer examination, he would have had to admit that it was completely kosher. So the poor soul remained unredeemed and had to wander about in the world some more. It appeared before the celestial court and lodged a complaint against the holy rabbi: he was responsible for the fact that it was still unredeemed, for it really had had the grace of being purchased by a god-fearing man for the sabbath. But the pious rabbi spoiled the whole thing with his decision; may the celestial court therefore condemn him.

The celestial court determined that the pious rabbi should make another gilgul to deliver the soul in his new existence. And the unredeemed soul once again entered into a bird, namely the chicken that the pious scholar was to eat at his wedding feast. As the scholar began to eat the chicken, the poor soul was immediately redeemed; the man, too, had nothing more to do on this earth since he had fulfilled the purpose of his life. Blessed is his soul, that fulfilled everything it was supposed to do at such a tender age!"

Learn from this that one should not grieve if a pious man dies young. For the Lord is just and knows what's good for the human soul.

The following tale treats a similar theme:

The Brief Marriage[17]

A scholar from Safed once wanted to move to another city; therefore he went to the wise rav to tell him of his decision and to take his leave. He had hardly entered and taken a seat and hadn't even opened his mouth before the rav beat him to it and said: "Wise Sir, you want to move to another city!" "Yes." "Do you want to know what will happen to you there?" asked the rav. "Yes," was the reply. "Well then, know that in that city you will marry the daughter of a very rich man and you will receive a very great dowry as well. But you will be married to her only for about six months, for then she will die and you will inherit only six hundred gold pieces from all these riches, and not a penny more." The scholar said, "I can't help but ask why it will be exactly six months and six hundred gold pieces and no more?" The rav explained: "Know that in a previous gilgul this woman was a man like you and you were his business partner for about six months. During this time he embarrassed you sorely with his company and later dragged you before the non-Jewish court and cheated you out of six hundred gold pieces. That's why you will now have your pleasure at her expense for a corresponding six months, to equal the time he vexed you, and in the end you will inherit the six hundred gold pieces he once cheated out of you."

In these two tales, but even more so in the second type which will be discussed below, death is actually redemption, a sign of the successful atonement and expurgation of sin; such a death can be accepted with ease.

In the second type of tale, the main interest focuses on an animal which reveals itself as the habitation of a human soul in gilgul, like the hen in the previous tale. This kind of existence in an animal (as well as in plants and minerals, by the way) is considered to be an especially severe punishment for sin; the sooner it ends with the death of the animal, the better. Only after the animal's death can the soul reincarnated in it enter its next gilgul on a higher level or, more happily, find its way to eternal rest. If the animal is one Jews are allowed to eat, its ritual slaughter and solemn consumption, most preferably during a sabbath meal, serves to elevate the soul that sunk to the level of the beast. Unclean animals, on the other hand, can be released from their shameful existence and delivered to rest by holy deeds, by prayer and by the actions of a miracle worker. Then one can "thank God," as the elder Samsa does (*Stories*, 90), or one can react the way the owner of the cat-lamb does, who presumes that the butcher's knife would spell redemption for this creature (*Stories*, 296); even Gregor knows he "would have to disappear" (*Stories*, 136). The close relation between Kafka's animal figures and the gilgul stories seems to be particularly grounded in the fact that Kafka's stories are neither fables nor metaphors. Instead, what are obviously human fates are depicted in animal bodies. These animal existences represent the mortal or spiritual life of sinful humans unable to enter into their eternal rest.

The following tale is very reminiscent of Kafka's half-cat, half-lamb creature, for here too a ram (or a lamb, as a parallel version has it) is the focus of the story. This animal sheds tears like a human and confides in a man:

The Tame Ram[18]

One evening, as they [Luria and his students] were sitting and studying, a large ram opened the door, entered the room, went up to the Rav [Isaac Luria] and whispered into his ear—and this in front of all his companions. The Rav answered him and said: "Go in peace, I'll do as you request." The ram went out, and everyone present was greatly astonished. The Rav then said to Rabbi Hayyim Vital: "Get up and go and buy the ram at whatever price they demand of you, and bring it to me." He said: "Sir, how shall I recognize him?" "Go along, he will give you a sign." Rabbi Hayyim Vital got up and went to a herd on the edge of the city. Immediately the ram ran up to meet him and pushed its horn into his belt. The shepherd tried to drive the animal away but failed to do so. Rabbi Hayyim Vital asked the shepherd: "Why are you hitting him, I want to buy him!" The shepherd laughed: "His owner is very rich and will not sell him." "I will go to him," said Rabbi Vital, and he went. He spoke with the owner, who demanded the price of fifty rams for this one. He gave it to him and took the ram with him.

The Rav then sent word that all the shohetim should gather before him, and they all came. He instructed each one to sharpen

> his knife. The Rav took one knife from them, and all the slaughterers examined it. Then he said to the ram: "Lie down on the ground and make your confession!" The ram did as it was bid, and they all noticed how it wept. When he finished his confession, the Rav said: "Stick out your neck!" and again the ram obeyed. They wanted to bind him as was the custom, but the Rav said it wasn't necessary because he voluntarily offered his neck. Then he told Rabbi Sophina that he should slaughter, and he told him the verses he should silently recite while doing so. The rabbi did as he was told and afterwards wanted to examine the lungs. But again the Rav felt they needn't do this either, for the ram had already assured him that his entrails were perfectly kosher.
>
> The Rav commanded that nothing but the animal's blood and excrement be discarded. His hide should be used to make Torah and tefillin scrolls, and his horns should be fashioned into shofars and all his flesh should be brought before the Rav. He then summoned a scribe, who wrote the verses down, and he sent them along with a piece of the meat to the scholars who wanted it so they might eat while meditating on these passages. After everything was done, the Rav's companions asked him what it all meant.
>
> And he explained: "The ram was once a shohet. One day the goyim forced him to do his work quickly and he failed to notice a tiny irregularity on his blade. This meant that he gave out some meat as kosher which in fact was not [because of the jagged edge]. This caused the Jews to eat non-kosher meat.
>
> "Then the ram came to me and begged me to perform tikkun, an act of rectification, for him. He asked me to have him slaughtered and to be especially careful with the knife, for if the knife were unfit, he would have to return to gilgul. And that's why I performed the tikkun for him!"
>
> His companions were left in fear and trembling. And during the night the ram appeared to the Rav in a dream and said: "May your spirit rest in eternal life, just as you have given me peace!"

Kafka's story about that strange hybrid between cat and lamb ends with the owner's reflections cited at the beginning of this chapter: "Perhaps the butcher's knife would be a deliverance for this animal." He then continues this train of thought: "However, since it is an heirloom, I have to deny him of it. As a result, it will have to wait until it breathes its last on its own, even if it does look at me at times with eyes that seem almost human, eyes that beg for an understanding act" (*Stories*, 296).

The animal in this story obviously yearns for redemption via the knife, just like the ram in Luria's tale. A normal animal in the natural state, and be it ever so much of a mongrel, certainly has no desire for any such deliverance. The animal's death wish, thus, lies beyond the realm of the natural, experiential world, and the same can be said of Kafka's cat-lamb. Is it its loneliness in the animal world? Such loneliness is at least one indication that this creature has nothing in common with the rest of the animal world, whereas it does feel itself much closer to the human world. But even there we would be hard put to find a death wish. Be that as it may, the fact remains that the animal feels comfortable in its owner's presence. "It feels best when snuggled up against me" (*Stories*, 292).

This half-cat, half-lamb creature empathizes with its human owner, it shares his joys and sorrows—man and beast united in the joint alliance so typical of the Lurianic tale. When its owner suddenly falls ill one day, the animal weeps: "Once when I had reached an impasse in my business and in everything having to do with it, as can happen to anyone, of course, and I was ready to give it all up, I sat in the rocking chair at home and abandoned myself to this mood. The creature was sitting on my lap, and as I just happened to glance down at it, tears were falling from its enormous whiskers.—Were they mine? were they his?—Did this cat with the soul of a lamb possess human ambition as well?"

It seems as if the owner of the cat-lamb had not yet realized the true depth of the alliance that bound him and the animal together; this would explain his decision to deprive it of deliverance by the butcher's knife. Has the development of the cat-lamb, which is the focus of the beginning of the story, not progressed far enough as to enable the owner to realize the complete significance of his relation to the creature? At any rate, in the passage with the tears, the "I" of both partners, of man and beast, almost merge into one. Will the owner be ready for the redemptive act only when he recognizes the "heirloom from the previous generation or even from generations before that" as his own responsibility resulting from an entanglement in this type of joint liability?

When seen in terms of the gilgul theme, Kafka's tale might be interpreted as the story of an entanglement in sin that was neither occasioned nor recognized by the person in question. Nevertheless, it places him under the obligation of performing the redeeming act within the context of this mutual liability (of souls). The life of former generations which extends into his own time in the form of this hybrid creature obligates the owner to redeem it. This is one interpretation of the story that has a painful actuality, particularly in Germany.

Three additional gilgul stories are reprinted in the Appendix; they all revolve around the expurgation of this type of guilt-laden inheritance from the past via an understanding "redeemer." In the one case an enormous frog bumps into the Baal Shem Tov in a desert into which he has wandered. The "hero" of the story is a student who did not take his religious duties very seriously in the beginning, starting with washing his hands before meals. As a result he was reincarnated into a frog in order to atone for his sin with a water punishment. The blessing or the piety of a person in later generations could have effected his deliverance— but he was barred from human society for a long time. It took the Baal Shem Tov to come as the redeemer in order to effect atonement for the former transgression. The release of the soul dwelling in the frog resulted in the latter's immediate death.

The second tale tells a similar story.[19] Here a debtor dies without having been able to pay off his debts to a creditor. He was reincarnated into a horse to expurgate the remaining debt. The soul dwelling in this horse was prematurely delivered of its debt, again with the help of the Baal Shem Tov, who tore up the obligatory note that just happened to still exist and persuaded the creditor to forgive the man what he owed. Once again, redemption is accomplished via the actions of later generations; in this case, too, the animal dropped dead as soon as the act of atonement was performed.

It is always thus mutual liability between generations that has to help bear as well as atone for the sin that transcends the generations. Within this alliance, the person bears an obligation for the transgressions of previous generations; in other words, for sins he did not commit himself. Kafka once expressed this same view in one of his aphorisms: "Sinful is the state in which we find ourselves, independent of guilt" (*Wedding*, 36f). Of course, here the thought is clothed in the language of neoplatonic mysticism, a point we shall pick up again later on.

In his impressive and detailed discussion of the animal figures in the works of Franz Kafka, Karl-Heinz Fingerhut expressed the opinion that the "ancient Jewish idea of the animal as a proxy sacrifice unconsciously motivated the author to conceive many of his literary 'scape-goats' in the guise of animals" (282). I think there is a more obvious explanation for Kafka's use of animals, and that is the idea of reincarnation. For one thing, the idea of the scape-goat played by no means as important a role in Kafka's contemporary Judaism as is usually ascribed to the scape-goat theology then current among Christians. On the other hand, the idea of an animal-man in gilgul was very widespread precisely within the Eastern Jewish folk belief. But there is another, more important consideration. The belief in animal reincarnations lifts the animal out of its natural physical distance from the human and raises it into the spiritual sphere of the human soul. An animal whose body harbors a human soul is an integral part of human society; it is, ultimately, a person in metamorphosis, and this introduces connotations that are totally alien to the concept of a scape- goat. Such animal-people seek human companionship and assistance and expect human solidarity. Like the ram in the tale discussed above, they emerge out of the animal world only to be completely absorbed into the community of man. The life of a person in an animal is not an animal life, but human life in a particular form, human life in judgment. But even here the distinction between this life and human life in a human body is only a relative one, for every human life is a life in judgment and in gilgul, even if it should occur more frequently in the shape of human beings than in that of animals. The difference between the two in reality is restricted to the physical realm. Psychologically, human gilgul and animal gilgul make up one unified community that must complete the work of redemption through atonement via common efforts performed within the joint alliance that exists for that very purpose.

As far as the inner life is concerned, both forms of existence are one and the same. It is perhaps this awareness that served Kafka as bridge for what Fingerhut calls his "depiction of his own [human] inner life in the disguised but universally valid apperception of the 'condition humaine' in the puzzling animal figures in his stories" (59). This is all the more likely, since it is the spiritual relationship of man with man and animal with man that forms the basic prerequisite for encounter and mutual assistance when viewed from the perspective of gilgul. Only if both sparks stem from the same spiritual root of Adam, the macro-psychic Primal Man, will they be capable of such a "meeting" and such mutual assistance (Scholem, *Godhead*, 232). Kafka's scepticism regarding a "conscious separation of the 'real' from the 'unreal'" (Fingerhut, 67; *Diaries*, 329, 546) is in itself one of the foundation stones of the belief in gilgul. What is ordinarily perceived as being unreal is to this way of thinking that which is most real.

What Fingerhut says of Kafka's phantastic animal figures is equally applicable to all Eastern Jewish gilgul stories, namely: "The actual existence and make-up of the 'world' that stands in opposition to the 'ego' . . . depends upon the name it is given. The fact that it can be metamorphosed by changing its name will be of tremendous significance in Kafka's later work" (85). All the animals or objects that play a role in the gilgul stories are transformed by the names given them by empathetic people who can see below the surface. The very recognition of a soul in gilgul dwelling in an animal or a mineral signifies its immediate "transformation"; it is no longer an external object, for, from that moment on, it becomes part of the human-spiritual world and its history. They have thus been removed from the purely animal or mineral world and enter into a human relation; they become people in metamorphosis.

Man's ability to transform his human environment can take on much more concrete forms, as the chapter on "Language and Reality" will show.

Fingerhut's conclusions concerning the animal figures in Kafka's works are equally valid for the traditional gilgul stories stemming from Lurianic Kabbalah. "A study of the animal figures in Kakfa's works indicate three points concerning the negation of the difference between reality and unreality that play a decisive role in his literature. The first is the elimination of distinctive characteristics between man and animal, so that men can become animals, animals can become men. The second is the loss of the universally recognized form or shape of the creatures. This loss is expressed in distortions of proportion or in hybrid cross-breeds of different animals. The third is the intrusion of phantastic animal figures into the mundane world of daily routine" (87). And: "The appearance of phantastic animal figures in Kafka's work occurs almost always according to the same formula: an animal intrudes into the mundane daily life of a person, a creature that does not fit in with the categories of this person's concept of the world. The reader thus expects shock and astonishment and is perplexed to find that the incomprehensible is accepted as if it were an integrating component of the normal" (118). Fingerhut's observations, of course, would have to be completely reversed in light of the reincarnation stories and their doctrine concerning the solidarity of souls in gilgul. Gilgul teaches that the man-animal is in fact neither unusual nor incomprehensible. It sees the man-animal as a truly integrated component of the normal, so that "someone in the know" finds nothing astonishing or strange about it. Gilgul animals can and ought to be accepted as "normal." There is no question but that these creatures occupy a pariah existence in the gilgul stories as well, a fact that Fingerhut mentions in connection with Kafka's animal figures (116, 107). However, in the gilgul stories, this pariah existence comes to an end the very moment the knowledgable and empathetic solidarity of the "related" soul returns the gilgul animal to the spiritual community of man-man through its word and deed. According to Fingerhut, Kafka's cat-lamb symbolizes "the total expulsion from the human as well as the animal world," because, like Kafka's other comparable animal figures, it lives equally as an outcast of the human as well as of the animal society, "as a non-animal . . . without ties relating it to the human being and the animals of reality" (107). Within the context of the gilgul stories, it appears equally excluded from the animal world simply because, as an animal-man, it flees from the society of animals. We saw this in the case of the ram that barged into the house of the rabbi in its search for human companionship, in the hopes of being recognized and once again taken in by them, be it only via the mercy of the butcher's knife. To quote Fingerhut once again: "Here the creature that yearns for redemption, just like a man, is bound to man in a partnership that actually can grant the individual a 'deliverance'"(267).

The opposite case of Dr. Bucephalus can be explained in this same context. It comes as no surprise that this man was an animal in a previous existence and still bears outward and visible traces of his past. He has the good fortune of being returned to the community of man-man from the lower level of animal-man. The same is true for the "great lady" Isabella in one of Kafka's narrative fragments (*Wedding*, 294). She was so great she had no equal among the narrator's circle of friends and acquaintances. This is because she is none other than the "dapple-gray, the old horse" that has "turned into a lady." She escaped from her stall, or better said, was released from it when "her days" were "accomplished." Even though her coat is still of a greyish-yellow material and the bluish veil of her hat flutters behind her, she is nevertheless now quite beautiful and enjoys human society (*Wedding*, 294f). Once again, a trace of a previous existence still clings to Isabella the lady.

On the other hand, the transformation of man to animal is always a sign of a particularly severe sin, just as K. H. Fingerhut observes in the case of the metamorphosis of Gregor Samsa into a vermin-like insect. "He [Kafka] uses [the insect] to give an important hint as to the reason behind Gregor Samsa's 'metamorphosis,' the change that has given rise to so much speculation [among readers and critics]: a confluence of personal sin with the 'negative [quality] of the times' which the weak person is not able to escape transforms the human being into 'vermin'" (214).

"An Animal Lives in the Thamühl Synagogue"

The animal in Kafka's fragment about the synagogue in Thamühl (*Wedding*, 288) ought to be mentioned in this connection, for it is truly an ancient animal known to generations, a timid beast: "Is it the memory of times long passed or the premonition of times to come? Does this ageless animal perhaps know more than the three generations that gathered in the synagogue, each in their own time?" (*Wedding*, 291)

This animal frightens the women especially, but even they would be loathe to lose it: "If they were more involved in their prayers they could forget the beast completely. The pious women would do this if the others, who make up the great majority, would allow it, but they always want to draw attention to themselves and the animal is a welcome pretense for them to do so. If they could have and if they had dared to do so, they would have lured the animal even closer to them, so that they might be all the more frightened" (*Wedding*, 290).

The animal Kafka depicts here is thus related to the feminine desire to count for something as well as the feminine desire to be the focus of attention. The pious women do not share these desires, but even so, it is this vain feminine attitude that directs to the animal whatever attention it does get in the story in the first place. At the risk of oversimplification, the animal owes its role in the story to the women's unvirtuous desire to please; were they all pious, there would be no commotion about the animal.

This theme as well as many of the motifs Kafka employed elsewhere are very reminiscent of one of the legends about the Baal Shem Tov. This particular tale focuses on the same fright on the part of the women in the women's gallery, except that here it is caused by one or more creatures whisking about the synagogue. Moreover, these creatures, the ones responsible for the furor, owe their existence to the egotism and lack of piety of the women (and one lascivious cantor). In this tale, as well as in Thamühl, attempts are undertaken to drive the trouble-makers out, and the immediate results would have been as unsuccessful in the Eastern Jewish legends as they are in Thamühl were it not for the miracle worker, the Baal Shem Tov, who ultimately masters the problem in these older versions. The same similarities and differences between Kafka's works and Eastern Jewish literature hold true here as they did in the previous discussion concerning the judgment tales: the human problems and their representation are ultimately the same, except that the solution for the pious Eastern Jew comes through the help of a miracle man or a charismatic rebbe, whereas this figure is painfully absent for the Western Jew called Kafka.

The hasidic story tells of two demons who were born of the lascivious thoughts of the women and the cantor leading the prayer in synagogue—in other words, they represent a mythological materialization of human egotism and lust. In the Eastern Jewish tale, the pre-kabbalistic topos of begetting demons had already been merged with the gilgul theme under the influence of the Lurianic school of Kabbalah. This being the case, it is no methodological faux-pas on my part to include this hasidic story within the context at hand. One final point: according to Luria, the faults that lead to reincarnation into animals are precisely arrogrance and lapses in sexual fidelity. Overweaning pride leads to gilgul in bees, sodomy to that in bats, adultery with married individuals leads to reincarnation into jackasses, with one's own mother into a she-ass, homosexuality leads to transformation into rabbits and hares, etc.[20] The dog has already been mentioned. In fact, even the Babylonian Talmud (*Megilla* 14b) named weasels with reference to arrogance, a fact demonstrated by the prophetess Hulda, whose name means "weasel" and who was guilty of the sin of pride.[21]

With this as background, the commonalities between the tale of the marten in the synagogue of Thamühl and the hasidic story of the demons in the synagogue of Izbors will be all the more apparent:

Two Demons in the Synagogue in Izbors

I heard the following tale from the rav of our community as well as from the rav of the holy community of Polonnoye. Two demons had been spotted in the women's section of the synagogue in the holy community of Izbors. The women were so afraid of them that they finally had to close the synagogue.

Shortly after that, Rabbi Hayyim, the rav and maggid of our community, went into the synagogue and by this he succeeded in driving the demons out. But they took their revenge and did harm to his two children. Then Rabbi Hayyim sent for the Besht, who just happened to be spending the night in his house of seclusion with his scribe, who was our teacher Tzvi. He instructed that the children be brought to him in his sleeping quarters. They were brought, whereupon they all went to bed; the Besht at the head of the table and the scribe opposite him, head to head. Before they fell asleep, both demons appeared in the house. They stood at the door and made fun of the way the Besht sang the sabbath song "Lekhah Dodi." The Besht jumped up and, sitting on his cot, cried to the scribe: "Do you see them?" The scribe certainly had seen them and covered his head with the Besht's pillow. All he said was: "Leave me alone."

By this time the two demons had moved to where the children were sleeping. Without hesitating the Besht jumped out of bed and cried: "Where do you think you're going?" Undaunted, they replied: "What's it to you?" and again began to chant the "Lekhah Dodi" the way the Besht usually did. Whereupon the Besht did what he did, and the two demons fell to the ground as if mesmerized.

As they began to beseech him, he ordered them to "See to it that the children are healed!" "What's done is done, and will not go away!" one demon announced, because they had gotten into the internal organs of the children, "and now we've come to make an end to them— it was only their good luck that Your Reverence was with them."

The Besht asked the demons: "How and why did you enter the synagogue?" They answered: "The cantor was accompanied in the synagogue by a bass, the very personification of an adulterer; whenever he sang, his lust directed his gaze solely to the women in hopes they might find him pleasing. And the women were attracted to him and lusted after him. We two demons, a male and a female, were created out of this lascivious union, and we live in the synagogue."

The Besht then banned them to a well in a place where no one ever went. (*H*, 105; *Praise*, 107)

Compared to this hasidic story, Kafka's tale seems little more than a fragment. However, if we examine the element missing in Kafka's tale when compared to its Eastern Jewish counterpart, it seems probable that Kafka intentionally ended his version at a point that would make it appear a fragment. Kafka's story lacks the element of the mighty miracle man who would have been able to remove the animal that owed its literary existence to the egotism of the women. Even so, Kafka's tale, too, tells of attempts, vain ones to be sure, at driving the animal out. The difference is that Kafka does not believe the realization of such a wish is possible and thus he leaves the synagogue in a state of ambiguity as to whether or not it is suitable for further use—the old animal remains in it.

In another brief hasidic tale the Baal Shem Tov opens the eyes of the community rabbi to the fact that the whole synagogue is full of demons, all of whom owe their existence to the iniquity of the resident cantor (*H*, 272; *Praise*, 255). In this case, too, help was at hand with the removal of the cantor. Kafka leaves the life of his Thamühl community in a state of blemish caused by the ineradicable sin of coquetry. To judge by the age of the animal, this sin has been handed down through the generations. The present generation is unable to escape this sin, except, of course, it should make proper atonement. This is why the animal stays, "and the majority of women probably would be unhappy if it should disappear" (*Wedding*, 290).

In this story, too, then, the animal is a symbol of a sin transcending the generations, a sin for which the community as a whole is responsible.

14
DIVINE JUDGMENT VIA THE WORD—"I NOW SENTENCE YOU TO DEATH BY DROWNING"

In "The Judgment," Kafka lets the elder Bendemann utter these words in reaction to the son who, he believes, is circumventing and controlling him and who has "buried" (*Stories*, 38) him, the old man, in a dark back room. The son Georg "felt chased out of the room. . . . He sprang out the door, something was driving him across the street toward the water."—An odd solution to a "father-son conflict."[1] It was this same strange tale, which Kafka wrote in one sitting one night in 1912 soon after Yom Kippur[2], that moved even Hartmut Binder to refer to the Jewish elements inherent in the story, and especially to the influence of the Yiddish theater, to a degree otherwise rare in his work. In Abraham Scharansky's play *Kol Nidre*, which Kafka saw toward the end of October 1911, "the father condemns his daughter to death; however, to keep a step ahead of him, she commits suicide"[3]. In Jacob Gordin's Yiddish play called *Gott, Mensch und Teufel* (*God, Man and the Devil*), with which Kafka was also familiar (cf. *Diaries*, 75; *Critical Edition*, 166), "Herschele, the main character, has fallen under the spell of money; he no longer respects his father, whom he later throws out of the house; he plunges into the excitement of worldly pleasures, rejects his wife and enters into another liaison, and leaves his best friend in the lurch, who in turn heaps accusations upon him. The result is Herschele's suicide."[4]

These references are certainly justified, even though they lack one additional element that Kafka himself describes as the "effect" of the sentence. In his own commentary on the story Kafka wrote on February 11, 1913: "The sentence has an effect only because he himself has nothing more than the image of his father," (*Diaries*, 186). Georg Bendemann does not commit suicide; instead, he is "driven to it. He was already holding fast to the railing, like a starving man holds fast to food" (*Stories*, 38). The father's sentence carries itself out, a fact that Binder also appreciates when he refers to Kafka's reflections in his letter to his sister Elli. Kafka wrote: "If they [the children] do not meet [the demands and deadlines set down by their parents], they will not be kicked out or anything like that . . . but cursed or consumed or both" (*Letters*, 345, 361). The words of the elder Bendemann are like a self-fulfilling curse, working its will against the will of the one rushing toward the water.

This theme of rebellion against authority and its consequences is an old (and not exclusively) Jewish theme. It even has its place in the Bible, where it appears as opposition and rebellion against religious authority, some of which, according to Jewish tradition, also accrues to one's parents. One need only think of the rebels who followed Korah in their opposition to Moses and who were subsequently swallowed up by the earth (Numbers 16), or of Miriam, whose rebellion was punished with leprosy (Numbers 12). Even the mockery of the scamps who teased Elisha, the Man of God, ended in a deadly curse:

> As Elisha was going up by the way, there came forth little children out of the city, and mocked him, and said unto him: "Go up, thou baldhead; go up, thou baldhead." And he looked behind him and saw them, and cursed them in the name of the Lord. And there came forth two she-bears out of the wood, and tore forty and two children of them. (2 Kings 2:23–24)

In a later Eastern Jewish folk tale it was once again irreverance toward a religious authority that cost the transgressor his home as well as his fortune: "He [a friend of his youth] made fun of his high sanctity. . . . But the man did not answer and held his peace. After a few days the friend of his youth returned home; a little while later his house burned down and he lost half his fortune."[5]

Georg Bendemann's mockery of his father died on his lips as well: "'Ten thousand times!' said Georg, in order to make fun of his father, but the words took on a deadly earnest tone before he could even utter them" (*Stories*, 37). In another version of the story that ends without the curse, the idea lurking behind such tales becomes even more evident: rebellion against divine authority automatically boomerangs upon the transgressor like a divine curse, and all the more so when such a person opens his mouth and speaks words of destruction. The Talmud tells of rabbinical scholars that they need only glance at a rebellious man for him to turn into a pile of bones.[6]

The curses of Isaac of Drohobycz, a contemporary of the Baal Shem Tov, have become almost proverbial examples of curses against the disobedient and the rebellious. Kafka learned of him and his magical powers after he wrote "The Judgment." He also heard a rather lengthy story about him from Georg Langer, a story he later noted in his diary on October 6, 1915 (*Diaries*, 300). It was the same Isaac of Drohobycz, the so-called *Tzaddik ha-Dor*, the leading tzaddik of the generation, whom, according to hasidic legend, no one could oppose with impunity. The early collection of legends about the Baal Shem Tov includes a similar collection of pertinent tales about Isaac of Drohobycz.

The Tax Collector's Disobedient Wife

> Rabbi Isaac of Drohobycz was accepted as the maggid of the community of Greater Horichov. Several weeks after he had moved in, it happened that a butcher owed the tax collector a certain sum. The tax collector was not at home at the time, so his wife confiscated the butcher's pillows and blankets.
>
> When the butcher's wife ran to Rabbi Isaac, crying and complaining about this, he sent for the tax collector's wife and ordered her to return all she had seized. But she didn't obey him.
>
> Then Rabbi Isaac cursed her, so that one of her children died on the spot.
>
> When her husband returned from his journey, she told him what had happened. "They named a new maggid who cursed me, and now our child is dead."

> In the meantime Rabbi Isaac had returned to his home in the community of Ostrohe where he served as maggid to Rabbi Yuspa.
>
> Since he was supposed to move to the community of Horichov, the congregation sent some wagons to help him transport his family and their belongings. What did the tax collector do? He sent a personal messenger with a letter for the Rabbi: "If you haven't started out yet, stay where you are. But if you are already underway, then turn back! For whenever you do come, you will be forced to leave." Rabbi Isaac sent him the following letter in response:
>
> "I shall enter the city the very moment they carry your bier out of it."
>
> And that's exactly what happened. The moment Rabbi Isaac drove through the gates of the city, the dead tax collector was being carried out the gate, and they couldn't pass through with the body. They had to push the wagon aside first before the mourners could continue on their way.[7] (*H*, 90ff; *Praise*, 87)

According to the golem legend, even Rabbi Löw of Prague was supposed to have said: "'The miscreants [who disobeyed the rabbi's orders] will receive their punishment from heaven!' And so it happened, for suddenly a black wart formed on the arm of the [rebellious] porter . . . Then the porter said that he received this as a punishment from God, because he did not heed Rabbi Löw's curse. He sent his wife and his children to the rabbi to beg forgiveness for him, but the latter would not receive him. He said: 'Let his death be his atonement!' The man died a few days later" (Bloch, 150f).

Finally, the legends of the Baal Shem Tov also tell of an instance not dissimilar to that of Georg Bendemann and his father, except that here it is not the father who delivers the sentence, but the Baal Shem Tov in his stead:

> *The Man Who Struck His Drunken Father*
>
> One day the Besht was visiting a particular community and had taken a room in an attic. As he looked out the window, he saw a man crossing the street. He ordered his servant: "Go quickly and bring this man to me!"

The boy ran and called the man. He was startled and afraid to go, but because he dare not openly defy the Besht, the man finally followed the boy. The rav greeted him with the following words: "You have committed a grave sin today." The man denied it and said: "What business is it of yours, Your Reverence?" The rav responded: "Do you mean to say you did not commit a grave sin when you struck your father?"

His elderly father was usually confined to the house, but on this day he had gone out to get some brandy and stayed away a long time. The man finally went out to see what had happened to his father, since he had not returned for such a long time, and he found him drinking from the spigot under the cask. Enraged, the son grabbed the spigot and hit his father over the head with it.

After the Besht confronted him with the truth, the man wept bitterly and implored the rabbi to help him atone for his sin. As a penance, the rav told him to fast Mondays and Thursdays, to stand where the mourners stand in the synagogue, and to do other things of the same sort.

The man willingly submitted to the penance, but the rav warned him that, God forbid he should alter any of them, he would not live to see the end of the year.

He worked hard at his repentance for some time until his mother began to mock the rabbi. She finally convinced her son to stop his acts of repentance. And what had to be came to be: the man did not live to see the end of the year, may the Merciful One save us!

This tale was told by the Rav of Torov, who witnessed the event himself. (*H*, 257; *Praise*, 240)

No measure is too drastic for the Eastern Jewish folk tale dealing with this theme. The sentence pronounced by the religious authority punishes disobedience, mockery and stubborness as well as the self-aggrandizement of all those who are relegated to a subservient position, and it does so mercilessly. This can be seen in the story included in the Appendix about the rich woman who ignored the admonishments of the community rabbi; because of her arrogance, she turned to stone the next day and fell down dead when the pertinent words in the rabbi's prayer were recited. Or take the case of the slanderer, whose sentence, like that of Georg Bendemann, was death by drowning!

Such connections between sin and punishment and the way they are formulated in these simple folk tales are indicative of the uncomplicated and scrupulous religious temperament of the broad masses and their offspring. They express a belief in the inexorable consequences of human behavior, a belief which Kafka, even if he had no way of knowing the individual tales, surely absorbed "with his mother's milk," particularly in a house in which the father-son relation was burdened by such a marked fear and strong guilt feelings. Right at the beginning of his *Letter to My Father*, Kafka wrote: "You recently asked me why I claim to be afraid of you. As usual, I didn't know how to answer, partly because of the fear I have for you . . ." (*Wedding*, 119).

In the eyes of the elder Bendemann, his son Georg was just such a rebel, a son not after his own heart (*Stories*, 35), one who neglected his father, who did not care for him, a forlorn old widower, and one who disgraced the memory of his mother (*Stories*, 36). All these reproaches are suggestive of Kafka's letter to his own father as well (*Wedding*, 119), rather like the way Georg's relation to his father resembles that of Kafka to his father down to the smallest detail and even into the very words he uses to express it. Like the authority figures in the legends discussed above, Kafka's father is "the ultimate authority [that] could appear almost without reason and carry me out of my bed at night and onto the back stairs, which proved that I was a mere nothing in his eyes" (*Wedding*, 122f). The words of the elder Kafka had the same destructive power over his son: "Your total lack of sensitivity concerning the sorrow and the pain you were capable of inflicting upon me with your words and your *judgments* was always incomprehensible to me; it was as if you had no idea of your power" (*Wedding*, 126). Like the word of the saintly men in the legend, the word of Kafka's father was "nothing short of a commandment from heaven" (*Wedding*, 126).

15

LANGUAGE AND REALITY—WRITING AS A FORM OF PRAYER

"Si Dieu le Père a crée les choses en les nommant, c'est en leur ôtant leur nom ou en leur donnant un autre que l'artiste les recrée" ("If God the Father created all things by naming them, the artist transforms them by taking their names away or by giving them a new one"). K. H. Fingerhut cited these words of Marcel Proust to describe Kafka's relation to the language of the narrator and to reality. "There is no longer any linguistic difference between the narrative world of the imagined and the fictional and the narrative world that mimics reality" (86). "The first-person narrator thus behaves like a creating god vis-à-vis the world; all the thoughts it produces immediately become 'reality'. Squirrels, for example, simply come into being if that's what the narrator desires just before falling asleep, or vultures, whenever he summons them from the air" (84).

This is somewhat reminiscent of Kafka's story about the walk in his "Description of a Battle," where the narrator says (*Description*, 20): "But since I, as a pedestrian, feared the exertion required to climb the hilly street, I made the path get flatter and flatter and finally sink into a valley in the distance. The stones disappeared before my will and the wind died down." Later he made a "massive and high mountain appear" (*Description*, 20). In his address to the landscape, the fat man said: "'But now—I beg of you—

mountain, flower, grass, bush and river, give me a little room so I can breathe.' A hasty transposition then took place in the surrounding mountains. . . ." (*Description*, 25). The narrator is quite literally creating his own world via language. Evidently, the way to do this is to name the names of that which one wants—at least this might be the obvious conclusion to be drawn from the conversation with the praying man, whom the narrator reproaches for having created a world to his liking via an arbitrary nomenclature: "Oh come on, what are you saying. Now I see, by God, that I did have an inkling about the state you're in right from the start. Isn't this fever, this seasickness on solid ground, a type of leprosy? Isn't it so, that, because of the heat, you weren't satisfied with the real names of things, that you couldn't get enough of it, and are now tossing off arbitrary names for them, one after the other? Quick, quick! But as soon as you pass on to other names, you'll forget these. The poplar tree in the meadow that you've named the 'Tower of Babel' because you didn't want to know it was a poplar tree, is again swaying without a name and you'll have to name it 'Noah, when he was drunk'" (*Description*, 32).

The recipient of this scolding obviously wants to create a world of his own with names of his own devising because he is unhappy with the existing world that expresses itself in its true names. We later learn (*Description*, 39) that these names actually did lend a certain creative power. Turning toward heaven and the moon, the man cries: "It is true, you are still superior to me, but only when I leave you in peace. Thank God, Moon, you're no longer the moon, but perhaps it's remiss of me to still call that which used to be named moon by the name of Moon. Why aren't you as frisky and haughty as you once were when I call you 'Forgotten Paper Lantern with the Strange Color'? And why do you almost disappear when I call you 'Our Lady of the Pillar'? And I don't perceive your threatening attitude anymore, Lady of the Pillar, when I call you 'Moon That Casts Yellow Light'! It really seems to me that it's not good for you when people think about you; you lose your courage and your stamina."

We have no trouble in recognizing the ancient biblical idea of creation via the word behind this conception of an arbitrary, world-creating language. The word is the power that brings forth the world. Even so, this idea alone would still not suffice to explain Kafka's relation to language, for the creative word of the Bible is exclusively the Word of God. Man does not share this power as far as the Bible is concerned. Once again it is the Kabbalah, or more accurately its Jewish predecessors in the ancient world, which first inserted the missing link here. The same ancient Jewish texts that passed the gatekeeper tradition on to the Kabbalah developed a theology of the Names of God which attributed creative powers not only to the Names of God mentioned in the Bible, but also and in addition, it attributed these powers to every word composed of Hebrew letters, even to "meaningless" combinations of letters and, finally, to each individual letter of the Hebrew alphabet itself. According to the authors of these ancient texts, God created heaven and earth with nothing other than these letters and these words, all of which they considered to be Divine Names.[1] This onomatological heirloom of hekhalot mysticism was taken over and further developed by the Kabbalists in the Middle Ages and by the hasidic mystics of the Rhineland in the thirteenth century.[2] It ultimately came to form the central theological concept held by the Baal Shem Tov, the founder of Eastern European Hasidism in the eighteenth century.

The Baal Shem Tov was the one who gave this theology of the creative word its final and most impressive expression. The comprehensible or incomprehensible *nomina barbara* and other chains of letters were for Baal Shem Tov not only the Names of God that had been fused together by means of creative power. This was his general view, but to his specific way of thinking language itself, the word and the thing thus designated were one and the same. To put it another and perhaps more accurate way, everything that exists is, according to its true nature, nothing but language. Thus, when the Creator uttered a word, the object designated by that word had already been named, and that means it had already been created. According to this idea, language is not merely the denotation of a material object which is otherwise differentiated from language. Instead, this view holds that the word itself is the object itself, while the visible physical object is only the external shell of the actual object, which is the word. The Baal Shem Tov once expanded upon this point by combining Genesis 1:6 with Psalm119:89:[3]

> And God said, "Let there be a firmament in the midst of the waters" (Gen. 1:6).
>
> And in Ps. 119:89 it is written: "For ever, O Lord, thy word standeth fast in heaven."

The Baal Shem Tov interpreted these verses this way:

The word that You have spoken, "Let there be a firmament in the midst of the waters"—these exact words and these exact letters are fixed and stand eternally in the midst of the firmament and are clothed in every firmament in order to give them life. As the Prophet Isaiah said (40:8): "The word of our God shall stand for ever", His words live and are fixed for evermore. Were the letters to disappear even for a moment and return to their source, all of heaven would literally become null and void, and would be as if they had never entered into existence. It would be as it was before the utterance [of the Creator], which commanded: "Let there be a firmament."

And so it is with all creatures in all upper and lower worlds, even with [our] physical, material earth. Were the letters of the Ten Creative Utterances [mentiond in Genesis] which brought forth the universe during the Six Days of Creation—were these letters to disappear for even one moment, all would return to total nothingness.

This is what Ari [Isaac Luria] meant when he wrote that there is a type of soul and spiritual vitality even in the real world, in stones and in dust, and this is the vesting of the letters of the words of the Ten Creative Utterances which infuse the mineral world with life and bring it to existence so that it emerges out of the void that was before the Six Days of Creation.

Even though the word "stone" was not named in the Ten Creative Utterances of the Torah, its vitality still derives from them and does so via the combination and substitution of the letters in keeping with the 231 possible combinations described in the *Book of Creation*.[4] The word "stone" emerges out of such manipulations of the Ten Creative Utterances, and this word is the spiritual essence of the stone. The same holds true for every created thing in the cosmos. It is their names in the holy language, the letters comprising the word, which form a chain originating in the Ten Creative Utterances of the Torah by means of the substitution and rearrangement inherent in the 231 possibilities. The links in this chain descend from one level to another until they arrive at that particular creature and invest themselves in it in order to give it life. . . . The power and the spiritual force necessary to create something out of nothing and

> to vitalize the world reside in the Creative Utterances of the Torah, for the Torah and the Holy One, blessed be He, are one.

Linguistic creation, or creation via the word, which is what we are talking about here, is not a creative process involving two stages, as it were, the first of which being the spoken word and the second being the object coming into existence. What is happening here is rather like what happens in a fairy tale, where gold coins fall straight from the hero's mouth. The creative act described here is a creation by language and a language creation, whereby the spoken word itself is the essence of the object. Like the Torah, the whole world is nothing other than a single speech, a spoken text. This structure of the universe comes about, as spoken language itself tends to come about, via the application of an already existing inventory of sounds or letters. New words and sentences come into being via ever new combinations, and the result is: a new world. Remarkable in all of this is the fact that this process of linguistic creation does not always proceed anew from a void. Rather, it makes use of the 'linguistic material' already available, changes it and makes new creatures out of it—the same way mountains become valleys and the moon becomes a lantern in Kafka's story. In another passage in the same legend, this creative linguistic material that existed ever since the Creation is directly identified with the twenty-two letters of the Hebrew alphabet (Gowortschow, I:39f).

As a creation itself, the linguistic process of creation is nothing other than a transformation of the creative power of language that God brought forth out of nothing. In other words, it is the use of the language God created. Or, to stay with the words of the Baal Shem Tov, God Himself is this creative language, a thought already conceived by the ancient Hekhalot mystics.[5] The creative process is thus nothing other than a linguistic self-unfolding of the Godhead.

Let it be said parenthetically that the Baal Shem Tov also includes the human being in this ontology of names. A person's own name is that person's actual being. To name a person is to create that person (Gowortschow, I:89): "We have learned from our master, the Baal Shem Tov, that a person's name is the essence of his life. As in the case of all beasts and birds and wild animals, his name, too, reflects the worth of the spark of the Torah inherent in the letters. And this name is rooted in his being for ever."

Compare that with what Kafka wrote in a letter to Grete Bloch on March 3, 1914 (*Felice*, 510): "I don't like to see my name written and automatically assume the same holds true for the people I am close to. What is contained in the name is to be taken for granted as far as the person is concerned."

If we stay with the kabbalistic view that the world is language, a view that was shared by the Baal Shem Tov and his teachings, the next logical step would be to assume that man as a speaking being also shares in this linguistic creative power. In fact, the Talmud already ascribed such an ability to Bezalel, the biblical architect of the Tabernacle in the Wilderness and the patron saint of Jewish fine arts. The Baal Shem Tov did not hesitate to refer to it (Gowortschow, 39, par. 11): "As the twenty-two letters [of the Hebrew alphabet] make up the words of the Torah and of prayers, so also do they make up all material things of this world, for the world and all that is in it was created by means of these letters. As the tractate *Berakhot* (55a) in the Talmud says: 'Bezalel knew how to combine the letters with which heaven and earth were created.' The only thing is that the letters are vested in the material things of the physical world, in various skins, coverings and shells."

A parallel tradition compares the interconnectedness of physical being and the letters with that ancient and medieval philosophical conception of material and form, according to which material is looked upon as pure potential, as pure possibility to receive real existence, whereas form, which clothes the material, transforms this potential into reality. Form, accordingly, is that which actually lends existence, and material is the potential preparedness to attain form and thus to attain existence (Gowortschow, I:39, n. 10): "Human beings consist of material and form, and so do the letters of the alphabet. [For example] the body of the letters is the stone, but the [formative] spiritual principle, which comes from the ten sefirot and is the Light of En-Sof [the eternal Godhead] and rests in Him, is the divine spiritual force in the letters, and that is the form and the soul of the letters."

According to the continuation of this text, the following point is important for man's participation in this linguistic process of creation: "This should be the target of one's mystical contemplation when studying the Torah and during prayer. The essence and purpose of such devotion is to draw this spirituality [of form] and this Light down from the upper levels and into the letters . . . so that the letters can ascend to a high level and turn the request into reality. All of this is accomplished by studying and reciting the Torah and the prayers . . . , in order to preserve the tzaddikim from all evil."

In other words, when a person concentrates his mystical contemplation during prayer or during the study of the Torah on the spiritual principle of form inherent in the letters, he is capable of realizing his own wishes by means of his own personal creative process. When understood in these terms, prayer is not man's request before God, it is not the request of the weaker before the stronger; prayer in this sense is man's participation in the personal creative power of language. He can use this power to turn his desires into reality, just as God once created the world and now maintains it by continuing to create it anew every day. Here prayer becomes the mystical magic of language.

Dov Ber, the successor of the Baal Shem Tov and leader of the third generation of Hasidim, also known as the Maggid of Mezhirich, described the building of the ark by the patriarch Noah in much the same terms (Gowortschow, I:119, par. 15):

> "A light shalt thou make to the ark" (Gen. 6:16) so that the ark [the Hebrew word for ark, 'tevah', also means 'word'], the word which a person repeats in the study of the Torah and in prayer, gives light. For every single letter contains worlds and souls and God. Then they [the letters] ascend on high and combine and unite themselves, one with the other and finally with God; after that the letters couple and combine, and out of this comes a tevah, an ark and a word.

It is this mystical-magical power inherent in the language of the words that compose a prayer that moved Ephraim of Sodilkov, the grandson of the Baal Shem Tov, to say that one should aim the prayer directly at the letters of the prayer themselves, which is to say, "at the mystery of the Godhead [contained] within them, because it is only by means of these letters that one can speak the words with true devotion. In this way, all sentences of the court will be sweetened at their root [that is, will be turned to the better]" (Gowortschow, 124). Finally:

> When a person recites the words of a prayer with total concentration and self-surrender, all the intentions in the word are gathered together, for each letter is a complete world in itself. And when a person recites the word with total concentration, he awakens all the upper worlds with his recitation, and with the help of these worlds he can perform mighty deeds. Therefore, let each person pray with great devotion and inner concentration, because that is the way he will bring about mighty deeds in the upper regions, for each letter stimulates the upper world. (Gowortschow, 124f)

Thought is also mentioned in this connection in addition to the spoken word, and it is understood as being the kabbalistic meditation that accompanies the word (Gowortschow, 125–131).

This list of supporting documentation could go on and on. All of them express the one central idea that it is the word of man in prayer that lets him share in the divine creative power of language. Moses Cordovero writes in his *Pardes Rimmonim*:[6] "The fourth way to learn the Scripture [that is, the way of the Kabbalists] is [via a knowledge of] the spiritual nature and the true being of the letters, a knowledge of their combinations and the [disclosure] of how they relate to one another. Whoever probes the depths of this art can create a universe."

It is surely no great leap from this creative language of prayer to Kafka's much-quoted dictum concerning his own writing. He describes the literature he creates via language as a world of his own, one in which he alone might live, with the words: "Writing as a form of prayer" (*Wedding*, 252).

We can certainly assume that Kafka, the Jew from Prague, knew of this tradition of the creative power of language. After all, Prague was the home of the legendary Kabbalists Liva Ben Bezalel, that is Chief Rabbi Löw, whom every child in the city knew as the creator of the golem. According to many but not all of the versions of this legend (Scholem, *Symbolism*, 255), a slip of paper bearing the Hebrew word EMeT, "truth", is what vitalized the golem in the first place and which, by removing the E, left the Hebrew word "met", "death," behind, which word caused the golem to sink back into a clump of mud. This very slip of paper is indication enough of the creative power of language. Kafka had an even closer knowledge of the golem theme, though, and this fact is substantiated by his own attempt at writing a golem story, even if his attempt never did get beyond the fragment stage (*Diaries*, 310). Still, this fragment may perhaps provide another indication that Kafka, too, identified the word with the object. Kafka's Rabbi who formed the golem said of the clay he used: "It was so hard that even squeezing it hardly stained one's fingers, and its taste—for the inquisitive had to approach it with their tongues as well—was bitter . . .

"Bitter, bitter, that is the operative word. How shall I solder fragments together to produce a living story?"

Besides the slip of paper (which does not appear in every version of the story), it is the rabbi's ritualistic production of the golem described in a popular Yiddish-Hebrew version that places specific emphasis on the creative power of language and makes it the focus of the whole idea behind the golem. In fact, this ritual was part of the story long before the appearance of the Eastern European version of 1909 mentioned above. The narrator was a storyteller as well as a man known as a collector of hasidic tales, Yehudah Yudel Rosenberg.[7]

What follows is his version of the story about the creation of the golem; it's reproduction here may serve to show how even those unfamiliar with the teachings of Kabbalah may still learn some of its basic tenets from such folk legends:

How the Maharal[8] Made the Golem

The Maharal made a dream inquiry[9] to the effect that the power [of heaven] might enable him to resist the [hostile and anti-semitic] pastor. He received the following answer from heaven in the form of an alphabetical acrostic [following the order of the Hebrew alphabet]: *A*ta *B*ero *G*olem *D*abbek *H*a-hemer. *W*e-tigsor *S*edim *H*abbel *T*orfe *I*srael [*Y*ou *M*ake a *G*olem, *G*lue *T*he clay *t*ogether. *A*nd *f*ell the *T*ransgressors, *ST*rike those who *T*ear *I*srael apart].

The Maharal remarked: "These ten[10] words contain [letter] combinations whose power can always be used to create a living golem out of clay."

The Maharal secretly summoned his son-in-law, Isaac Ben Shimshon ha-Cohen, and his best pupil, Jacob Ben Chaim Sasson ha-Levi, and showed them the heavenly answer he had received to his dream inquiry. And he taught them the secret of making a golem out of the clay and the dust of the earth. He told them that he wanted to take them along to help him make the golem, because they needed the four powers of the four basic elements fire, air, water and earth to do it.

The Maharal revealed that he had been born with the power of the element air, his son-in-law with that of fire and his pupil Rabbi Jacob Sasson with that of water [while the golem itself would contribute the earth]. This was why the creation of the golem could only be carried out by these three men.

He told them not to tell anyone of the secret and instructed them regarding the tikkunim [kabbalistic meditations and penitential exercises] and the appropriate behavior they would have to observe during the next seven days.

On the 20th of Adar[11], 5340 [1580] all three men left the city of Prague at four o'clock in the morning and went to the Moldau River. On the banks of this river they looked for and found a place with clay and mud. Out of the mud they fashioned the shape of a man, three ells long. They drew the face, hands and feet of a man lying on his back.

Then they took their positions at the feet of the golem, their faces turned toward the golem's face. First the Maharal ordered his son-in-law to circle the golem seven times, starting on the right to his head and moving from his head to his feet on the left. He also gave him combinations of letters that he was supposed to recite as he walked around. They did this seven times. After they finished the first seven circumambulations, the body of the golem turned as red as a glowing coal.

Then the Maharal ordered his student, Rabbi Jacob Sasson, to circle the golem seven times in his turn, and he gave him different combinations of letters to recite. When he had finished, the fire went out, for water had now entered the golem's body, and it gave off steam. He also grew hair as of a 30-year-old, and nails grew on the tips of his fingers.

Finally, the Maharal himself made seven circles around the golem, and when he was finished all three men recited the Scripture verse: "And He breathed into his nostrils the breath of life, and he became a living soul" (Gen. 2:7), for as it says in the *Sefer Yetzirah* [*Book of Creation*], one's breath must be composed of fire, water and air together.

> The golem opened his eyes and looked about, astonished. Then the Maharal said with a commanding voice: "Stand up!" And the golem got up jerkily onto his feet. They dressed him in clothes they had brought with them, clothes that were appropriate for a servant of the court. They even put shoes on his feet.
>
> In brief, he had become a man like other men: he saw and heard and understood. The only thing he couldn't do was speak. At six in the morning, still before the break of day, four men turned toward home . . .[12]

As a point of interest I should mention the fact that Kafka himself occasionally engaged in "kabbalistic" letter games to underscore the identification of the characters in his texts with those of real life, with himself—or: should one say, to create them? In doing so, Kafka employed the same practices as did the Kabbalists before him. For example, if two words or two names of biblical heroes have the same numerical value or if their names can be equated by rearranging the letters, the Kabbalist considers them identical or at least united in their essence. In his *Pardes Rimmonim*[13], Moses Cordovero tells how the Kabbalist uses language to attain a knowledge of the divine mysteries as well as how he can use alphabetological methods to discover the inherent interconnectedness of all things:

> Knowledge of the mysteries of our Holy Torah is gained by [making] word combinations, numerical value reckonings, letter transpositions, acronymic and teleonymic word formations; by interpreting the middle letters of a word, the beginning and the end of a verse, by skipping over letters and by making different letter combinations. . . .
>
> The letters are the building blocks [derived] from the divine power of the insight [that] . . . one stone does not build a house, but two stones do build two houses. If, for example, a person combined two letters, two words will result from them, each one a house. If one combines A and B, for example, one gets AB and BA ["father" and "to come"] [etc.]

By producing combinations such as these, the Kabbalist discovers the essence of the object lying hidden beneath its surface; he sees commonalities and essential relationships. At the same time he is also effecting a corresponding change in the divine world, which in turn sets the creative process in motion and reaches all the way down to the lower ranks of our mortal sphere. Kafka himself tried his hand at finding inner relationships and identifications within objects by means of such letter games. He takes the identical number of letters as well as the corresponding positions of the vowels in the names Georg Bendemann and Franz Kafka as an indication of the fact that the one shares fundamental commonalities with the other—which in fact is true, as the previous chapter demonstrated. The observation that concludes these letter games in Kafka's diary seems to want to indicate that Kafka had not planned on these correspondences beforehand, but, like a kabbalistic exegete, he first discovered them after the fact. He thus obviously believed that the correspondences he was initially unaware of between the two individuals found their own expression in their own names, a fact he was only able to state *ex post facto* during his kabbalistic reflections.

Kafka made these observations on February 11, 1913 (*Diaries*, 186):

> Georg has as many letters as Franz. The "mann" in Bendemann only intensifies "Bende" and stands for all the as yet unknown potentialities of the story. On the other hand, Bende has just as many letters as Kafka and the vowel "e" is repeated here in the same positions as is the vowel "a" in Kafka.
>
> Frieda has the same number of letters as F. and the same initial letter; Brandenfeld has the same initial letter as B. and a certain relation in meaning as well through the word "Feld." Perhaps the thought of Berlin may even have had some influence and the recollection of the Mark Brandenburg may also have played a role.

Compare that with the preface to the Yiddish-Hebrew chapbook *Kav ha-Yashar* mentioned above. There the author, Tzevi Hirsch Kaidanover, says:

> I called the book *Kav ha-Yashar* (*Measure of the Righteous*) for two correct and expedient reasons. The first is that I have

> presented "Kav" [numerical value = 102] chapters before you in keeping with the numerical value of my own name, "Tzevi", which also amounts to 102. And if one rearranges the letters, the word "ha-Yashar" reveals my civilian name Hirsch; the letters of the one are within the letters of the other.

Moses Cordovero adds in his *Pardes Rimmonim*: "Gematria is when the numerical value of the Hebrew letters is the same. . . . For example, Rasiel has the same numerical value as Abraham. Even the number of letters is the same, each has five letters. . . . Thus they are of equal value, the one with the other."[14]

Even Kafka's sensitivity to the graphic form of his initial "K" testifies to an awareness of the identity between a name and the person bearing it, something we have already seen with reference to the Baal Shem Tov. Kafka says: "I find the K.'s ugly, they almost disgust me, but I still write them; they must be characteristic of me" (*Diaries*, 375). The process of infusing the graphic form of a letter with all sorts of contextual, ethical and ontological interpretations likewise extends deep into ancient Jewish mysticism, for the shape of the letters was just another part of the mystical universe of significance inhering to the Hebrew alphabet. To quote Moses Cordovero once again:[15]

> The letters of the Torah can not be traced back to an agreement made among human beings. On the contrary, they are spiritual and their external shape alludes to the innermost essence of their being. This is why the ancient scholars were so precise about their explanation of the essence and the form of the letters, with their spikes, their crowns and their components, for they all refer to a recognizable spiritual essence, namely: to the upper sefirot. Each letter has a spiritual form and a glory that emanates from the world of the sefirot, a glory that descends like a chain from one level to another. . . . By pronouncing a letter, a person awakens its spirit, and the breath of his mouth turns into holy forms that rise up and unite with their root in the heavenly regions.

The fifteenth century Kabbalist Moses Botarel provides a particularly instructive example of the interpretation of the shape of a letter:[16]

> The form of the letter "alef" is a reference to God's name, for the top of alef has the form of the letter "J," and the middle axis of the letter has the shape of the letter "W," and the foot is again a "J." The numerical value of these three letters is 26, and that is the same as the numerical value of the Name of God, YHWH.

According to all of this, then, the very form and shape of the letter represent spiritual realities, in this case the very essence of God, which the talmudic tradition expresses in the tetragramm, YHWH. Moreover, this name also symbolizes God's mercy and compassion. Moses Cordovero, for example, says that the first six letters of the Hebrew alphabet represent absolute compassion, the seventh through the tenth stand for simple compassion, letters eleven through sixteen (K falls within this range) stand for the mixture of compassion and judgment, while the remaining letters, seventeen through twenty-two, stand for absolute judgment. With reference to the letter "Kaf," which also corresponds to the German "K," Cordovero has this additional remark to make: "The K comes from the side of strength, that is, of judgment, as it says in Ezekiel (21:19): 'Smite thy hands [kaf] together.' Thus K is also called sin." Kafka, Joseph K. and the land surveyor K., Karl Rossmann,—according to this they would all succumb to strict judgment. A coincidence?

Kafka's relation to language as a creative power in which man also has a share, and be it as the language of prayer or of writing, whereby even the shape and the form of the letters are meaningful and whose inherent interrelationships reflect existential structures and bring forth creatures, all fits in seamlessly with the linguistic world of Jewish mysticism and Kabbalah. This may explain why life and language are identical for Kafka and why he attributes a religious weight to writing as a form of prayer.

16
JOSEPHINE THE SINGER; OR, THE MOUSE PEOPLE

"In Kafka's 'Josephine The Singer; or, the Mouse People,' a narrator who is obviously one of these mouse people writes about one of their outstanding artists, namely the singer Josephine" (Zimmermann, 75). Hardly anyone even vaguely familiar with the well-known stereotypes of Jewish history—the preservation of the people despite persecution—can help but share the impression D. H. Zimmermann presents with this statement: "This people . . . that has always managed to save itself somehow, regardless of how great a toll such preservation exacts, a toll that makes the historian—and in general we tend to neglect historical research completely—freeze with horror" (*Stories*, 192). This is a valid observation, even though K. H. Fingerhut maintains that the parenthetical remark about neglecting historical research must be taken as proof to the contrary (Fingerhut, 202f). From a Jewish point of view, the concluding sentence of the story naturally elicits astonishment; there the narrator expatiates as follows: "Perhaps we might not feel we were missing very much, but Josephine, delivered from the mortal travail which she felt all chosen people had to endure, will be cheerfully absorbed into the countless ranks of our people's heroes, and, since we don't record history, she'll soon be forgotten like all her brothers in a heightened state of deliverance" (*Stories*, 203). It appears that Fingerhut is quite correct in interpreting this observation as proof that Kafka did not have the Jews in mind when he spoke of the mouse people: "The great individual as a 'minor episode in the eternal history of our nation,' a person soon forgotten in 'a heightened state of deliverance': such a phenomenon is totally alien to the Jew's awareness of history" (Fingerhut, 203). History certainly plays an important role in Judaism; the biblical and ancient talmudic profession of faith in God as Israel's Deliverer from Egypt is founded in historical fact. But within what secondary literature sees as Judaism's at times almost mythical awareness of history the following fact is frequently ignored: kabbalistic or mystical Judaism is not terribly interested in actual history. For these people history is at most the cyclical repetition of a stereotypical event, an event that oscillates back and forth between good and evil. They see history as a reflex of the inherently divine state of unity or separation which, like a pendulum, is constantly shifting back and forth. The adepts of those forms of Kabbalah that stress the mystical union with the Divine, and these include for the most part significant aspects of Hasidism, are not interested in history as a consequence of irretrievable and unrepeatable events that may or definitely will lead to redemption. This explains, for example, why Zionism was not a viable option for this mystical conception of Judaism, for in the latter one attained redemption by stepping out of history by means of the personal/mystical upward surge toward the *unio mystica*—and not via historical or political activism. A person may attain this mystical deliverance despite his existence in exile; its elimination therefore was no longer a real or primary goal. The mystic looked upon the end of personal exile at most as the result of his personal mystical deliverance.[1] Both schools of kabbalistic thought, the cyclical as well as the ahistorical unio-mystical, were spread far and wide by the expansion of Hasidism and Kabbalah in eastern Europe.

More important, however, is the fact that historical research did not play as great a role as the topos of Jewish historical consciousness might suggest in the religious consciousness of everyday life and in the traditional talmudic training of the yeshivas, where the "orthodox" elite of rabbis and rabbinical scholars were educated. Furthermore, whatever historical awareness does exist in these circles is sooner directed to the collective history of the nation and less to that of the individual hero. The heroes who figure in this collective historical consciousness of the general Jewish population are primarily biblical figures: the patriarchs, Moses, David and Solomon, as well as Esther who protected her people against the plots of Haman, and finally even the post-biblical heroes of the Maccabean wars, Jehuda the Maccabee, his father Mattathias, the mother with her seven sons who defied religious persecution. On a somewhat lower level one finds references to Rabbi Akiba and nine additional martyrs from the period of the Bar-Kochba rebellion against the Romans at the beginning of the second century of the common reckoning. These latter stories actually became the models determining the depiction of medieval martyriologies. The sole purpose of these reports is not to relate the deeds of "heroes;" they aim instead to impress upon the reader's mind the stereotype of Jewish martyrdom in a form closer to the litany. The post-classical period produced very few if any historical hero stories focusing on individual champions of the nation. In other words, it hardly knew champions of the type Josephine claims to represent. These medieval chroniclers were much more interested in the history of the scholarly tradition, in the development of the talmudic commentators, or in individual family chronicles which again focused in on the scholarly tradition for the most part. Traditional rabbinical literature, which follows the model of the Talmud, is less interested in the recording of actual history. In this sense it can probably be said of traditional Judaism that "we don't write history," especially since a national history of the Jews scattered throughout the four corners of the world only began to be contemplated again with the emergence of the scholarly study of Judaism in the wake of the Enlightenment.

On the other hand, stories about individual redeemers of the Jews have existed within the sphere of the Holy Roman Empire (in the German, Italian and Spanish languages) and later in the Slavic regions of eastern Europe ever since the late Middle Ages. As we shall see, much of what is said of Josephine applies to these heroes as well. But even here, in these redeemer stories, there can be no talk of "historical research" in any real sense. This is because the potential individuality of the heroes of these tales is completely concealed behind the repeated stereotype, so that the individual can in fact "be cheerfully absorbed into the countless ranks of our people's heroes" (*Stories*, 203). What actually happens is that the stories of the liberating acts of these redeemers are passed on from one "hero" to the next—their names are as interchangeable as the deeds they perform and as the nature of the catastrophe that calls them forth. Deliverance from the repressive acts of a non-Jewish potentate or of some other anti-semite is thus always cast in the stereotypical prototype of Haman's plots against the Jews and their rescue by Esther and Mordecai. One result of this is the fact that a whole series of local Purim celebrations grew up around the traditional Purim festival that originally recalled this deliverance; one such local version is the Purim Vinz in Frankfurt on Main, which commemorates the successful outcome of the Fettmilch Uprising of 1614. The story of these heroes' deeds, then, as passed on by folk tradition, was thus no more "alive" than the people's current recollection of them. In other words, the reported heroic deed, historically speaking, had no greater historical reality than the memory of it. The forces supporting the memory were the same ones that gave form to the reports. The detached skeptic, the persona Kafka assumes in his "Josephine" story, is thus quite justified in asking: "Was her actual piping significantly louder and more animated than our memory of it will be? Was it actually more than mere memory, even during her lifetime? Could it be, perhaps, that the people in their wisdom valued Josephine's singing so highly, simply because it could never be lost that way?" (*Stories*, 203). Kafka's observation about the relation of the report to the reported is equally applicable to the Jewish tales of the redemptive deeds of miracle-men. Popular belief created the topos of the redeemer and maintained it through the centuries, transferring it in the course of history from one to another historical figure like an official robe that could be draped over the shoulders of the successor as soon as the incumbent took it off.

The narrators of these "hero stories" were well aware that the hero of the tale was basically capable of doing nothing more than what the popular memory of him itself could do. In his *Major Trends in Jewish Mysticism*, Gershom Scholem describes the situation this way:

> When the Baal Shem had a difficult task before him, he would go to a certain place in the woods, light a fire and meditate in prayer—and what he had set out to perform was done. When

> a generation later the "Maggid" of Meseritz was faced with the same task he would go to the same place in the woods and say: We can no longer light the fire, but we can still speak the prayers—and what he wanted done became reality. Again a generation later Rabbi Moshe Leib of Sasov had to perform this task. And he too went into the woods and said: We can no longer light a fire, nor do we know the secret meditations belonging to the prayer but we do know the place in the woods to which it all belongs—and that must be sufficient; and sufficient it was. But when another generation had passed and Rabbi Israel of Rishin was called upon to perform the task, he sat down on his golden chair in his castle and said: We cannot light the fire, we cannot speak the prayers, we do not know the place, but we can tell the story of how it was done. And, the story-teller adds, the story which he told had the same effect as the actions of the other three. (*Major Trends*, 349f)

The interchangeability of the individual hero figure and its absorption into the "ranks of [folk] heroes" ultimately produced the idea of the Tzaddik ha-Dor in Jewish folklore. This is the Righteous One or "champion" of the generation, and the idea was already prefigured in its own way in the Talmud with references to the *Hasid ha-Dor*, the miracle-working holy man of the generation.[2] "If someone had performed a conjuration and he wasn't heard, let him go to the Hasid ha-Dor, and let him pray for mercy for him."

This same figure appears again in the form of "the Great Man of the Generation" in a report on the after-effects of the Frankfurt Fettmilch Uprising of 1614 before the gates of the Judengasse in Worms. According to the chronicler Liva Kirchheim, the following miracle occurred as the mob from Worms besieged the Judengasse:

> The Lord our God took pity on us and our children and rescued us from their hand, since fear and terror had fallen upon the people [before the gate]—for among us was the Great Man of the Generation, namely the sublime leader, the jewel of the nation, our Master and Rav, Gedaliah, who was a Baal Shem. By calling upon the Names of God, he saw to it that the Judengasse was filled with warriors who went about in their armor with all sorts of weapons and materials for making war.

> When our enemies saw them on the wall, they were struck with terror.[3]

The Eastern European hasidic folk tales call this kind of leader-figure the tzaddik ha-dor. According to Elimelech of Lizensk, the theologian of hasidic tzaddikism, there are, at least in theory, other "lesser" miracle men or tzaddikim who either work together with this one or are believed to be dependent upon him. Kafka knew of such theories from his friend Georg Langer, who told him at least two stories of this kind, and surely not without the necessary background information. Kafka recorded them in his diary on October 6, 1915. Kafka was familiar with the role such hero figures played within the consciousness of the Jewish people from one of the two tales and probably from some other of his favorite hasidic stories, not to mention what he learned from his visit to the wonder-rabbi in Zizkov[4] and from his acquaintance with the Rebbe of Belz in Marienbad. At times, and particularly in the hasidic traditions surrounding these miracle men, the relation between them and their people was described with a give-and-take similar to the one that characterizes Josephine's relation to the mouse people.

In a small volume of Eastern European legends I managed to find a more expansive and probably more imaginative Hebrew version of the more important of the two stories about the tzaddik ha-dor that Kafka noted in his diary. I should add here, by the way, that one of the characteristics of the folk tale is the fact that various versions often differ considerably from each other and that no one version can be considered the "original." The most that can be said is that each version represents a different approach to the same material. This particular version will follow the one Kafka noted in his diary on October 6, 1915 (*Diaries*, 300):

Kafka's Version

> Every hundred years there appears a supreme tzaddik, a tzaddik ha-dor. He need not be well known, doesn't have to be a wonder-rabbi, and yet he is still supreme. Baal Shem Tov was not the tzaddik ha-dor of his day; that role was allotted to an unknown merchant in Drohobycz.
>
> The latter heard that the Baal Shem wrote amulets, as did other tzaddikim as well, and he suspected that the Baal Shem

> was a follower of Shabbetai Tzevi and that it was his name he inscribed on the amulets. For this reason and without having met him personally, the tzaddik ha-dor, although far away, deprived the Baal Shem of the power of his amulets. Baal Shem soon discovered the impotence of his amulets—even though he had never inscribed anything other than his own name on them—and learned in due course that the Drohobyczer was the cause of it. One day—it was a Monday—when the Drohobyczer entered the town where Baal Shem lived, the Baal Shem let him sleep through one complete day without his noticing it. As a result, the Drohobyczer was always a day behind in his reckoning. Friday evening—he thought it was Thursday—he wanted to return to celebrate the holidays at home. He sees the people going to temple and realizes his mistake. He decides to stay here and goes to the home of the Baal Shem, who that very afternoon had instructed his wife to prepare a meal for thirty persons. When the Drohobyczer comes, he sits down to eat right after the prayers and in no time at all eats all the food that had been prepared for thirty persons. But he isn't satisfied and demands more to eat. Baal Shem says: "I expected an angel of the first order; for an angel of the second order I was not prepared." Whereupon he had all the food in the house brought to the table, but even that wasn't enough.

The Hebrew version in the 1856 anthology *Mif'alot ha-Tzaddikim* reads as follows:

> The rav and holy tzaddik, our teacher Rabbi Isaac [Drohobyczer] once journeyed through the city of Mesibos. While there, he heard of the miraculous power of the Baal Shem Tov's amulet, and he believed that the Besht accomplished this by magically invoking the Holy Names [of God as well as of the angels]. That's why the following words slipped out of him: "If one uses the crown, may it disappear"[5], which is to say, this miraculous power has to disappear and be lost to him. From that moment on the Baal Shem Tov's amulet was deprived of its miraculous power, and from then on they were useless and nothing could be done about it.

This continued for a full twelve months. When the Baal Shem Tov realized that his amulets were no longer effecting cures, he pursued the matter and discovered it was the result of the words of the tzaddik rav Rabbi Isaac. The Baal Shem Tov instigated an action of his own which requited Rabbi Isaac's deed twice over.

It happened this way: while the rav, Rabbi Isaac, was on one of his journeys, he got confused about the counting of the days and was convinced that Monday was Sunday and so on, until he came to Thursday, which he believed to be Wednesday. The next day, which he thought to be Thursday although it was actually Friday already, he arrived in the city of Mesibos. His intention was to travel on and spend the sabbath in a nearby town. Still believing it was Thursday, he took his time about continuing his journey, since he was sure he still had two days' time to get to his destination by the sabbath.

He passed the time comfortably in his hostel, praying, eating and resting again from the toils of his journey, all the while thinking he still had close to a day and a half for the short trip.

But when he got up, he saw that the table in the hostel had been set in a festive manner, complete with the sabbath bread and the candles ready to be lit in commemoration of the sabbath. He was confused and completely nonplussed. He asked the master of the house why everything had been prepared as if for the sabbath since it was still only Thursday. Everyone answered at once: "But today is the eve of the sabbath, Friday afternoon!" He couldn't believe it and went outside; there he saw people hurrying to the *mikveh* with their sabbath coats over their arms, and many were even returning already. He finally realized that what they had said was true, and he returned to the house to prepare to welcome the sabbath.

Meanwhile, the Baal Shem Tov came to him to invite him to share his sabbath meal. The Baal Shem Tov wouldn't give in, even though the Rabbi didn't want to accept the invitation and said: "But look, the house master has prepared all sorts of delicacies in my honor; how can I be so rude as to render all his preparations vain?" But the Baal Shem Tov replied: "I've already asked the master of the house and he has agreed; as a favor to me he will forego his honour and bear the loss."

The Rabbi continued to prevaricate with all sorts of excuses and finally said: "Actually I eat an enormous amount before I'm full. Your invitation will surely not suffice." The Baal Shem Tov assured him: "I have prepared enough food for you." And he didn't cease until the Rabbi finally agreed, whereupon he went with the Baal Shem Tov to his house.

They sat down to the sabbath meal, and right after the *kiddush* [the blessing of the wine] Rabbi Isaac placed a silver medaillon engraved with the Name of God on his thumb. This was his saintly habit every time he sat down to eat. He focussed his attention on the Holy Name throughout the entire meal.

As he began to eat, all the dishes they had prepared were placed before him, and he left not so much as a crumb for the other guests. He ate everything they had prepared. When he had finished, he said to the Baal Shem Tov: "Didn't you promise me there would be enough? I'm still hungry and there's no food left."

The Baal Shem Tov replied: "Alas, I prepared enough food even for the angels, but not for the seraphim!," whereupon the rav put the silver medaillon away and from that moment on he couldn't eat another bite.

Toward the end of the sabbath, during the third meal that accompanies the sabbath queen's departure, the Baal Shem Tov asked the rav: "Why did you deprive me of the power to do wonders with my amulets? That power was given to me to help people."

The rav, Rabbi Isaac, answered him: "It is forbiden to make use of the Holy Name!"[6] The Baal Shem Tov responded: "There is not one single Holy Name written on my amulets, and I use absolutely no invocation, just my own name: Israel Ben Sara Baal Shem Tov."

The Rabbi didn't believe him and cried: "How can your name alone bring about such great and awesome deeds?" Several amulets were placed before him, and he opened them and saw that the Baal Shem Tov was telling the truth.

Rabbi Isaac said to him: "If you give me a new sabbath robe, I'll restore the power of your amulets to what it used to be."

> The Baal Shem Tov gave him a robe, as he requested, and Rabbi Isaac opened his mouth and spoke: "Lord of the World, if this man can earn his living with his own name, why should that bother you? Restore to him the power of his amulet which bears his name only." And so it happened.
>
> From that day on the Baal Shem Tov was once again able to work mighty and awesome wonders with his amulets. And everyone present marvelled that this man had the power to pervert the will of the Baal Shem Tov. The Baal Shem Tov explained it this way: "What can I do? For the time being Rabbi Isaac is still the Tzaddik ha-Dor, the Tzaddik of the Generation, and all the world obeys his word. I too must keep my peace, even though many of his deeds do not please me. Even when he lectures on an exegesis of a passage in the [kabbalistic book] *Pri Etz Hayyim* (*The Fruit of the Tree of Life*), the true meaning of which I understand much better than he, I have to hold my tongue.[7]

It is impossible to try to compare and contrast these two versions in the hopes of learning something about Kafka's intentions because we do not know whether the differences between them were already present in Langer's tale or were first introduced by Kafka himself. Clearly, however, a great deal can be ascribed to the editing that went into the diary entry. Langer's version is based on a story similar to the one cited above, even though Kafka's retelling of it lacks some significant details, such as the reinstatement of the "magical power" of the Baal Shem Tov's amulets, which is, of course, what leads to his triumph over the tzaddik ha-dor in this confrontation. Regardless of the exact wording of Langer's version, we may still assume that many of the details concerning the magical power of names and the ability of such a man to act as a champion as described here will have had their origin in Langer's tale. A few years earlier, on December 25, 1911, Kafka wrote even more details concerning the use of amulets during a circumcision "in Russia" as well as about the vigil meant to keep the demons at bay (*Diaries*, 132).

We can conclude from all of this that Kafka had accurate information about the true nature of the Eastern European miracle men, be they Hasidim or non-hasidic Kabbalists like Rabbi Löw in

Prague. Much of this information was gleaned from Kafka's own observations—even if, as Max Brod maintains, they led him to draw the derisive and summary conclusion that it was all "crass superstition" (Brod, *Kafka*, 187):

> In those days I spent a lot of time together with my Kabbalist friend Georg Langer at the house of a wonder-rabbi (the Rabbi of Grodeck). He had fled from Galicia and was living in the Prague suburb of Zizkov in dark and unfriendly rooms that were always filled with people. Particular circumstances in my life had brought me close to a kind of religious fanaticism. It's worth noting that Franz, whom I took along to one of the "Third Meals" at the close of the Sabbath with its whisperings and hasidic singing, actually remained quite cool. He was unquestionably moved by the primal sounds of an ancient custom, but on the way home he said: "To tell the truth, it was a bit like being with a wild African tribe. Crass superstition." There was nothing offensive in this statement, but surely a tinge of sober defense. I understood him well: Franz had his own personal mysticism and he couldn't just take over ready-made rituals from others. (And yet, the impression was strong enough and had its effect. The beginning of the golem story in the diary seems to be based on it.)

I think Brod's opinion accurately reflects Kafka's relation to the magical world of the Kabbalah with its leader and hero figures. Kafka records Langer's tales in his diary with the same mixture of interest and detachment, careful to maintain an objective and accurate representation as far as the essential points are concerned, and he refrains from adding any commentary of his own. His own report of their visit to the Zizkover Rabbi on September 14, 1915 reflects the same oscillation between attraction and repulsion that this so very naturalistic eastern European world elicited in him (*Diaries*, 297):

> With Max and Langer Saturday at the wonder-rabbi's. Zizkov, Harantova ulice. A lot of children on the sidewalk and on the stairs. An inn. Upstairs completely dark, blindly groping along step by step with outstretched hands. A dimly-lit room as at

> twilight, greyish-white walls, several small women and girls standing around, white kerchiefs, pale faces, hardly any movement. Impression of bloodlessness. Next room. Everything black, full of men and young people. Loud praying. We squeeze into a corner. We'd hardly had a chance to look around before the prayer was over; the room empties out. A corner room with two window-walls, two windows each. We're shoved up against a table to the right of the rabbi. We protest. "You're Jews, too, aren't you?" The rabbi exudes the strongest possible paternal nature. "All rabbis have a savage look," says Langer. This one in a silk kaftan, underpants visible underneath. Hair on the bridge of the nose. A fur yarmulke which he constantly shifts back and forth. Dirty and pure, the peculiar characteristic of people who think intensely. Scratches his beard, snorts through his hand and onto the floor, eats with his fingers—but when he momentarily rests his hand on the table, one can see the whiteness of his skin, rather like the whiteness one believes to have seen only in the phantasies of childhood. Of course, back then one's parents were pure, too.

A similarly detached and yet not unsympathetic relation characterizes the ties between Josephine and the mouse people. From what the hasidic texts tell us, this relation was not all that different from the one that existed between the hasidic rebbe or miracle man and his congregation. Josephine is the master of an art form that basically belongs to the whole people. This is as true of the magical powers of the Baal Shem, the "kabbalistic magician of the Name" as it is of the related practice of singing passages from the Holy Scriptures.

The *Sefer Hasidim*, the thirteenth century *Book of the Pious*, originated in the Rhineland; the Baal Shem Tov, who came from the east, used it as a guide. In a section dealing with practices employing the Holy Names of God, the foundation stone of the power possessed by Jewish miracle men like the Baal Shem, it says that every honest and god-fearing Jewish family man can learn this art. It adds the caveat, however, that those who haven't studied these names properly can do a great deal of mischief and harm with them.[8] The important point is that, although such a miracle man and leader of his people occupies a privileged position among them and is looked upon as their redeemer, all his powers derive ultimately from an art that is, in principle, accessible to all.

The same holds true for the idea of the tzaddik. This idea is related to that of the Eastern Jewish miracle man, but certain religious and phenomonological distinctions should be made with respect to the Baal Shem. As a Kabbalist theurgist, the tzaddik is capable of drawing blessings upon his fellow man down from the divine Source of Light and from the divine Life Force.[9] If I may be permitted a parenthetical observation: the remarks of the dog in Kafka's "Investigations of a Dog" are reminiscent of this type of theurigical skill: "To my mind, tilling the soil serves to produce both kinds of nourishment and will always be absolutely necessary; sayings, dance and song, on the other hand, have less to do with the nourishment of the soil in a narrower sense. Their main purpose is rather to draw nourishment from above. Tradition supports me in this view. Here the people seem to correct science . . ." (*Stories*, 358).—Moreover, in the Kabbalists' view, this theurgic ability which uses prayer, meditation, song and, among the Hasidim, dance as well, to draw divine blessings down to the material world to enhance its health and prosperity, is accessible to every Jew. In fact, the very name of the person who possesses this skill, tzaddik, proves the point, for it means nothing more and nothing less than "the righteous one" and has been used to define the ideal of normal "bourgeois" piety throughout the thousands of years of Jewish tradition. Naturally, there is a great difference between a talmudic tzaddik and a kabbalistic tzaddik. The former is a man who has been acquitted before the bars of the celestial court on the grounds of the overwhelming preponderance of his merits on the balance with his transgressions. The same applies to the kabbalistic tzaddik, but he enjoys the additional gifts of mystical meditation and the ability to practice theurgy. The decision to apply the ancient name to this new quality is also in keeping with the circumstances, for, according to the Kabbalah, every Jew can and should reach this goal of direct contact with the Godhead via theurgy.

For the Kabbalist, song is an important element of this theurgical ability; however, over time and only in relatively rare cases has the term come to mean a type of chant somewhat similar to the

Western model. It is generally more reminiscent of the oriental sound of the Torah cantorials and the prayer chants of the synagogue, rather like the "sing-song" that accompanies the study of the Torah. It can also be said to resemble the *Niggun*, the wordless song, that characterizes the language of the pious Jew, rather like the piping of the mice in the parable of the mouse people.[10] In the words of the fourteenth-century *Sefer ha-Peli'a*: "One draws down the spirit of the living God by means of familiar melodies, the twenty-three melodies in which the Torah is chanted. People say these melodies are the accents for the cantorials of the Torah (ta'ame tora)."[11]

The liberating and redeeming power of song (a power also Josephine claims for her singing) which looks and sounds for all the world exactly like the song everybody sings (even Brod mentions it in his report) can also be found in hasidic folk tales, and it plays a pivotal role in the legend of the Baal Shem Tov (*H*, 9; *Praise*, 12):

> Soon after [the youth Baal Shem Tov] hired himself out as a teacher's assistant. As such, he accompanied the school children into the bet midrash and the synagogue, where they sang "Amen, may His great name be praised" [part of the kaddish], the Kedusha and Amen in a pleasant voice. This was his duty, and it was a holy task to work with these children, for their breath is a breath free of sin.
>
> Whenever he accompanied the children, he led their singing with a pleasant voice and such deep delight that he could be heard from far off, for his devotion ascended to the heights where it was received as purely and delightfully as was the song of the Levites in the Temple. It was a time of joy in heaven on high.
>
> "And Satan came also among them" (Job 1:6), for he realized just where he stood. He began to fear for his own existence—had the time come already that he should be swallowed up by the earth?
>
> Satan disguised himself as a sorcerer; when the Besht passed by with the children, singing in his pleasant and enthusiastic manner, the sorcerer transformed himself into a wild beast, a werewolf, and fell upon them so that they all

scattered in their fright. Some of them even became so sick that, God forbid, the daily "offering in the temple" had to be abandoned.

It so happened that the Besht now recalled the words of his father: he should fear nothing, for the Lord was with him. This thought filled the Besht with renewed strength in God, the Lord. He went to the men of the house, to the fathers of the children and spoke earnestly with them, entreating them to entrust their children once again to his care. He would resist the Evil One and kill him in the name of the Lord. After all, why should the children, who are such a treasure, be kept away because of him? The fathers were persuaded by his words, and the Besht armed himself with a hefty rod. As it happened, as he was leading the children along, singing pleasantly amidst the joy and exultation, the beast once again fell upon them. The Besht confronted him and struck him so fiercely on the forehead that he collapsed dead on the spot.

The next morning they found the dead body of an uncircumcised sorcerer lying stretched out on the ground.

According to this legend, the song the innocent school children sang under the direction of their charismatic teacher brought the messianic redemption closer, which was to lead the way toward the end of Satan and the reestablishment of the Jerusalem Temple cult.

According to those who know, the song mentioned in Brod's report as well as in the legend quoted above has absolutely nothing to do with art. Beauty and aesthetics play a peripheral role in such singing. What is important is the person's total absorption in his singing: he falls into it with heart and soul. It should not surprise us, then, if Kafka had this Jewish folk music in mind when he wrote his parable of the mouse people: "Of course, it's only a kind of whistling. Why not? Piping is the language of our people. Many of us whistle our whole life long and never know it, but her whistling is freed from the constraints of daily life and it liberates us for a little while. There's no question but we wouldn't want to miss these performances" (*Stories*, 196f).

The hasidic tales also tell of the singing and dancing of their masters and how they elevate, and be it ever so briefly, whoever happens to witness these events into the mystical sphere of timelessness, which is to say, into the mystical sphere of temporary deliverance:[12]

> The rav, our teacher Rabbi Baruch of Mesibos, a saintly man, fear-inspiring like one of the seraphim, the grandson of the holy light of Israel, which is to say of our master the Besht, blessed be his memory, was the brother of the venerable author of the book *The Banner of the Tribe of Ephraim.*
>
> Everybody knows the story they tell about him, the miracle that happened whenever he started to sing The Song of Solomon on the eve of the sabbath after the mikveh.
>
> At those times he burned like a fire, and his ecstasy blazed to heaven.
>
> The Kabbalists said of him that his own soul bore a spark of the soul of King Solomon, peace be with him.
>
> Whenever he started to sing this song, it always turned out that he burst into flames and rose up like a torch, and no one could come close to him because he would have sent him into a swoon and divested him of his corporality. And this is because anyone who is not accustomed to devekut [the mystical state of communion with God] and the abandonment of corporality becomes dizzy and dies from it.

Rabbi Baruch falls into ecstasy while singing the Song of Solomon; his soul departs from his body and pushes the physical world aside, so that, liberated from all material qualities, it might cleave to God, which is to say, enter into the unio mystica. This ecstatic exit of the soul was believed to lead to death in extreme instances. Ever since the Middle Ages, such a departure has come to be called "death in a kiss"[13]. More important for our purposes, however, is the tale that follows this prefatory remark. This tale tells how the mystical act can communicate the mystical experience to those listening to the singer and lead them to a vision of God as well. In other words, it can inspire them with a new divine vitality:

> Our teacher Tzevi, the holy rav of Siditshov, blessed be his memory, told the following tale:

One day while in Mesibos he hid in a room with ar in order to hear the Song of Solomon from the ve mouth of the rav, the memory of this Righteous One b eternal life. As the latter fell into an ecstatic state an sing the song with total abandonment, the Hasid saiu . holy rav, our teacher Tzevi, blessed be his memory, that his thoughts were being distracted by the fire that burned within him. And when he came to the verse: "He hath brought me to the banqueting-house, and his banner over me is love. Stay ye me with dainties, refresh me with apples, for I am love-sick" (Song of Sol. 2:4–5), one could actually see how the fire blazed about him. The Hasid, who was with him, fled, because he couldn't bear the great and awesome fire, for he "perceived the thunderings and the lightenings" (Exod. 20:15) and the whole house burned with fire. Rabbi Tzevi, however, took heart and gathered all his strength in order to listen to the voice of the "Angel of the Lord", until he finally came to the verse: "I am my beloved's, and his desire is for me" (Song of Sol. 7:11). At this point he was ready to pass out except that the holy one, our teacher Rabbi Tzevi, blessed be his memory, said to himself: "Come what may, I want to give my life to the Lord in love, to hear the words of the living God as at their revelation on Sinai, even if, God forbid, my soul should leave my body. I am ready to do the will of my Creator, blessed be He."

A new spirit from on high poured out over him, and he saw the fire of the Lord of Heaven blazing in the house—it couldn't be measured, it couldn't be described and it couldn't be told. So he stood there until he recited the words of the Scripture: "For love is strong as death, jealousy is cruel as the grave. The flashes thereof are flashes of fire, a very flame of the Lord" (Song of Sol. 8:6).

He almost passed away, God forbid, out of pure ecstasy and desire, but the Lord came to his aid until he had finished the song.

The singing these texts talk about refers to the traditional chantings of the Torah to which all sorts of folk songs and wordless melodies have been added in the meantime. Even so, in spite of an uninterrupted Jewish vocal tradition and many medieval

…usical culminating points,[14] Jewish musical life was considerably hampered by a series of strict rabbinical prohibitions, with the result that instrumental music remained as good as banned from the synagogue because of the prohibition on work on the sabbath. In addition, the only music that was tolerated on "worldly" occasions were religious hymns, and this as a sign of mourning for the destroyed temple.[15] Compared to the role music and singing played in European culture, music as an art form played hardly any role at all in synagogal and traditional Jewish life, and this in spite of the cantors who were held in high esteem by the members of the congregation. When seen through the eyes of a Western European, then, one might easily come to the same conclusion about synagogal folk music as about Josephine's singing: "During such periods we would certainly never tolerate a really professional singer, should one ever find his way to us, and we would unanimously reject the foolishness of such a performance. May Josephine be spared the realization that the very fact we listen to her at all is evidence against her singing" (*Stories*, 194).

Josephine's piping wails, however, not only stand for song in its narrower sense, but, in general, for her ability, as she sees it, to "give us new strength during such times" (*Stories*, 197). "Josephine thinks she's the one who's protecting the people. Her singing supposedly saves us from a dire political or economic situation" (*Stories*, 192). This is precisely what countless hasidic tales about miracle men and leaders of Eastern European Judaism claim to do. Elimelech of Lizensk, the theoretician of Eastern European tzaddikism and the man whose works Georg Langer studied, discusses this power of the tzaddik in his homilies, thus providing the theological underpinnings for what the folk stories later elaborate upon:[16]

> One of the essential duties of the tzaddik is to see to it to bring about everything. That's why he's called "Master of the House", because he provides the world with plenty just as a father provides the members of his household with their sustenance. And God has nothing to do, as it were, because the tzaddik can accomplish everything by means of his own actions and behavior.

Elimelech of Lizensk puts the tzaddik in the position Josephine claims for herself in the passage quoted above: "Josephine . . . thinks she's the one who's protecting the people. Her singing supposedly saves us from a dire political or economic situation" (*Stories*, 192).

On the other hand, the people also feel they have to take care of Josephine (*Stories*, 191), and in fact "the people thus look after Josephine the way a father cares for a child. . . . One might think that our people were not very good at performing such parental duties, but in reality we attend to her, at least in this case, admirably. No one person could do what the people as a whole are capable of doing in this regard. Of course, the strength differential between that of the people and that of the individual is so great that all the people have to do is draw the protégé into the warmth of its proximity for it to be sufficiently protected" (*Stories*, 192).

The hasidic tzaddik, who, in Elimelech's words, claims possession of all and sundry powers, is, again according to Elimelech, just as dependent as Josephine upon the "care" of the whole group; without this care his own powers would count for nothing. This is because the power of the tzaddik exists only as long as all of Israel submits itself in obedience to the will of God by fulfilling all of God's commandments. This means that the power of the tzaddik is once again ultimately founded in the collective strivings of the whole group. Should this be lacking, the tzaddik is powerless and God Himself will once again have to step in and help out.[17] "If, God forbid, [Israel] fails to perform the will of God, then He Himself has to be after them, so that they turn their attention to His Holy Torah . . . , for it is incumbent upon God Himself to see that He provides His people with plenty."

When the people sin, the channels of the river of life that provide the divine abundance that flows out over the world via the tzaddik become clogged. In such a case, even the tzaddik is unable to effect any changes.[18]

Elimelech says it is also the people's faith in the tzaddik in addition to their obedience in fulfilling God's commandments that finally transforms his potential powers into actual deed:[19] "It is only due to the simple folk among his people that he is able to effect change and bring about a true union in the upper world . . . , all because they believe in him." The hasidic teachings of Jacob

Joseph of Polonnoye, the Baal Shem Tov's most loyal disciple, as well as those of Elimelech, stress the fact that a connection and a community must exist between the people and its tzaddik. Martin Buber took this same teaching from Hasidism and applied it to his sociological utopias, a fact that can be seen, for example, in the spontaneous contribution he made during the discussion period following a lecture by Gustav Landauer.[20] With their insistence upon this reciprocity between the tzaddik and his followers, the ideologues of tzaddikism raised a demand that Josephine in turn required of her own people (*Stories*, 198):

> For a long time now, perhaps even since the beginning of her artistic career, Josephine has struggled to be excused from all work out of consideration for her singing. In other words, she should be relieved of all responsibility for her daily bread and whatever else has anything to do with our battle for existence, and this responsibility—probably—should be passed on to the people as a whole.

It was the first hasidic author, the Jacob Joseph of Polonnoye mentioned above, who established the ideological basis for such a demand. According to his theology of mystical community, the tzaddik, the rebbe, is considered the soul of his community, and the community, in turn, is looked upon as his body. Jacob Joseph says that this division of being shared by the tzaddik and the community corresponds to a similar division of function. By means of his contemplations and his ecstatic ascents into the realms of the Divine, the tzaddik provides his community-body with celestial blessings and mystical union with the Godhead. The community-body, on the other hand, like the body of an individual person, is ever ready to provide the community soul, the tzaddik, with its necessary physical and material needs.[21]

> The wise man passes wisdom on to the generous, and the generous man passes some of his wealth on to the wise man.
>
> The one[22] who brings down [divine blessings] is called a tzaddik. . . . The wise man . . . lets it flow to those on a lower level. . . . But the rich are charitable toward the poor, and these

> are the scholars. And the world persists in the fact that they were all created as an alliance. This is to teach us that the world insists upon the one giving something to the other. Let him who possesses wisdom pass wisdom on, and he who has wealth pass wealth on.

This rather general delineation of the wise man and the rich man takes on a very precise meaning within the context of Jacob Joseph's homilies: The wise man is the spiritual man, in ancient philosophical terms the "form"-person, which is to say the ecstatic or tzaddik, or, in other words, the rebbe. The rich man, on the other hand, is a person of the professional world and daily routine, the person oriented toward income and the necessities of life; in philosophical terms the "material" man.

Amplifications such as these show that the hasidic author asks for the same thing that Josephine wants when she claims that she, who saves and sustains her people through her singing, bears such a heavy load with her redemptive activity on behalf of her people that they must assume responsiblity for providing her "daily bread." Many texts depict the hasidic tzaddik as a man whose thoughts and being are totally preoccupied with the upper world through his ecstatic cleaving to God (unio mystica). This is the way he looks after his people's prosperity, but the result is that he has neither time nor freedom to attend to his own material needs. On the other hand, the community can devote itself completely to sustaining his day-to-day existence, for he provides it with all its spiritual needs. The community must reciprocate therefore by providing for the rebbe's physical well-being. According to the considered opinion of Jacob Joseph, these two elements of the mystical *corpus communitatis* are mutually dependent upon each other through the order God planned for His creation; the world is only then in the proper order God wanted when each side fulfills its responsibilities toward the other.

Kafka was well acquainted with this Eastern Jewish hasidic way of life, for he frequently witnessed its practice among the followers who clung to their miracle-rabbi. If we keep this in mind, his "Josephine" reads in places like a rather frivolous treatment of this Eastern Jewish symbiosis. Even so, tones of melancholy and acknowledgement can be heard again and again throughout the story, a reflection of Kafka's approach/avoidance conflict vis-à-vis this way of life. It underscores his conclusion that this pious and mutual "self- deception" in the end does have its good sides for daily life: "And even if [her singing] doesn't dispel the misfortune, at least it does give us the strength to bear it. . . . Of course, she doesn't rescue us and doesn't give us any strength. . . . And yet, it is true that we listen to Josephine's voice with more attention than usual in times of trouble. The threats that hover over us make us quieter, less supercilious, more accepting of Josephine's bossiness; it gives us pleasure to gather together, it gives us pleasure to press up against each other . . ." (*Stories*, 192, cf. also 197).

Kafka continues: "It's easy to play the great hero of this people, accustomed as it is to suffering, not sparing itself, quick to decide, well acquainted with death, only apparently anxious in the atmosphere of daredevilry in which it constantly lives, and moreover, as fruitful as it is presumptuous—it's easier, I say, to play the great hero of this people after the fact, a nation that has always managed to save itself somehow, regardless of how great a toll is exacted . . ." (*Stories*, 192).

This is precisely what a whole series of "hasidic" stories tell about their heroes. Put in slightly different terms, these stories occasionally make the retroactive claim that the hero warded off a threatening danger or brought about the rather good ending of some catastrophe that had just occurred. The two tales of the Baal Shem Tov cited above belong to this genre; the third such legend reads as follows (*H*, 198; *Praise*, 180):

> I heard the following tale from the rabbi of the holy community of Polonnoye: When a war broke out between the Greeks and the Ishmaelites during his own lifetime, the Besht said: "I saw two angelic warriors battling one another. The one of the Ishmaelites was the superior warrior, whereupon the one on the side of the Greeks retreated in great danger. I realized that a great danger for the Jews could arise from this, God forbid. So I prayed that it should be otherwise, that the Greek warrior should gain the upperhand. There were only two Jews whom I couldn't rescue from their hands."

In contrast to the contention Max Brod maintains in his study, *Franz Kafka* (234), I want to repeat that these references to parallels between Kafka's Josephine and the world of Eastern Jewish thought are not meant to say that Kafka wanted to use this story to thematize the "Jewish question." What I do mean to say is that Kafka could very well have had the Eastern Jewish world in mind when he sketched the image of the mouse people in "Josephine" as well as the image of its self-proclaimed hero, neither of whom are overly fond of each other, but neither of whom necessarily want to part company, either. The hasidic source could shed a great deal of light upon this peculiar relation between Josephine and her people, but Kafka carried this relation over and applied it paradigmatically to human society as a whole. Nevertheless, the web of relationships between a community and its champions is more clearly visible in the small hasidic community than anywhere else within the society in which Kafka lived. The life of this community, which he witnessed and in which he participated more than once, could very easily have served as the source for many of the views expressed in "Josephine."

Kafka described his Marienbad visit with the Rebbe of Belz in a letter he wrote in July, 1916. In many ways his report reflects the same important insignificance of the figure of the rabbi that also applies to Josephine. On the one hand there is the trust in the rabbi: "The sight of his back, the sight of his hand resting on his hip, the sight of the curvature of his broad back—all of that inspires confidence. The calm, happy confidence I perceive is also [reflected] in the eyes of the whole group." The rabbi leaves the house during a downpour: "It was raining extraordinarily hard, even for this rainy season. It hadn't rained exactly at this time [when the rabbi used to go out] in perhaps the last fourteen days. Langer felt it would surely stop, but it didn't; instead, it rained even harder. Langer said that it had rained during his outing only once before, in the woods, but then it stopped right away. This time it didn't stop" (*Letters*, 144, 142).

The whole description of this outing conveys the contradictory nature of the relation between the rabbi and his community—the latter expected everything of him, but was required to assist him in even the most banal of routine matters. The whole group of disciples accompanying him took everything, even the most insignificant utterance of their master, seriously and stood ready at hand to be of service to him.

Langer told Kafka a great deal about life in the court of the Rabbi, the admiration he enjoyed, the expectations people held of him; he also knew of their "success." Enough observational material for the affectionate skepticism on the part of the narrator in "Josephine."

17
THE APHORISMS—BETWEEN THE TWO TREES OF PARADISE

Kafka's aphorisms do not present a unified system of thought; they are better described as a collection of ethical and ontological reflections, as well as contemplations on the theology of sin. What pulls them together and unites them into a whole is perhaps the fact that they all seek to express the inherent but fundamentally contradictory nature of human existence. Nevertheless, among these disparate thoughts are several that are unmistakeably related to a single, larger context. They might be described roughly as a semiplatonic mysticism, even if Michael Schreiber does make the not completely justified observation that "the actual experience of the unio mystica and the announcement of it has no place in [Kafka's] work" (Schreiber, 259). Despite Hasidism and despite the Kabbalah, which was so deeply influenced by neoplatonism, elements of such a semiplatonic mysticism alone are certainly not sufficient demonstration of a Jewish background to Kafka's thoughts. Nor is his use of biblical topoi in the aphorisms any more indicative on their own, for they could just as easily have found their way to Kafka via Christian mystics such as Meister Eckhardt. On the other hand, Kafka's thoughts about the two trees of paradise are more telling. These two trees were interpreted in astonishingly similar ways in Kafka's aphorisms and in the hasidic source that Georg nger, Kafka's authority on kabbalistic matters, knew from his wn understanding of the first books the Rebbe of Belz recomnended he read at the beginning of his studies. The one under consideration here bore the title *No'am Elimelech* and was written by Elimelech of Lizensk (1717–1787), one of the original disciples of the central figure of the second generation of Hasidism, Dov Ber, the Maggid of Mezhirich (1710–1772).[1]

This fact may justify our attempt to interpret the other metaphysical statements within the context of hasidic mysticism, and particularly those of the Maggid and his student Elimelech. Kafka was familiar with the preacher and important elements of his teachings from his own reading of Buber's *Maggid* (*Diaries*, 362: May 12, 1922) and no less certainly from his conversations with his friend Langer.

In Aphorism No. 54 (*Wedding*, 34), Kafka sketches a mystical-cosmic "salvation story." One could describe it as the quintessence of the mysticism of the Great Maggid: "There is nothing other than a spiritual world; what we call the material world is the evil in the spiritual one, and what we call evil is only a moment's necessity in our eternal development."

According to the mystical theology of the Maggid, one of the fundamental theologists of Hasidism, the Godhead "created" the world because He wanted to have His "pleasure" in the love His creatures bore for Him. In other words, God conceived and realized the idea of creating the world simply out of his desire for the love his creatures, his children, would show for him. The necessary transition from the infinite, all-encompassing and all-filling absolute being of God to the boundedness of the temporal world and its individuals, however, was only possible if the Godhead initially limited its infinity in an absolute restriction to the divine nothingness. God contracted His fullness into a nothingness, a void, and it was this absolutely restricted nothingness that became the divine creative force[2] that brought forth all material existence.

In a reversal of the Lurianic concept of the breaking of the vessels, the passage of God's infinite Oneness through the void and into the multiplicity of individuals meant nothing other than a splitting up of God's Oneness into the variety of individuals in this world. This rupture of the divine Oneness is the *felix culpa* of creation, without which there could not have been any being outside of God. The rupture of the unity was the *sine qua non* of creation, even if this break did establish a sinful claim to autonomous being on the part of individuals outside of and juxtaposed to the Godhead. Kafka's Aphorism No. 83 (*Wedding*, 36f) is a precise expression of this relation: "Sinful is the state in which we find ourselves, independent of guilt."

In this sense, the physical world is the evil in the spiritual world, and this evil is in fact only one necessity "of our eternal development" (Aphorism 54). Without this sin, without the evil of the dissolution of the One into the many, the goal inherent in the creative intentions of the Godhead could never have been attained, namely: the loving return of His children to the Oneness of God. This love, of course, is what God wanted to "delight" in. This then is the end point of the "eternal development" initiated by the act of creation. In the words of the Maggid (*Maggid Devaraw*, c. 73, 126):

> The break was necessary for the world! [If it hadn't happened], every single thing and every attribute would cling to the root [to God, to nothingness], and in their own eyes they would be as nothing, for the universe would have no existence! If, for example, the [lower] world of action were to cling constantly to the Creator, without forgetting Him for even an instant, everything would be without existence and not present, for they would all be clinging to the root, to nothingness. They would then perform no deeds, either, for they would think themselves nothing, too. Their whole existence would be completely absorbed out of pure fear and shame before the root and they would cling exclusively to that root, to the naught. And this is true of all the universe.
>
> This is why the break was necessary, because, thanks to it, the root was forgotten and everyone and everything could raise its hand and complete its work!

The fact that the world forgot God is the world's sin, but at the same time it is also that which made its independent existence possible. If the world were truly aware of its root—and thus redeemed from sin—, it would immediately dissolve into its root and no longer exist. This tension is the original incongruity inherent in the world; it is the sinful state without sin or guilt.

The way out of this sinful state can only lead through self-dissolution, through total abandonment of the world and the giving up of one's own independent ego: "The works of the righteous are greater than the work of the creation of heaven and earth. For the creation of heaven and earth was a creation of being out of nothingness. The righteous, however, make nothing out of that which is" (*Maggid Devaraw*, 24).

In sociological as well as mystical terms, this path leads initially to quietism, to an absolute indifference with respect to worldly events and societal roles, to an awareness of one's own insignificance and nothingness:[3] "To the degree that a person sees himself on the level of nothingness and of 'what am I actually?' . . . he heals all breaks, which is to say, the fallen worlds are reestablished and reascend, thanks to the person who stands on the level of [nothingness] and of 'what am I actually?'" (*Maggid Devaraw*, 109)

A person attains this level "when a person thinks he is dust and impotent without the strength of God, so that that which he does do is an act of God" (*Maggid Devaraw*, 12).

In Aphorism Nr. 90 (*Wedding*, 38) Kafka weighs "Two possibilities: to make yourself unendingly small or to be it. The second is accomplishment, in other words passivity; the first beginning, in other words, activity."

Despite this dichotomy that the world and its individuals perceive between divine unity and temporal diversity, there is actually only one single spiritual world. Kafka expressed this idea in Aphorism No. 62 (*Wedding*, 35): "The fact that there is nothing other than a spiritual world deprives us of hope and gives us certainty."

According to the Maggid, there is in fact and in reality only one spiritual world, namely the Oneness of God, which is unquestionably hidden from the eyes of man, but which nevertheless still represents the single true reality. This is why the Maggid, too, believes there is ultimately no ontological root for evil but only an epistemological one. Kafka says: "Evil is an emanation of the human consciousness in certain transitional states. The material world is not actually appearance; appearance is the evil of the material world, and this evil, of course, is what shapes the material world for our eyes" (Aphorism No. 85, *Wedding*, 37).

The Maggid uses similar terms to describe man's evil eye, his false regard for the world which is the base of evil in the physical world. In actual fact, however, the temporal, material world is not evil, because the single spiritual world reveals itself within the material world to those who understand it properly. After all, it is only because of this spiritual world that the material world has any existence in the first place. The proper way of seeing things reduces the material world to nothing compared to the spiritual world. This proper view of the world is its dissolution into nothing, into the infinite Oneness of God (*Maggid Devaraw*, 124):

> If a person has a good eye, which is to say, wisdom, [then] when he looks at something, he knows that this object is as nothing before God, which is to say, that this object is in truth null and void without the divinity of God which dwells within it . . . and without Him it truly is nothing.
>
> When [a person] looks in this way, he draws additional life force from out of the Godhead, which is the source of life, and down into the thing he is looking at. He does so by fastening the object onto the absolute nothingness out of which all being arose, as a being [that arose] out of nothingness.
>
> However, if a person has an evil eye, [then] when he looks at an object, he is astonished by it and thinks: "How beautiful this object is!"—and thus he turns the object into something independent [of God]. . . . When a person looks in this way, the object becomes separated from its life force, which is to say, from the Godhead. It is the very nature of the break that each object claims of itself: "I am my own king", [which is to say, I am an independent ego].

"Only evil has self-knowledge," says Kafka (*Wedding*, 62), completely in keeping with this train of theological thought. Martin Buber says the same thing of Aaron of Karlin, another pupil of the Maggid, who showed a nocturnal visitor the door because the latter responded to the question "Who's there?" with the pronoun "I." After all, "Who is he who makes so bold as to call himself 'I', which only God may do?"[4]

This is the dialectic of temporal existence that links existence as sin on the one hand and self-dissolution as the return to the divine vacuum on the other. It is also what makes the world and its human inhabitants appear evil or good in accordance with the individual's "awareness" of his self as an independent being or as a non-being, as something encompassed within the Oneness of God.

As a student of the Dov Ber, Elimelech of Lizensk describes this state of man between individuality and all-encompassing unity, between sin and self-dissolution, as man's situation between the Tree of Knowledge of Good and Evil and the Tree of Life (Nigal, 24):

> "And the Lord God commanded the man, saying: 'Of every tree of the garden thou mayest freely eat'" (Gen. 2:16).
>
> This is hard to understand. Why did He tell them what they were to eat . . . ? Moreover, He initially offered "of every tree of the garden [thou mayest eat]," that is, they might also eat of the Tree of Life.
>
> And why, after they had eaten of the Tree of Knowledge of Good and Evil, were they then forbidden to eat of the Tree of Life?
>
> I think we have to understand it this way:
>
> In the beginning, [man] occupied a high level in the upper world—a level that is called the Tree of Life. This is why God commanded him to eat of the Tree of Life, so that he might remain in this sanctity for ever. And this is why he was forbidden to eat of the Tree of Knowledge of Good and Evil—for these are the lower worlds—so that he might not become physical-material.
>
> However, after he had eaten of the Tree of Knowledge of Good and Evil, he fell from that highest level and became physical-material. This is why God forbade him to eat of the Tree of Life. After he had become physical, and good and evil were in him, he was no longer worthy of touching the Tree of Life until such time as he had first climbed back up from the lowest to the highest level, step by step.
>
> It follows, then, that after the Fall, man has to serve God from one level to another, from the lowest to the highest.
>
> And this is the meaning of the Scripture verse [where God says to Abraham]: "Get thee out of thy country" (Gen. 12:1), namely: "Go to your higher root, [the one] from which you were cut off."
>
> [The words] "out of thy country" [mean]: the most important aspect of your beginning to return to the upper root is the humility

> that lets you realize how lowly you are, "for dust thou art" (Gen. 3:19) . . . "Get thee out of thy country" so that you might not think of your country and the house of your father and might go to your root in the higher realm . . . for everything comes from Him.

Man in the temporal world, material/physical man, exists in a state of sin on the level of the Tree of Knowledge and is therefore separated from the Tree of Life. Only after man leaves the material world—or, in the words of the Maggid—only after man leaves his individuality, will he return and eat again of the Tree of Life. Only then will he have abandoned corporeality.

I believe Kafka had the same thing in mind when he wrote Aphorism No. 83 (*Wedding*, 36): "We are sinful not only because we ate of the Tree of Knowledge, but also because we have not yet eaten of the Tree of Life. Sinful is the state in which we find ourselves, independent of sin."

Kafka's aphorism about the two-fold truth (*Wedding*, 80) also fits in here:

> There are two kinds of truth for us, represented by the Tree of Knowledge and the Tree of Life. The truth of the active and the truth of the quiescent. In the first, good is separated from evil; the second is nothing other than the good itself, it knows neither good nor evil. The first truth was given to us in reality, the second only intuitively. That's the sad part of it. The happy part is that the first truth belongs to the moment, the second to eternity; therefore the first truth is extinguished in the light of the second.

The truth of the Tree of Life is the truth of the dissolution of the individual in the Infinite Oneness of the Divine—this is the eternal truth. Once having been attained in the temporal world, it leads to stillness, to quietism. The truth of the Tree of Knowledge, on the other hand, is the truth of this world of discrete individuals, of activism, of the separation between good and evil; it is the temporary truth of this world. Once man comprehends the truth of the Tree of Life, this other truth fades away in the light of the truth of Oneness, of the elimination of opposites. This is the truth of the Tree of Life, the eternal truth which is present in the unity of all being.

It is this Janus-faced quality of knowledge that Kafka addresses in another of his aphorisms. One type of knowledge, that which is acquired from the Tree of Knowledge, is an obstacle to eternal life; the other type, that of the Tree of Life, is a step toward eternal life. Kafka too sees the latter type as leading to the dissolution of the self (*Wedding*, 78):

> "If . . . , you must die," means: knowledge is both a step toward eternal life and an obstacle to it. Should you want to attain eternal life after you have acquired knowledge—and you will not be able to do anything but want this, for this desire is what knowledge is—[then] you will have to destroy the obstacle, which is yourself, in order to build the step, which is this destruction. The expulsion from Paradise, therefore, was not a deed, but an event.

Yet another similarity can be found in Kafka's understanding of the eternal truth that leads to the dissolution of the individual and opens the gates of access to the ultimate Oneness. His description calls upon images derived from neoplatonic Jewish philosophy and mysticism; ever since the Middle Ages this has been known as "the divestment of corporeality."[5] Kafka says (*Wedding*, 77):

> Before appearing before the Most Holy One, you must take your shoes off, and not only your shoes, but everything: your travelling clothes and baggage, and that includes your nakedness and everything that is under your nakedness, and everything concealed beneath this, and then the kernel and the kernel of the kernel, then whatever is left and then the rest and then even the appearance of the everlasting fire. It is only the fire itself that will be absorbed and that lets itself be absorbed by the Most Holy One. Nothing can resist Him.

As in the philosophical and mystical descriptions of ecstasy, here too the ego, completely stripped of all corporeality, is absorbed by the Holy of Holies and dissolved in Him. Compare this with the description Leone Ebreo alias Judah Abravanel gives in his *Dialoghi d'amore*[6] of the ascent to divine beauty:

> . . . when we abandon our tangible clothing and physical passions, not only in that we [learn to] despise their meagre beauty . . . but that we also hate it and flee from it, since it hinders us from arriving at that which is truly beautiful and upon which our weal depends. In order to see it [the beautiful], we have to put on spiritual garments, clean and pure, . . . for when our mystical communion with God arrives at the highest beauty and the highest Beautiful One, our love for Him is so strong that we abandon everything else . . .
>
> . . . so that we loose ourselves in meditation [Italian: *contemplatione*] to such a degree that our mind . . . unites so closely with God and clings so completely to him that it perceives itself as a spark and a part of God.

The corresponding description of the Maggid (*Maggid Devaraw*, 38f):

> . . . and when man clings to the Holy One, blessed be He, . . . he becomes man, for the Holy One, blessed be He, undergoes several self-constrictions through various worlds so that He becomes one with man . . . and man must strip himself completely of all physicality until he ascends through all the worlds and becomes one with the Holy One, blessed be He, until he has been completely removed from [physical] reality: only then will he be called man.

We have already mentioned the fact that the existence of evil in the world is essentially dependent upon man's view of or awareness of it. If man looks at the world with the proper knowledge, it no longer need appear evil to him because he abolishes the world contemplatively before the infinite Oneness of God. On the other hand, if man looks at the world with the knowledge of the Tree of Knowledge, which only aims to separate and differentiate and which perceives the world as an entity independent and separate from God, then the world is evil. Thus, man's relation to the world is an ambivalent one; everything depends upon his attitude toward it. The very same world can serve him as a start toward the correct or the false knowledge. This is probably what Kafka had in mind when he wrote Aphorism No. 105 (*Wedding*, 87):

> The means whereby this world leads us into temptation are simultaneously the guarantee that this world is only a transition. Properly so, for that's the only way this world can seduce us and it accords with the truth. The worst part, however, is that, after having been seduced, we forget the guarantee, so that the good has actually lured us into evil; the sight of the woman has lured us into her bed.

Another of Kafka's aphorisms (No. 79) is also pertinent to this theme, for it formulates, as it were, a central topos in hasidic folk literature. This theme holds that sensuous love—all forms of sensuality, in fact—ultimately derive from divine love (*Wedding*, 36): "Sensuous love takes the place of the divine; it couldn't do this on its own, but since it unconsciously possesses an element of divine love within itself, it can."

The ambivalence expressed here between metaphysical surety on the one hand and a desire for the things of this world on the other corresponds precisely with the Maggid's view. He follows closely the hasidic principle that everything in this world, the beautiful as well as the bad, owes its life and thus its seductive powers to the spiritual force dwelling within it; its goodness or badness is solely dependent upon whether the person succumbs to temptation or holds fast to the surety in his mind.

The Maggid seems to be more optimistic than Kafka on this point and gives his disciples a contemplative tool that is meant to help them extract the surety from temptation:[7]

> "May their belly be filled with what thou hast seen for them" (Ps. 17:14)[8]. [This means] that one should avoid looking at the good tangible things, and particularly at beautiful women, for men look at them to satisfy their own desires. By looking this way, they serve only themselves, and this self-serving is idol-worship . . .
>
> The words "what thou hast seen" refer to what you look at for your own purposes: a beautiful woman, for example (or tangible things, and that is called "what thou hast seen")[9], because you are looking only for yourself (at its realness for the sake of its realness) . . .

Instead of this, one should look at things this way:

> If you suddenly and inadvertently notice a beautiful woman, turn your attention to the following considerations:
>
> Where did she get this beauty? Would she still have this face if she were dead? (Then she would be the personification of ugliness!)
>
> This beauty then inheres to her via God's force that floods her being. This divine flow lent her the strength of beauty and freshness! Thus we find that the root of beauty is the power of God.
>
> Why should I let myself be attracted to a part? It were better for me to cleave to the root and the taproot of the universe, for that is where all beauty resides.
>
> The same applies for looking at all material objects. When we look at a vase, for instance, we should think:
>
> Where did this vase get its charm and shape? The answer: the raw material is waste, but the charm and the shape are the spiritual elements and the vital force inhering to this vase, and this, too, is a part of the Godhead on high (for the vital force of every material object is part of the supreme Godhead).
>
> And so, when you eat, be aware that the taste and the sweetness of the food derive from the higher vital force and the higher sweetness which are themselves the source of its own vital force.
>
> This vital force is also present in the mineral world, for we see that constancy and duration are aspects of the mineral world. Thus we find that the vital force of God on high is everywhere.
>
> If you learn to look at things this way, your gaze will be tied to thought and your looking will serve the Divine Eternal (En-Sof). And this is a good way to dispel doubts and all desires.

According to the Maggid, it is this mystically contemplative way of perceiving the ultimate unity of all being hidden behind every temporal manifestation that enables a person to recognize the eternal surety, the spiritual force that makes up the All in All. On the other hand, this force also lies concealed in temptations, for it is the indwelling spiritual force that lends such temptations their seductive powers in the first place. One should therefore not be tempted by the sight of a woman in her bed, but should better use that image to move on to a mystical contemplation of divine beauty. Kafka's view of man's ability to concentrate on the divine light in this way is considerably more pessimistic:

> If we look at ourselves through eyes tainted by worldly things, we are like passengers on a train that derailed in a long tunnel at precisely that spot where we can no longer see the light at the beginning but the light at the end is so tiny that our eyes have to keep searching for it. The result is that we are no longer sure of beginning or end. In the confusion of our senses or in the hypersensitivity of our senses we find ourselves in the midst of veritable monsters, and, depending upon our mood and the severity of our injuries, in the midst of a charming or wearisome kaleidoscopic show (Aphorism No. 50, *Wedding*, 34).

This last quote concludes our discussion of the esssential parallels between Kafka's aphorisms and hasidic mysticism. To my mind, the correspondences in detail as well as in the entire mystical conception justify the assumption that this literature had a profound influence on Kafka's aphorisms, despite his skepticism regarding man's ability to actually take the liberating step toward this way of seeing. The fact that the authors cited above were all known to Georg Langer, the friend who introduced Kafka to the life and thought of the Hasidim in the first place, only serves to support this assumption. Buber's writings could have conveyed essential fundamentals of this thought as well, even though they are couched in a misreading of philosophical terms to a certain extent. Nevertheless, I must stress the fact that Buber systematically diverted the transcendental reference point of this thought into an intrinsically personal one in the sense of an affirmation of temporal existence and of the daily routine of human life. Such an understanding is worlds apart from the genuine hasidic way of thinking.

Despite the many demonstrable parallels between Kafka's aphorisms and hasidic thought, there still remains a fundamental difference. Kafka draws the same theology, cosmology, and mystical anthropology as do the hasidic mystics, but his own mysticism is in a crisis stage: it has lost sight of the light at the end of the tunnel. This explains why man seems capable only of succumbing to "temptation," but not of holding fast to the "surety" in his mind.

And yet, on the other hand and in spite of this hopelessness, Kafka seems to think there is a logical connection between hopelessness and hope or even certainty. In Aphorism No. 62 he writes (*Wedding*, 35): "The fact that there is nothing other than a spiritual world deprives us of hope and gives us certainty."

Where the spiritual world removes hope while simultaneously giving certainty, hopelessness can perhaps be interpreted as a sign of the existence of that spiritual world.

This may also have been the meaning behind Kafka's aphorism that speaks of faith as one way to express trust in the metaphysical even though it remains hidden. Here Kafka describes belief in a personal God as one of the ways man expresses his unconscious yearning for something indestructible within himself. In other words, faith appears here as just another of those acts of desperation people turn to in order to be able to live in the face of emptiness. Kafka interprets this desperate act as the expression of the individual's unconscious need to believe, without which he could not live. In this faith, in this desperate attempt on the part of mankind, then, Kafka seems to see one effect of that spiritual force long lost to view—in rather the same way that sensuous love discloses for the Maggid the continuing effects of divine love: "The human being can not live without an enduring faith in something Indestructible within himself, even though this Indestructible as well as his faith in it can remain permanently concealed. One of the ways to express this hiddenness is the belief in a personal God" (Aphorism No. 50, *Wedding*, 34).

Man's desperate attempt to believe in a personal God grows out of an ignorance of the real, true state of affairs: it is a consequence of the hidden nature of the Indestructible. This is why it gains such a positive meaning for Kafka. Man's false relation and his false human striving—in other words, his belief in a personal God—are founded in the hidden nature of the Essential, just like the love that has turned to sensuality. Abiding in both is still a spark of divine force, a view Kafka shares with the Hasidim. Like the hasidic thinkers, Kafka, too, is obviously wrestling with the attempt to discover the force of something eternal, something divine in the vanity and the oppressive reality of the material world. This search also includes an attempt to hold on to the wrong approach and to misunderstanding as a sign of inherent meaning.

Gershom Scholem's Kafka-poem juxtaposes this mysticism of nothingness as the true world against the deception of material reality in the following stanzas:[10]

Schier vollendet bis zum Dache
ist der große Weltbetrug.
Gib denn, Gott, daß der erwache,
den dein Nichts durchschlug.

So allein strahlt Offenbarung
in die Zeit, die dich verwarf.
Nur dein Nichts ist die Erfahrung,
die sie von dir haben darf.

So allein tritt ins Gedächtnis
Lehre, die dein Schein durchbricht:
das gewisseste Vermächtnis
vom verborgenen Gericht.

* * *

The great deception of the world
is total and all-encompassing;
Grant then, Lord, that he who is
consumed by your Nothingness may awaken.

Revelation knows only this way to penetrate
and illumine the time that has rejected you.
Your Nothingness alone is the only knowledge
such times may have of you.

The truth that shatters all appearances
enters into human awareness by no other route:
the legacy of which we are most certain
[is that of] hidden judgment.

18
KAFKA WITHOUT END—YET ANOTHER INTERPRETATION?

Kafka's work has been subjected to many different interpretations ever since critics first started to read it. Some think of Kafka as a theologian in a writer's garb; for others he is the bard of nihilism and a "God is dead" theology, or else the herald of the decline of the mythological-metaphysical tradition. Some critics on both sides of the Atlantic see in Kafka nothing more than the author of his time, the writer who describes the "Age of Anxiety"[1]; they see him as the witness of the alienation of modern man who keeps God's commandments without believing in God.[2] The "psychoanalysts" found fertile ground in Kafka and have produced a bumper crop of interpretations based upon depth-psychology. His representation of totalitarian power structures of the eastern or faschistic ilk catch the attention of critics with a political agenda. On the other hand, many other authors feel they have to emphasize the socialistic element in Kafka's thought; similarly, sociological interpretations make their own contributions to the view that sees Kafka as the spokesman for the social pariah. Cynical is the appropriate adjective for Catholic interpretations like that of Ignaz Zangerle: "The latter-day Jewish writer Kafka is a *homo religiosus* who denies the *anima naturaliter Christiana*. He remains caught up in the space between the original Revelation and the Revelation of God in His Son Jesus Christ. Kafka's world is the world of limbo . . ."[3]

ax Brod, who quite rightly insisted upon a consideration of the ish element in Kafka and who never tired of referring to Kafka's owing interest in Judaism, produced an image of Kafka[4] that in its pologetic simplification and its emphasis on the "positive" hardly attests to a deeper understanding of the man. Walter Benjamin's sarcastic remarks about this work were not unjustified: "The biographer's position itself is one of total *bonhommie*" (*Briefe*, 757). We can not join Brod in reclaiming Kafka for Zionism or in calling his "positive relation to community" one of his central concerns—nor will it do to divide Kafka's work into judgment and grace, or into the confessions of the confused (in *The Trial*) and those of the believer (in the aphorisms). Heinz Politzer had good reasons to stress the fact that *The Trial* and the aphorisms both express an essentially identical "world outlook"—even if Kafka, as we have seen, spoke different "languages" and applied different systems of Jewish mysticism in both of these genres. When seen in this light, Politzer's blunt evaluation of Brod's interpretation of Kafka does not seem unjustified: "The original sin of all Kafka interpretations can be traced back to Max Brod, namely: the direct translation of poetic images into the language of theology, philosophy or psychology and the resulting reduction of its literary value which is necessarily associated with such translations. Max Brod turned the work of Franz Kafka into program music" (*WdF* (1973), 216).

The majority of the critical views mentioned above seem to support Politzer's view about Kafka's post-war reception in Germany: "Soon after the end of the war the first volumes of Kafka's work appeared through Fischer in Frankfurt as the licensed edition of Schocken Books New York, and the German readers did what their predecessors abroad had done before them: they saw their own reflection" (*WdF*, 12). Thus, Politzer's summary, positive and negative at the same time, remains: "Kafka's world of images is composed of symbols, even of symbols of closure, that nevertheless lead to no conclusion; these symbols represent finely honed keys, but there is no lock in sight which they might open. The essence of Kafka's work lies in the futility of arriving at conclusions and of making decisions" (*WdF*, 9).

Wilhelm Emrich's monumental study, *Franz Kafka*, produced an understanding of the writer's works that, at least in the case of *The Trial*, arrived at conclusions quite similar to what has been said here, even though Emrich started out with a completely different set of assumptions. "The World as a Court of Justice" is the title of one of his chapters. Of course, a considerable difference arises when Emrich sees judgment as "a reflection of K.'s psyche," when he sees judgment as "the expression of his own inner state" (*Critical Study*, 323); when the gatekeeper legend is understood in the following way: "The liberating breakthrough or the world system of laws is always possible—possible, that is to say, when man inquires into the determination of his own existence instead of staring, as if hypnotized, at the menacing 'power' and superiority of the world. Then liberation from the 'world' would be possible even during life on earth" (*Critical Study*, 329).

It is most probably interpretations such as these that Heinz Politzer had in mind when he said: "Finally, one would have to ask whether the basis of Emrich's whole mode of thinking weren't floating in the air, whether his interpretation of *The Castle* did not itself represent a castle in the air, so to speak. Is it at all appropriate to measure the ka[f]kanic Jew Kafka against the standards of classical German aesthetics and its tradition?

"The writer derived from a different existential basis as did Kleist, for instance, regardless of how closely related he might have felt to the Prussian Junker in his never overcome oedipal tie to his background. Kafka came from Prague, this European lightning rod in which Slavic, Jewish and German history were inextricably entangled, the city of the Hapsburg Emperor Rudolf II, of Rabbi Löw and the golem, a city constantly besieged by intruders but never conquered in its innermost being" (*WdF*, 14).

With these words Politzer paved the only road that held any promise of hope. This approach would expose the foundations of Kafka's buildings and end the reliance on castles in the air that owed their being to the individual position of the respective critic. This is the sentiment behind Politzer's challenge: "A solid positioning of Kafka within the German-Jewish context has yet to be made" (*WdF*, 220).

The interpretation of Kafka should not be allowed to deteriorate to reception history, and the best way to avoid this is to try to discover the presuppositions Kafka brought to his work. The fact that Judaism was one of the major presuppositions should no longer be open to doubt. And yet, just how seriously many Kafka scholars still take the Jewish side of this author can be seen, for example, in Joachim Unseld's detailed study of *Franz Kafka. Ein Schriftstellerleben*[5], which limits its treatment of this topic to a few telling remarks: "Franz Kafka's attitude toward Judaism was very ambivalent, and a brief discussion of it can hardly be expected to present a clear picture." Or take his reference to Otto Pick in his anthology called *Das jüdische Prag*, where he states: "Kafka never betrayed 'what faith' he ascribed to. And as late as 1922 Kafka described to Brod his 'lack of any solid Jewish footing under his feet'" (149f).

As if such a complaint were not itself a clarion call that here speaks a man who is searching for his Judaism but is loathe to content himself with a "bourgeois" version of it. Unseld's book follows up on the various human contacts in Kafka's life but fails to even mention Georg Langer and contents itself with the meaningless reference to the "Prague actor and friend of Kafka, Jizchak Löwy"[6] (88), both of whom played a pivotal role in Kafka's Judaism. Also lacking is any mention whatsoever about the countless and unmistakeable comments concerning "Judaica" in Kafka's letters and diaries.

The same can be said of Werner Kraft, who discusses Kafka's "A Dream" fragment in a chapter entitled "God": "Here we have a reference to Kafka's attitude toward Judaism, although and precisely because it does not appear in the body of work he himself authorized, nor does it appear in the novels of his literary estate. ... Any attempt to infer a specifically Jewish content from this work is extremely precarious, just as all Protestant and Catholic interpretations have missed the mark as well."[7]

One may well wonder at times just what it was that led an author like Günther Anders to contest the Jewish element in Kafka, a topic about which he obviously knows very little. Anders' book on Kafka is one of the best, but we still have to wonder where he gets the arrogance to write: "Only a few theses about Kafka can actually be as unequivocally confirmed as the one that maintains that Kafka's 'religiosity' had no direct connection with the Jewish religion" (95). Anders does not tire of returning to this viewpoint again and again: "To claim Kafka as the continuator of the Jewish religion and Jewish theology is completely and absolutely off the mark" (93, cf. 94).

Was Scholem so wrong when he said in his "Ten Unhistorical Statements about the Kabbalah": "Kafka's delineation of the boundary between religion and nihilism is unsurpassed. That is why his writings, the secularized representation of the kabbalistic conception of the world, possess something of the rigorous splendor of the canonical for many of today's readers—they possess something of the Absolute that breaks into pieces" (270). Granted, Scholem does insert the parenthetical phrase "unknown to him" [that is, to Kafka] before the words "kabbalistic conception of the world," without asking himself how such a concurrence might have come about. In any case, Scholem does pose the question: "Is it some sort of psychic attraction that brought Kafka to such concurring ideas one hundred years later?" The presentation of the parallels and correspondences as well as the discussion of the paths that could have or did bring Kafka into contact with such traditions make up the bulk of this present study. They demonstrate beyond any doubt that the answer is more than mere emotional attraction. In his here frequently cited poem about Kafka's *Trial*, Gershom Scholem depicts Kafka's view of the world in explicitly kabbalistic terms, and he does so in a way that presupposes much more than coincidental overlappings.[8]

Kafka thinks Jewish. This can be stated unconditionally if we understand that his Judaism is considerably different from Brod's bourgeois Zionist version. Let me expand briefly upon this final point once again.

The most important finding of this study is the fact that Kafka's *Trial*, "The Judgment," "In the Penal Colony," and several other scattered fragments treating the theme of judgment were written under the direct influence of the Jewish High Holy Days, the "Days of Awe." This period is so called because, according to Jewish holy day liturgy, it is the time when all people, each individual person, stand before the Divine Throne of Judgment. A balance is struck during these days, sin and virtue are weighed against each other and everything conceivable is done to attain justification before God's tribunal. This annual judgment decides the life and the fate of the individual until the next New Year.

Kafka was always keenly aware of the significance of these days, and frequently dealt with it in his works on the judgment theme. This fact leads to the obvious conclusion that—at least as far as *The Trial* and the other pieces named above are concerned—wherever Kafka speaks in them of judgment, sin, atonement and justification, he is working from the direct context of a Jewish theology having to do with judgment and sin; in other words, from a religious context. This context presupposes a transcendental, divine court of law whose decisions have a direct effect upon human life. On the other hand, this is not to be construed as a subjective court of conscience, nor is it a guilt complex vis-à-vis his father. (For the exegetes of the Jewish-Christian model involving the fall from grace and ultimate salvation, let it be mentioned parenthetically that Jewish judgment theology knows its own paths to redemption via divine grace and has no need to yearn—as people like to believe—for Christ to deliver them from their "Jewish anguish.")

An essential tenet of ancient Jewish judgment theology was the fact that justice and grace are inseparably combined in God himself, which is to say, in the figure of the Divine Judge. According to the Talmud and the literature that grew out of it, this combination of justice and grace is what ensures the continuation of creation.

The Kabbalah's mythological manner of thinking and speaking dissected these two fundamental elements of Jewish theology into an expanded hierarchical court system which ranged from the mythologically conceived Godhead, its manifestations in the ten sefirot, and on down to the smallest detail of the world. The intermediate celestial hierarchies with their motley court personnel and their labyrinthine subdivisions merge into the terrestrial, everyday life of human beings via the confusing interchangeability that characterizes their lowest levels. This includes celestial participation in human sordidness, perfidy, and spite. The judicial hierarchies are this way because they are themselves a reflection of human wickedness. Human life in this world, therefore, is a life anchored in constant judgment. Human life and its history are judgment, they oscillate in cycles between damnation and temporary acquittal and end with execution.

This judgment, and this must be emphasized again, is divine judgment; to quote Rabbi Löw of Prague, it is God's way of ruling on earth. The labyrinthine court, the confusions, the night and the smut of the courts are thus God's rule in the world. Against this background, any search for nihilism in Kafka's prose misses the point. The perception and appreciation of the fact that man is abandoned to this court is tantamount to a perception and understanding of God and His authority.

Faced with the generally sinful state of mankind before God, any justification of man in the strict sense of the word can be attained only by illegal means (in theological terms: by means of an act of grace). The offers of protection and bribery the Kafkaesque judicial hierarchy makes can be looked upon as absolutely adequate offers of grace within the frame of an extreme awareness of the sinful nature of man and of the hopelessness of ever attaining real justification. These offers of grace have their own frequently unseemly parallels in the Eastern European folk tales.

Against a Jewish background such as this, it is inappropriate to see Kafka's *Trial* as the expression of the abandonment and the delusions of man while seeing the "Indestructible" in his aphorisms, which is the way Max Brod looks upon them (223). Both of these works betray the confounding fusion of light and darkness against a kabbalistic background, or, in other words, they protray the light concealed in an utterly impenetrable darkness. If we accept the view of the *conditio humana* as a state of constant judgment, then this means nothing less than to look at man before God.

The world view Kafka expresses in his aphorisms would surely be diminished if one were to follow Brod's example of distorting the dark side of this world they express by rendering it as something cute. Kafka's aphorisms, like their hasidic counterparts, portray the situation of man before the Eternal One in its total ambivalence; they show it as the human condition situated between sin and redemption.

This study introduced two groups of texts for comparison with Kafka's works, and both ultimately depict the same basic human condition. The first group dealt with the judicial hierarchies. These texts describe the human condition in judgment between sin and repentance in the language of mythology, whereas the hasidic conception, which was compared to Kafka's aphorisms, uses a more philosophical/mystical language to describe the same situation.

Politzer, too, noticed a similar correlation between Kafka's narratives and his aphorisms: "Each one of Kafka's aphorisms can be spun out to produce a necessarily fragmentary novel. Each one of his longer fragmentary narratives can be summarized in an aphorism. Like Novalis, Kafka demonstrated the inner relationship between the aphorism and the epic fragment."[9] In other words, *one* thought and two different ways of expressing it. This is why Politzer is so vigorous in his emphasis on the uniformity of the world view in Kafka's aphorisms and in his literary work, which, as was mentioned above, also applies in a similar way to both of the mystical traditions preceding him. As far as the latter are concerned, however, the difference is not an aphoristic-epic one, but rather a philosophic-mythological one. In his Kafka-poem, Scholem combined both kabbalistic conceptions into one strand as well.

The prominent theme in the hasidic doctrine most closely related to Kafka's aphorisms is the idea that mortal life, human life, or to put it in even more extreme terms, all being outside of or next to God, is by definition sinful. Only God in his Oneness is "sinless." In keeping with this view, the emergence of additional individuals outside of God necessarily means a disintegration of the Oneness of Being, a break of the One into the many. Human life is inconceivable without this *felix culpa*. It is sinful without guilt, and with that human life is constantly in judgment or, to put it in kabbalistic terms, it is in a constant state of separation. The end of judgment and thus redemption is the dissolution of the human claim to individuality in the only legitimate ego, which is God.

The philosophical/mystical language of the Hasidim thus says basically the same thing as does the mythological language of the Kabbalah mystics who place human existence under the authority of the all-encompassing judicial hierarchies. According to both systems, man escapes the court, and thus life, by giving up his ego, by renouncing all insistence upon his own individuality, by death and dissolution in the mystical nothingness of the Godhead.

It is this dualistic-dialectical world view of Jewish mysticism that seems to have influenced Kafka's apparent vacillation between "nihilism" and "confidence in faith" and which explains the contradictory nature of the critical reception of Kafka's works. Jewish mysticism speaks of God in a way in which the light of God is barely visible, veiled by the darkness of the world.

Günther Anders gave one of the chapters in his little book on Kafka the following heading: "Kafka is a Marcionite. He does not believe in no God, but rather in a bad one" (87). As Anders sees it, Kafka answered the question of theodicy this way: "'Granted the existence of evil—how are we to imagine the powers that created or govern or even enjoy evil?' The answer: 'As bad powers. As a bad God.'" (88) Here Anders sees the Marcionitic idea revived in Kafka, the doctrine of an evil, finite, bad creator-god. "And the correspondence is all the more remarkable since with Marcion this creator-god (unlike the God of Love) is at once the God of 'Law', the God of the Old Testament. With Kafka, too, the divine authority, the law and 'meanness' coincide." Naturally, Anders could not have known just how close he comes with this statement to the kabbalistic conception described above, which is rather ironic considering how vehemently he denies the Jewish element in Kafka. The only difference is that in the Kabbalah, this "bad" outward shape of God does not result in a bad God. The Kabbalists' God, sublimely exalted above the meanness of the world, the *deus absconditus*, the "En-Sof", as well as the *deus revelatus*, the Adam Kadmon or the ten sefirot, can only communicate with the sordid lowliness of the world when he divests himself of his greatness and conforms to that baseness. This is why the lowest levels of the judicial hierarchy resemble the darkness, the mire and the opacity as closely as Moses Cordovero said they did.

The Kabbalists did not take up the demiurgic-gnostic consequences of the manifestation of God in judgment or of his judicial authority, not even when this dualism penetrated deeply into Jewish thought as it did in the Zohar and in the Lurianic school of Kabbalah. For the Kabbalists, this dualism always remains subordinate to monotheism: even evil is in its own way part of God's manifestation.

A misunderstanding of this conception of the fusion of light and darkness, of the inner and outer aspects of the Godhead is what earned Kafka the reproach of Marcionism and what led to Brod's division. And yet, the coexistence of Kafka's "nihilistic" and "confident" statements can hardly be understood in any other way, unless one wants to accuse him of vacillating between two extremes.

This kabbalistic antithetical-dialectical world view is represented in Kafka's works, as I have said, in different means of expression. In *The Trial* and related narrative texts, Kafka employs the language of a "mythology" that has been transposed into the world of the modern metropolis. In his aphorisms, on the other hand, like the hasidic mystics, he reaches for a more abstract diction.

If we look at *The Trial* on the one hand and the aphorisms on the other as representing the two differently constructed poles of Kafka's world view, and if we acknowledge the fact that these two poles correspond well with the two traditions of the Kabbalah discussed above, then we may confidently proceed to the next step, which is to interpret the numerous other symbolic and thematic parallels that exist between Kafka's narratives and the kabbalistic and hasidic stories against this background. The fact that Kafka did not simply reproduce this Jewish-kabbalistic world view but creatively combined it with new and modern thinking has already been established.

The similarity between Kafka's symbols and images and those of the Kabbalah can be generally ascribed to the "mythological" manner of speaking. This includes, for example, the role women play within the judicial hierarchies, the relationship of court personnel and the accused; it includes particularly the gatekeeper tradition together with the man from the country as well as a whole series of animal stories which obviously relate closely to the Lurianic tales of reincarnation, all of which are themselves part of the judgment theme.

Standing, as it were, between the two strands of the kabbalistic tradition is Kafka's conception of language, which merges seamlessly into the kabbalistic doctrine of the Divine Names and the alphabet as the elments of the divine creative language. Man as the bearer of a name, and particularly as a speaking and praying being, participates in this creative process. Like God, man can bring forth the new by using language in a creative way, and he can reign as judge over other beings in the same manner.

Despite man's sharing in the creative power of language, however, the kabbalistic belief in the power of theurgy seems to have entered a crisis stage with Kafka. To cite Scholem once again:[10]

> Abandoned to forces
> that invocation can no longer touch
> no life can unfold
> that does not sink back into itself.

Here we do encounter a definite difference between Kafka and the Kabbalah. The Kabbalist believes unswervingly in his ability to exercise his influence on God, or else he believes equally unswervingly in the rebbe of the Hasidim who can do this for him. Kafka's "heroes," on the other hand, are sooner seen exhausting themselves in hopeless activity. And yet, at times Kafka seems to be able to glean some sense from even this useless endeavor, and be it only a consoling self-deception concerning the ultimate efficacy of human action.

APPENDIX

Source Texts

RE: THE KABBALISTIC DEPICTION OF THE CELESTIAL COURTS

Pardes Rimmonim, "The Gate of the Halls"[1]

THE FIRST HALL from the lowest to the highest is called SAPPHIRE. The overseer in this hall is called Tohariel [God of Purity]. He stands at the gate to this hall together with several angelic overseers, and all are flaming fire: they hold firey scepters in their hands and are all eyes.

When a soul, ascending on high, is found to be deserving and worthy of entering, they open the gate for this soul and it enters. But if it is defiled, they push it back.

An overseer and several avenging angels are stationed before this hall, and they push the soul until it plunges into gehinnom, where it is judged for twelve months.

The same thing happens to prayers. In the case of a community prayer, once it has penetrated the skies and arrived at the gate of this hall, it is immediately taken up and brought to the realm of lightning. . . . Here it is detained by the overseers until all of Israel has finished the prayer. Then all the prayers are placed in the hand of the angel Sandalfon, who weaves them into crowns for his Lord. From there they are led along and are used to crown the head of the Righteous One, who is the foundation of the universe [= Sefira IX].[2]

The prayer of an individual, on the other hand, is tested . . ., and if it is found fit, they let it in. If not, they shove it out, and it plummets from there into the lowest heaven and is given over to the angel Sahadiel [God of Witness].

THE SECOND HALL is called EZEM HA-SHAMAYIM. . . . There are three gates in this heaven, one to the south, one to the north, and one to the east, in the middle. The gates to the south and the north are locked and two guards are placed over them, both of whom answer to the highest overseer called Orpaniel [The Illumined Countenance of God]. He is positioned in the middle above the eastern gate and rules over the three winds of the world, south, east and north; all the souls of those who were executed by the court or killed by the nations are under the aegis of these overseers. . . . And this Orpaniel is the power over life and compassion, and the power of the [evil] shells bows down before him. . . . However, if the world is judged while the [evil] shell is reigning, this light [Orpaniel] is locked in, and the world is judged.

Standing next to this spirit are the robes of the righteous who are climbing upward because they want to behold the countenance of the Lord of Hosts. Once they have gotten so high as to show themselves, an overseer called Zadkiel [God of Justice] comes, and this angel takes the robe, the robe this man earned for himself by keeping the commandments, for a person earns the robe commensurate with his efforts. He wears this robe until he comes to the river of fire, where the soul is purified and washed and sometimes scorched in the river, in which case, it does not ascend any higher that day. . . .

Among those lights and spirits are several courier angels with jurisdiction over matters of this world . . . , and they are the overseers of the mighty court that examines the righteous ones with hair-splitting precision, and they stand ready to chastise in this world as well as in that one. . . . When the soul ascends and comes before the angel Jofiel, the latter quizzes it on the wisdom of the Torah it has learned. He rewards the soul . . . commensurate with the efforts it made in studying the Torah . . . , and if it could have gleaned more than it did from the Torah, the angel shoves the soul back down again into the lower hall with ignominy and shame. There they singe this soul, and it burns and yet is not consumed by the fire and is singed and is yet not consumed, and thus it is judged, all day long, regardless of the good works it has, simply because it did not concern itself with the Torah as was fitting and proper.

[In a second account of these halls, another tradition (49a) adds the following: "It is here the angels who rule over the deeds of mankind and who are charged with tempting them have their habitation."]

THE THIRD is the HALL OF SPLENDOR. It is loftier and more splendid than the two previous ones. This hall has four gates facing the four winds of the world.

At the southern gate stands a guard called Malkiel [God-King]. He rules over all the verdicts pronounced against men to judge them. When they [the verdicts] come down from the higher tribunal, they fall into the hands of this overseer. Under him are two scribes, Shamshiel and Kemuel, who write out all the verdicts that have come down against mankind to judge them. While the scribes are doing this, the overseer detains these verdicts so that they do not find their way into the hands of the angel Sangadiel, who stands to the left of the first hall and rules over those of the other side, who stand ready to accuse mankind and occasionally even to judge them, God forbid. . . . This is why this courier angel tries to write them down, and while doing so, he also keeps an eye out for their virtues and whether there might not be yet another advocate-angel for them . . . who might mitigate the harsh verdict.

Nevertheless, after all the guilty verdicts have been written down at this gate, Gasriel [God of Judgment] takes them and brings them to the second gate in the east, where they meet an overseer called Asriel [God's Help]. The name of each gate is identical with that of its overseer. The keeper of this gate seals the verdicts, be it for life or for death. . . .

On Yom Kippur, this gate remains locked until the afternoon prayer has been completed. Following this afternoon prayer, a spirit from the Hall of Justice, the fourth hall, awakens and the gate is opened. The angel on duty together with two assistants, one to his right and one to his left, puts his seal to life or death. They hold all the verdicts in their hands, and they seal them. . . .

The third gate in the north is where announcements are made about the chastisements that were meted out to the sinners, be they diseases or humiliations—all the sentences that do not lead to death. This gate is guarded by Kafziel [God of Anger]. He is charged with closing the gate over the judgment of a person so that his atonement is not accepted unless it should be total. . . .

In the middle of this hall, beneath the lantern of Ahadiel . . . is a hall with four gates facing the four winds of the world. Ten overseers are posted at each gate, forty in all, and they take and receive the verdict from the Hall of Justice, which is the tribunal . . . , and they chastise the soul that needs chastisement, and this soul is scolded until the days of its reprimand have passed. These forty banish every person who says a despicable thing, in which case his prayer does not ascend on high for the next forty days. This is also the way they banish anyone who has committed a transgression worthy of this ban. Ten heralds go forth every day into all the heavens, and they announce and cry out: "Beware this one and that one, for he is banished because of this and that sin." And for every day that he is banished, his prayer is also banned from appearing above, and his soul doesn't ascend during the night, either.

THE FOURTH HALL is called THE HALL OF JUSTICE. This hall stands ready to guard the paths of the Torah. In this hall are judged all virtues and all sin, every single reward and every single punishment, for everyone who either honors or violates the laws of the Torah.

There are four halls in this hall, each one different from the other. . . . There is a light called Sechutel [Justice God] here, and it gets its name from him. . . . This is where all the trials of mankind are held . . . every day.

Four guards stand at the four gates in these four halls; we will have more to say about them later on. The hall that contains these four . . . has an overseer called Sansinia, and to the left above him has been placed an overseer who takes the judicial matters from him in order to disseminate them in the world. . . . When the trial is over in the Hall of Justice, this gate-keeper stands up and announces the verdict to the twelve avengers standing at the twelve gates. These stand up and announce all the verdicts that came down in this hall. . . .

There is one light that encompasses all others; it is called Sechutel, and from this one light emerge seventy more . . . , and from their midst emerge two that stand and bear witness constantly. This is the mystery of it all: the seven eyes of the Lord whose gaze sweeps throughout the whole world . . . [and which are seven angels], watch over the doings of mankind; into them are engraved images of everything that happens in this world, be it bad or good. When they ascend, the two lights look at them and see what has been engraved upon them, and then they attest to it before the seventy, and they judge the righteous and the sinful, for good and for evil, for acquittal or for damnation.

These seventy-two lights stand in the middle of the hall . . . and opposite them on the right are another seventy-two lights and on the left likewise seventy-two—all together 216 lamps, and they are all encompassed within that one light. . . .

It is no secret that the ones on the right refer to the [sefira] of grace and the seventy-two on the left refer to the [sefira] of judgment and that those seventy-two in the middle refer to the [sefira] of mercy[3] which draws a balance and pronounces the verdict. This is why the main tribunal lies with those in the middle and they are the most hidden. . . . Then yet another light issues forth which illuminates and sparkles toward the four winds which are the four halls. This light produces three other lights, which are the three courts that divide amongst themselves the judicial matters of the world below, concerning wealth and property, disease, healing and the like. . . . Standing at one of the gates is an overseer by the name of Gasriel [Judgment God]. He is charged with announcing the verdicts that come down from the angel stationed above the hall on the impure side. The verdicts are announced by this angel. Heralds go forth and announce them in all the heavens, in those of purity and those of impurity.[4] The verdict goes from mouth to mouth, from heaven to heaven, until it even reaches as far down as the birds, and they spread it among men. . . .

Standing at the second gate is an overseer called Dahariel, who is charged with gathering the virtues of mankind so that they may be judged for the good. If a person is lying on his sickbed, this angel carries his virtues in, and if these good deeds outweigh his sins and the scale tips in favor of virtue, this angel communicates this to the overseer at the gate to the third hall, who is called Padael [Acquittal God], and he announces it by saying: "Deliver him from falling into the Pit; I have found an expiation for him!" And from there the verdict descends one level at a time until it reaches this world. . . . To the left of the third gate stands an overseer by the name of Gadiel, who has jurisdiction over the guilt and the sins of mankind and brings them to the balance scales at the fourth gate. There they are weighed against the other, transgression against virtue.

Below this overseer at the right of the fourth gate . . . stand several angels ready to rescue a person from the left side [of evil] if his merits tip the scale. However, if his sins should prevail, several angels who answer to the left overseer proclaim the matter to several avenging angels, who hasten over and take his soul. . . .

Another angelic being oversees all the requests mankind makes as well as all their prayers. Each and every request is detained in this hall for forty days, and every day this angelic being emerges and takes the requests and places them before the seventy-two lights, and they judge [the request]. The light that is called Sechutel examines the request to see if it is worthy of being fufilled or not. . . . In sum, then, one can say: all trials and all verdicts are processed in this hall, except for three, namely: those having to do with the blessing of children, the duration of life and material well-being. These three are not handled by this Hall of Justice, but rather by the higher one, namely by the power which is called Massal, Lucky Star.[5] Even though they are not handled by this hall, they are nevertheless judged here; should there be an acquittal, it comes from above. . . .

THE FIFTH HALL is called THE HALL OF LOVE. This is the hall responsible for the support and duration of life as well as the lower halls.

Standing at the gate of this hall is a guard by the name of Sanegoria [Advocacy Lord]. He stands there to speak on behalf of Israel so that the left side should not rule over her. . . .

THE SIXTH HALL is called THE HALL OF DELIGHT because upon it depends the period of approval and benevolence of every matter, request and every prayer. . . . Four lights face the four winds, one to the south, which is on the right and is called Michael, the Advocate of Israel, the one who defends her so that she will be rescued from the accusations of the [evil] shells. . . . A second light stands on the north side, and this one receives the verdicts from the fourth hall, known as the Sechut Hall, and passes them on to the gatekeeper so that he might pass the verdict on to the angels standing on the impure side, for he sucks from the side of the Gebura [the Sefira of Judgment] and is therefore called Gabriel. Many a time it is he who judges a person himself, in which case the person is not delivered to the shells, but suffers chastisements of love instead. . . .[6]

[Gabriel is called that] because he comes from the left side [of the sefirotic system, which is the side of judgment]. and every one who originates on the left side is called that, which is to say, everything that flows forth out of the court is called night because the attributes of night are the attributes of the court.

THE SEVENTH HALL is called THE HOLY OF HOLIES. . . . In it is Sandalfon . . . , who exercises his strict discipline over the earth from his position in heaven between two heroes who rule over the form of the fetus in its mother's womb. He gives them all the spirit of life and he kills all creatures on earth with his drawn sword of fire. . . .[7]

[This traversal through the Holy Halls of Purity is followed in the Zohar as well as in Cordovero's works by a description of the impure twin of this system of halls, namely the Hall of the Shells[8].

After[9] having said in the previous chapters everything that is recorded about the holy angels, we should also know that God made the one in opposition to the other. Just as there is a holy and a pure side, one of justification, of decency and of good behavior . . . , so is there also that side of the shells which is the corrupted impurity, and that is accusation. From this side comes the accuser as well as that which makes man deviate from the straight path and leads him to the path of that which is not good. When this happens, they [the forces of this left side] ascend and make accusations against the person and defile him.]

THE[10] FIRST HALL is called PIT, an empty pit. And whoever comes to enter there finds the support of no one who might take him by the hand so that he shouldn't fall. Instead, they all give him a shove that makes him tumble in. Keeping watch in this hall is an overseer by the name of Duma. He stands in this hall, outside the gate of the first holy hall, together with several avenging angels, in order to seize the souls that the holy angel Tohariel tosses away. . . .[11]

He stands ready to lure mankind away from the good paths so that they look toward adultery and prostitution, for he does as his name says [Duma also means "the one suspected of adultery"]. All the avenging angels that are with him walk ahead of people so that they can direct their eyes toward transgression. This overseer is also called Sarsaris, for he is the Sarsur [mediator] of transgression. He also stands at the grave, and when the body is consigned to the grave, he breaks the body's gaze because it once followed his advice. This is the way of the [evil] shell, it lures us downward, then climbs up and makes an accusation on high; then it descends again and takes the person's soul. . . .

THE SECOND HALL is called THE DEN OF INIQUITY. It is impure and lies in darkness. This hall has three gates facing three sides. At one gate stands an overseer called Asatiria. Under him are several thousand and several thousand thousand overseers who watch over those people who spill their seed in vain; they will not see the face of the shekinah.[12] These people come and soil themseves in this world; and in the hereafter, when their soul escapes [in death], they [these overseers] seize it and bring it up to themselves to judge it. They are called "the boiling ejaculation". . . .

Standing by the third gate is an overseer called Sangadiel. He has been placed over all those who defile the holy covenant of circumcision and penetrate one of the daughters of foreign peoples. As for all those who perform unclean acts with foreigners, they are marked with the shapes of those women with whom they have sinned. These shapes are also engraved upon this overseer and on the many thousand overseers beneath him. When a person's soul is liberated [in death], it is defiled by these shapes engraved upon it, and they are wrapped around the soul in this hall. . . .

It can also happen that all of those [impure] spirits that originated from the wasted ejaculations go forth from this hall draped in human form in order to lead mankind astray. . . .

THE THIRD HALL is called OFEL [Mists of Evil]. . . . There are four gates to this hall, and each one has an overseer assigned to it. Standing at the first gate is an overseer by the name of Katritia, who stands in the power of anger when judgment is meted out over the world. . . .

The second gate is guarded by Nagdiel. He has under his command several thousand and thousands of thousands of avenging angels. They all stand before the third holy hall ready to receive the verdicts of the court. Once he has received the verdicts, he descends back into the two preceding halls, namely into the Den of Iniquity and the Pit, where he has several thousand and thousands of thousands of avenging angels who all wander about in the world to execute the verdict, God forbid!

Angiriyon stands in front of the third gate. He has been put in charge of the burning malaria in one's bones and over all sorts of foul diseases that cause the body to glow and to burn. . . .

Standing at the fourth gate is an overseer called Asakra, who is charged with the killing and the death of infants. . . .

THE FOURTH HALL is called SIN and TERRESTRIAL MIRE, and in keeping with it man's evil instinct[13] is called Stumbling Stone.

This hall is so named because it stands opposite the Hall of Justice. All the sins of man as well as all his frivolous transgressions are collected here. The avenging angels gather them together and bring them to this hall, and on the day of judgment, at New Year's, when they weigh sin against virtue, if the scale of virtue tips the balance to the side of holiness, then they keep him and his sentence reads: Life! But, if the scale of sin predominates, then the sin spirits grab him and cry out: He is ours, he is ours! And they rejoice at his expense and condemn him to death.

Listen to this: the way a person behaves in this world determines the rewards that flow down upon him from above. If he follows his impure instinct and commits a sin, the spirit of impurity will pursue him and help him defile himself even more and will induce him to commit further transgressions . . . .

This hall contains all those who are called foreign gods and they are the ones who seduce mankind with the pleasures of this world, with adultery and prostitution. Reigning over all these foreign gods is a spirit called Other-God. He lures the Torah scholars into the bet midrash with evil and alien thoughts and with all sorts of impurities and says to them: What are you doing standing there, wasting the days of your youth with learning and squandering your strength? Is it not better to enjoy yourself in your youth with adultery and fornication? . . .

This hall decides for the worst over all things except the blessing of children, the support and the duration of life, which are decided higher, in the other halls. But they come down to this hall, and from there the accusers go out to do evil, be it that a person has fewer children, be it for death or for poverty, may the Merciful One protect us! . . .

THE FIFTH HALL is called SHEOL (The Dwelling Place of the Dead). The evil instinct receives its name in keeping with the nature of this place: "Uncircumcised One". . . .

In the midst of this hall stands a spirit that lurks along the highways and byways in order to see whichever person disobeys the laws of the Torah. They then betray that person on high and sow enmity between the upper and the lower worlds. They all stand around to lure man away from the good path and toward the evil one. Then they ascend and make accusations against him and kill him, and they remove him from this world and from the other. . . .

THE SIXTH HALL . . . has four gates and in those four impure forces: one is Death, another is Evil, the third is the Shadow of Death, the fourth is Darkness. They remain forever doing evil and making accusations. . . .

Scripture says of this hall (Prov. 27:6): "Faithful are the wounds of a friend, but the kisses of an enemy are importunate." Gathered together here are all the kisses and temptations and carnal desires of fornication and adultery, for whose sake man is driven out of this world as well as of the other . . . , and all these temptations originate with the spirit of this hall. Scripture says of this spirit (Prov. 7:11)): "She is riotous and rebellious, her feet abide not in her house", for she goes out to seduce man. And after she has seduced him, she lets him taste of bitterness, "the cruel poison of asps" (Deut. 32:33), and she seizes his soul with her sword, which drips with three drops [of poison]. . . . In this hall abide all those who make accusations against a man and seduce him with clothes and garments and induce him to curl and comb his hair, wash his body and groom his face so that women will take notice of him. An overseer with the name of Saktofa is put in charge of this group. There is also another overseer in this hall who is called Mirror; he helps man gaze at himself, groom and prettify himself, whereafter man looks in the mirror and cloaks himself in pride and arrogance and vulgar attitudes. Through these actions he arouses another force called Asirta, who has been given charge over all dreams. She shows a person a body by which he lets himself be attracted, and thus causes him to lose his soul. This overseer arouses yet another who is subservient to her, and this one goes down and arouses in the lowest hall, where Askara is, the woman with the name of Lilith, the mother of demons. If the person's carnal desires have been excited, Lilith unites with Asirta. With every new moon this Mirror awakens with Lilith, and now and then they manage to injure the person and he plunges to the ground, is overcome, and is violated. All of that was set in motion by this Mirror, and all because of the pride with which he gave himself airs. . . .

THE SEVENTH HALL is the HALL OF THE WINE DREGS, which make a person drunk. . . .

Actually, one might think that these [seven] halls are the halls for the [evil] sefirot-shells [in keeping with] that which was said in the previous section. But clearly the sefirot are encompassed by the halls and the halls and the shells are one and the same. And corresponding to these seven are the seven types of evil instincts [in man], and these drives get their power from these seven. This is why the evil instinct has seven names: Evil, Impure, Abomination, Hater, Stone, Stumbling Stone, the Northerner. Gehinnom has seven chambers corresponding to these seven instincts where the sinner is punished in seven ways. These chambers are called: Pit, Den of Iniquity, Duma (The One Suspected of Adultery), Terrestrial Mire, Sheol, Shadow of Death, Lowest Earth.

The one corresponds to the other. Opposite purity is impurity, opposite fitness is that which is unfit, opposite the permitted is the forbidden, opposite justice is sin. "God hath made the one over against the other" (Eccles. 7:14).

Re: The Animal Stories

A Frog

One day the rabbi [Baal Shem Tov] sank into such a deep meditation that he spent three days and three nights in that state without realizing it. Finally he noticed that he had wandered out into a great desert, far from his house. He was quite puzzled by this, but concluded that it was not without meaning.

While he was thinking these thoughts, an enormous frog appeared, so huge that the Besht almost failed to recognize it for a frog. He asked: "Who are you?"

"A scholar whose soul was reincarnated into this frog," was the reply. (The Besht said: "You are indeed a learned man!" And by these words alone he gave him a great lift.) The man then went on to tell how he had spent the last five hundred years in this shape. Even though Ari, Isaac Luria, blessed be the memory of this holy tzaddik, even though he had performed acts of tikkun for all souls, because of the enormity of this particular man's transgression Ari had expelled him and banned him to a place where no one ever came, [and thus] where no one could perform tikkun for him.

The Besht asked the man what he had done. He explained that he once neglected to wash his hands and thus had not performed this customary ritual.

Satan brought charges against the man, but was turned aside: "He can not be brought before the court because of one single transgression except that one sin should drag another in its wake. If you are able to catch him committing another sin, this first one will be charged against him as well. However, if he should remember the Lord and repent of his sins, he will be cleansed of this one, too."

Satan immediately put him to the test; the man was led astray and did not resist the temptation. He did this repeatedly, a second, a third time, and more as well, until he had broken just about all the commandments.

The verdict came down to cast the man off and to take no more notice of his repentance from that moment on.

Actually, we know that he would have been accepted had he persisted in his repentance, for has it not been said: "Return, o backsliding children, except Acher!"[14]

As punishment for his sins, the man was cast off, but had he made wholehearted and urgent atonement, he would have been accepted, for there is nothing that can stand in the face of repentance and obstruct it.

But Satan had led him astray and turned him to drink, so that he had no time left to think of repentance; thus he committed every sin in the world.

And since the cause of all his sins was the first one of neglecting to wash his hands, his soul was condemned to gilgul. When he died, his soul entered a frog that lives constantly in water. He was also condemned to remain in a place where no one ever went, so that no Jew might pass by and give him a blessing or even so much as a good thought and by so doing draw forth the precious from the vile.

But the Besht performed a tikkun for the soul of this man and raised it so high that the frog lay dead on the ground. (*H*, 24; *Praise*, 24)

An Extraordinary Horse[15]

One day the rabbi [Baal Shem Tov] was staying with one of his followers in a village. The man prepared a feast in his honor. During the meal the rav chatted as everyone does about business, whether the master of the house made a living and how things were faring for him. The man explained that things were going well and that he had all he needed. Then the rav asked: "Do you have good horses? Let's go and see them!"

They went to the stables together, where they found one small horse that greatly pleased the rav. He asked the housemaster to give it to him as a present, but the man responded: "Sir, please don't ask for this particular horse. It's my favorite, and more dear to me than all the others. Every time things get difficult and when even three horses can't pull the wagon out of the mud, this one pulls it out all by itself. This has happened a few times already, and that's why I'm so fond of it."

About an hour later the conversation again focussed on the man's business and how things stood with him, and it turned out that he had many debtors. This time the rav asked: "Please show me your debtors' notes." The man showed him all of them. As he was looking through these obligations, the rav noticed one particular one and asked the man to give it to him as a present.

He responded: "Rabbi, why do you want this obligation, especially since the debtor died a long time ago and left nothing behind with which he could pay his debt?"

The rav persisted: "I want it nonetheless."

The man gave him the note, whereupon the Besht took it in his hands, tore it in two, and they both forgave the dead man his debt.

"Now," said the rav again, "go back and see how the horse is doing."

The man went to see and found the horse lying dead on the ground. He began to understand that all of this was not without meaning.

The rav explained it to him. "The man who owed you money but couldn't pay it was condemned to serve you well and to work off his debt in that way. His gilgul transformed him into a horse. That's why it pleased you so much and did all the heavy labor. Once he was released from his slavery, he returned to his rightful place; that's when the vital force of the horse was extinguished and it died."

A Dog and a Fish

Rabbi Nachman of Kosov had a relative called Rabbi Yudel from Chednov, whose father, Rabbi Joseph, was a maggid. Rabbi Yudel had the habit of not accepting anything from anyone. He lived by the toil of his own hands, and that work had to do with the iron trade.

One day he went to one of his mines, and since he wanted to spend the sabbath there, the master of the house said to him: "What might Your Reverence want to eat here? I have no fish, and you won't want to touch the meat because you couldn't check the slaughterer's knife. The best I can say is that not far from here is another mine where a rich man lives; surely he will have some fish as well as a shochet. Go to him, Your Reverence, that would be best!"

The rabbi followed his advice, and as he came to ford the shallow canal near the house, he found the water had risen considerably because it was the season of heavy rains or melting snow. They hadn't realized this and wanted to cross over anyway. At that very instant a dog ran up from behind and into the stream, where it drowned in the flood. The dog bobbed up and down and howled so bitterly that the pious man was overcome with compassion and his eyes filled with tears. He immediately realized that no one could cross over the water, and thus returned to the original mine. There he asked the housemaster to please take the trouble to get some fish for the sabbath. The housemaster went out and so pleaded with the fisherman that they actually returned with a glorious pike.

The housemaster said: "I've lived in this village for many years now, but I've never seen such a fish before!" They cooked the fish and prepared a number of dishes for their guest.

On the night of the sabbath, as the man was sitting at the table singing songs, he fell asleep. His father appeared to him in a dream and said: "Know that my soul was imprisoned in this fish through gilgul, and the informer whom I spent my life pursuing was making his gilgul in the dog that drowned in the stream. This drowning was his tikkun, for he drowned for you, my son, in order to save you! And I had to suffer gilgul in the fish because I persecuted him. You were the one who performed the tikkun for me, because your eyes swelled with tears at the sight of the drowning dog. And now pay attention, my son, to how you eat this fish!"

Later he visited the Besht who told him that he used to say that Rabbi Yudel was a reincarnation of the prophet Samuel. (*H*, 132; *Praise*, 133)

Re: Divine Judgment Via the Word

Rabbi Isaac Warns Quarrelsome Antagonists

The tax collector had a large family, and they hid their great hatred in their hearts because they feared him.

"And strife is like a leaking levee; once it is broken, the water spreads far and wide"[16], until the strife widened and no one who challenged the maggid was left alive. (*H*, 90; *Praise*, 88)

Deadly Perjury before the Court of Rabbi Isaac

One day two plaintiffs came before Rabbi Isaac, and he instructed one of them to take an oath so that the matter might be clarified.

The man's adversary burned with rage and protested against this decision because he knew perfectly well that the other man had lied.

Rabbi Isaac said to him: "What's your hurry? Let this decision stand. If someone lies to me, it always turns out that one of his children dies, and if he takes a false oath, he is the one to die. Do you want him to die on the spot? Wait a while; if he has lied, one of his children will surely die. That may make him regret his deed and thus save his own life!"

And so it happened. One of his children did die, and the man confessed the truth. (*H*, 92; *Praise*, 88)

The Haughty Rich Woman

In the city of Kovel there once lived a very rich man by the name of Rabbi Susman, and he held a very important position there.

As the rav was going home after prayers one sabbath evening, he heard someone in the synagogue reciting the prayer that ushers in the sabbath. He went to the bet midrash and summoned the assistant. He asked him: "Why are all of you in the synagogue so late in welcoming the sabbath?"

"Rabbi Susman was in the castle, and we were waiting for him."

"What if Rabbi Susman hadn't come back until tomorrow, would you have postponed welcoming the sabbath until then?"

When Rabbi Susman's wife heard of this exchange, she threatened: "If the rav is praying in the synagogue and they don't wait for my husband before reciting the 'Holy, Holy,' the 'Bless Ye the Lord' and the 'Amen,'[17] I'll lock all of you out of the bet midrash." As it happened, her husband used to pray in a spare room in the bet midrash where he could hear the "Holy, Holy," the "Bless Ye the Lord" and the "Amen."

When she got up next morning, she went to the tub to wash her face and hands. As she reached for the towel to dry herself, she suddenly froze, petrified like a stone. They ran quickly to the rav and caught him in prayer just as he came to the words "and cut off"[18]. He waved his hand, and she was dead. (*H*, 206; *Praise*, 193)

Fatal Disobedience

Another tale from Rabbi Jehiel from Kovel:

He ordered the Jews of the village to come to the city for the Passover holidays. It was his custom to always appoint two scholars whose duty it was to go from house to house and watch that the people purified their pots and pans properly in preparation for the holiday and baked the matzos in their presence.

It happened that a tax collector lived in the village, a learned man who paid no attention to the rav's order and thus did not go to the city for Passover. His innkeeper didn't go either.

However, when the tax collector went to the city during the intermediary days, the rav sent for him. He had hardly appeared before the rav said: "Since you did not celebrate the first days of Passover here in the city, you will be here for the last!"

And so it happened. When the tax collector returned to the village, he discovered his wife had died. He brought her to the city on the sixth day of Passover, and since it was already evening by the time she was buried, he had to spend the last day there.

The innkeeper died, too, just as they were reciting the consecration for the last day of the festival. (*H*, 207; *Praise*, 194)

Death by Drowning[19]

One day, a traitor slandered Rabbi Hayyim of Chernowitz and cast aspersions against him, God forbid, to the effect that he had committed a capital crime. Rabbi Hayyim was put in prison, and when the presiding officer summoned him for interrogation he allowed him the honor of sitting down almost as soon as he saw him.

One of those present said to the officer: "It is not fitting that such a prisoner as he should be allowed to sit!" The officer, however, replied: "The truth is written all over him."

He immediately declared him innocent and let him return home in peace.

On the way home, Rabbi Hayyim said to his followers: "I will not rest until the traitor does some harm to himself."

And so it happened: that very day the traitor went and threw himself into the river Prut.

"So perish all Thine enemies, O Lord!" (Judg. 5:31)

NOTES

Chapter 1 Kafka and Judaism

1. Two separate colloquia provided important incentives for this study. The first met in Frankfurt in December of 1986 under the direction of H. D. Zimmermann, Stéphane Mosès from Jerusalem, and myself. It focused on the topic: "Franz Kafka und das Judentum." The second colloquium took place in the Literaturarchiv in Marbach in the fall of 1990 under the direction of H. D. Zimmermann. I owe special thanks to the Fritz Thyssen Foundation which made this last conference in Marbach possible and whose research grant allowed me to make a study of Eastern Jewish literature, the fruits of which have contributed a great deal to this book.

2. Cf. also: Beck, *Kafka and the Yiddish Theatre. Its Impact on His Work* (1971); H. Binder, *Franz Kafka, Leben und Persönlichkeit* (1979), 296; Nagel, 123.

3. Cf. Zimmermann, 186ff.

4. For the many parallels between the authors and the movements mentioned here, cf. among others: Flasch (1989); Bernhart (1922); Grözinger, "Neoplatonisches Denken..." (1983), "Theosophie,..." (1986), "Osteuropäischer Hasidismus" in: *Theologische Realenzyklopädie*; Scholem, *Ursprung und Anfänge der Kabbala* (1962); Tishby (1988); Idel, *Kabbalah, New Perspectives* (1988).

5. Cf. Secret (1985); Benz (1958).

6. Cf. Harnischfeger (1980).

7. Cf. Buber, *Konfrontation und Koexistenz*, edited by N. Altenhofer, in preparation.

Chapter 2 *The Trial* and the Tradition of the Gatekeeper in the Kabbalah

1. Cf. Grözinger, "Schuld und Sühne" (1994).

2. The first edition of the work actually appeared in 1597 during its author's lifetime.

3. Babylonian Talmud, Rosh ha-Shanah (New Year), 16a.

4. *Shabbat* 32a.

5. Cf. *Kizzur Reshit Hokhma* (i.e. the abridged version), reprint of the 1912/13 edition, USA 1978/79, Chapter Jir'a 11:243f.

6. Cf. Grözinger, "Himmlische Gerichte" (1987).

7. The Kafka family seems to have enjoyed recalling such pious kabbalistic forebears. In the same entry he wrote about his great-great-grandfather (134): "An even more learned man than her grandfather was my mother's great-grandfather, who was equally revered by both Christians and Jews. His piety was such that, during a conflagration the flames miraculously skipped over and thus spared his house, while all the other houses in the neighborhood burned down." For more information regarding such fire protection among the Kabbalists, who would recite magical names of God to invoke angels, cf. Grözinger, "Wundermänner" (1991).

8. Re: vigil, cf. Pollack (1971), 19–22.

9. Kafka made his own attempt at a story based on the Prague golem legend, cf. *Diaries*, 310; cf. Scholem, *Symbolism* (1969); Idel, *Golem* (1990); Grözinger, "Wundermänner," 205, 220.

10. *Sefer Gevurot Adonai*, Honig and Sons (1980), 46, 178b.

11. Zohar, the main work of medieval Kabbalism, compiled in Castile in the thirteenth century, probably by Moses de Leon.

12. Cf. Kafka's aphorisms on this subject in *Hochzeitsvorbereitungen auf dem Lande*, where he takes up this kabbalistic tree-typology together with its kabbalistic connotations.

13. Cf. for example Jacobs (1972), 70ff.

14. Kafka certainly had similar Jewish depictions in mind when he noted in his diary entry of July 19, 1916: "Strange judicial procedure. The man condemned to death is stabbed in his room by the executioner with no other person present. He's sitting at the table and is finishing the letter in which he has written: 'Beloved Ones, O Angels, where are you hovering, unaware, out of the reach of my mortal hand . . .,'" *Diaries*, 361. On July 22:

> "Strange judicial procedure. The condemned man is stabbed in his cell by the executioner while no other person is allowed to be present. He's sitting at the table and finishing his letter or his last meal. There's a knock at the door; it's the executioner. 'Are you ready?' he asks. His questions as well as his instructions are prescribed for him, right down to the words and the sequence; he may not deviate from either. The condemned man, who had jumped up from his seat, sits down again and stares straight ahead or else buries his face in his hands. Since the executioner gets no answer, he opens his instrument case on the prisoner's cot, chooses the daggers and starts to sharpen various parts of their blades. . . ."

15. Here I am following the editions Lemberg (n.d.) and Sulzbach (1795).

16. Max Brod's as yet unpublished diary actually cites Margarita Pazi, who tells of Kafka's regular visits to the synagogue.

17. The burning of sinners is not reserved for the Roman Catholic hell, for the Jewish conception of the punishment of sinners also knows a purgatory, called Gehinnom, which will turn up again later on.

18. One might also mention the diary entry of October 21, 1921 here (*Diaries*, 340, *Critical Edition* 869): "It was impossible for him to enter the house for he had heard a voice saying: 'Wait until I lead you!' Thus he remained lying in the dust in front of the house, even though everything looked hopeless (as Sarah would say)." A second doorkeeper tradition based on the High Holy Days?

19. Rosh ha-Shanah fell on September 23; Yom Kippur began on the evening of October 1. The date in the diary should accordingly read October 2.
20. Cf. M. Pazi, "Franz Kafka, Max Brod und der 'Prager Kreis'" in: Grözinger et. al, *Judentum*, 81.
21. Cf. M. Pasley, "Handschrift" (1990).
22. Binder, *Kommentar* E (1975), 138; Steinberg (1962), 23ff.
23. Cf. Nagel, 118.
24. The story of the relation between Rabbi Meir and Aher (Elisha ben Avuyah) that Löwy mixed into his tale is found in the Babylonian Talmud Hagigah 15b. The simile of the kernel and the shell of the nut was meant to explain why the pious Rabbi Meir could learn from an heretic. Hagigah 15b has it this way: "How was it possible that Rabbi Meir could learn from the mouth of Aher? . . . In the west they say that Rabbi Meir ate the date and tossed the kernel away. Rabbah said: It is written (Song of Sol. 6:11): 'I went down into the garden of nuts, to look at the green plants of the valley.' Why are the scribes compared to a nut? This means: As the kernel is not repulsive even if the nut itself is covered with filth, so also is the Torah of the scribe not to be despised, even if he has sinned." The tradition of the sabbath ride: "One day on a sabbath Aher was riding a horse, and Rabbi Meir followed him in order to learn the Torah from his lips. The former said: 'Meir, turn back, for I can tell from my horse's stride that the sabbath border (which marks the distance one is permitted to go) reaches up to here.'—'You turn back, too', was Meir's response.—Aher replied: 'I have already told you that I heard from behind the curtain [of God's Throne] 'Return, thou backsliding Israel!' (Jeremiah 3, 12), except Aher." The legend about Akiva's late start to his studies is found in the extra-talmudic tractate *Avot de Rabbi Natan*, Vers. A c. 6, edited by Schechter (1967), 28.
25. It really was glittering marble stones, and only the one who was unworthy of a heavenly journey went astray here and thought it was water.
26. Cf. Grözinger, "Wundermänner," n. 32.

Chapter 3 When and How the Celestial Court Functions

1. Cf. the descriptions in the "Tractate on Gehinnom", translated by A. Wünsche, *Aus Isrels Lehrhallen*, five volumes, Leipzig 1907–1910
2. This according to the Albeck commentary. Normally this is translated "like counting sheep"; Cf. L. Goldschmidt's German translation of the Talmud, III: 565
3. Cf. Ganzfried (1988), 735
4. This passage comes already in Bl. 16a
5. Cf. Babylonian Talmud, Rosh ha-Shanah 16b and Tosafot on this point.

Chapter 4 The Ecstatic Ascent to Heaven

1. The Angel of Death is also the chief accuser in the celestial court, the Angel Samael or Satan.
2. Even the ancient Jewish hekhalot mystics brought new melodies back with them from their celestial journeys. They learned these tunes with great enthusiasm because the success of their journeys depended upon this knowledge. Some ecstatic celestial ascents also started in the middle of a song; cf. Grözinger, *Musik*, 308ff. The sabbath motifs introduced below, the additional sabbath soul and the two angels who accompany the pious man home from the synagogue at the beginning of the sabbath, are all pre-kabbalistic talmudic

teachings. To this day the orthodox still sing a song at the sabbath table at the beginning of the sabbath as a greeting for these two angels.

3. Cf. also *Praise*, 54–58.

4. It was actually the Talmud, as the rest of the tale makes clear. The Talmud, together with the whole of the extra-biblical Jewish tradition, makes up the Oral Tradition, which is also considered sinaitic. Without it, the Jewish conception of revelation is incomplete and incomprehensible.

5. The ceremonial evening service ushering in Yom Kippur; it begins with the Kol Nidre prayer, which absolves all vows made to God but subsequently forgotten. The purpose is to free people from the sin of unkept promises.

6. According to the hasidic concept of prayer, the letters and the words of the prayer are worlds of divine habitation. The prayer must pass through these worlds, which is tantamount to transversing celestial spheres.

7. "Kavvanah," inner devotion and steadfast intent; particularly among the Kabbalists this was understood as the mystical meditations that bind the words of the prayer with the nature of the Divine.

8. Cf. 27a of the Mesibos edition of 1817. The reference here is to the biblical prophet Ahijah of Shiloh (cf. I Kings 11:29). According to rabbinical/kabbalistic tradition, he was a teacher of Elijah (Jerusalem Talmud, Eruvin 5,1, 22b) and was well versed in the wisdom of the Torah and especially in mystical teachings (Babylonian Talmud, San 102a; also Ginzberg, *Jewish Encyclopedia* II, 389 and the Index to his *Legends*). Thus, unlike the usual custom in the rabbinical tradition, the Besht is not calling upon the worldly teachers of the Torah or upon traditional writings, but primarily upon the mystics and the Kabbalists for direct divine guidance.

9. In an addendum to the anthology of homilies prepared by his student Jacob Joseph of Polonnoye, *Ben Porat Josef*, printed in Pietrkov (1883/84), 255 .

10. Cf. *Machsor Kol Bo*, Nusach Aschkenas, reprint New York, 326, 328, 335.

11. Sermon No. 22 for the Ten Days of Penitence, Bl. 33a in the *Derusche ha-Zelach*, Warsaw edition (1886).

Chapter 5 "No One Else Could Enter Here, for This Door Was Meant for You Alone"

1. *Judentum*, 223

2. *Grundbegriffe*, 90ff

3. *Scha'ar ha-Gilgulim*, c. 17, *Kitve ha-Ari*, Tel Aviv 1962/63, 48f; cf. also Korez, Bl. 59a

4. The doctrine of the fourfold meaning has been traced back to the thirteenth century and was known under the acronym PaRDeS. Luria interpreted it within the context of his teachings on the transmigration of the soul.

5. Cf. Scholem, *Symbolism*, 44: "From here it was only one more step to saying that God Himself is the Torah, 'for the Torah is not something outside Him, and He is not outside the Torah'."

Chapter 6 The Gatekeeper Tradition As It Relates to the Description of the Court

1. Re: The gatekeeper legend, cf. Grözinger, "'Trübselige Meinung', sagte K." in: *Franz Kafka "Vor dem Gesetz"*, edited by M. Voigts, Würzburg 1994.

2. Cf. Ch. Eschweiler, 29, where he comes to the same conclusion on the basis of his analysis of *The Trial* in his attempt to reorganize the chapters of the book.

Chapter 7 The Status of Man vis-à-vis the Officers of the Court

1. This is the theological basis of the later Eastern European hasidic doctrine of tzaddikism with its passionate tzaddikim, who used this their superiority like pyknics on behalf of their faithful followers.

Chapter 8 The Human Face as a Reflection of Divine Judgment

1. Cf. Grözinger, "Sündenpropheten," 17–46
2. This genre of tales revolving around the figure of the prophet of iniquity goes back to the legends surrounding Isaac Luria, the founder of the Lurianic School of Kabbalah. Here is an example of a very brief and typical tale of such sin prophecy: "The rav, the saintly Kabbalist, our master Isaac Ashkenazi, said remarkable things when the Holy Spirit appeared upon him. One day an uneducated wine merchant entered his house. To this man the rav said: 'I see unpaid tithes on your forehead, woe is you!' The Jew began to weep and confessed the truth, whereupon [Isaac Luria Ashkenazi] gave him an act of atonement to do." (Benajahu, 360)
3. Moses Maimonides (1135–1205), commonly known as Rambam, one of the major codifiers of talmudic law. His halakhic code is known as the *Mishne Torah*.
4. According to Mondshayn (1982).

Chapter 9 The Kabbalistic Depiction of the Celestial Courts—History as Judgment

1. "I've forgotten to ask you right away which type of acquittal you want. There are three possibilities, namely: the real acquittal, the apparent acquittal and postponement." (*Trial*, 205).
2. Zohar I: Bl. 38a–45b; II: Bl. 244b–268b.
3. Sixth Impure Hall, cf. Appendix.
4. *Briefe*, 611f.

Chapter 10 The Incursion of Judgment into Human Life—Disease and Dreams

1. "There are three possibilities, namely the real acquittal, the apparent acquittal and postponement . . . I know of no real acquittal, but certainly of many interferences."
2. The late Zoharic text *Tikkune ha-Zohar* offers a similar but more detailed description (Appendix, *Tik*. 5, 142b). I shall cite several excerpts: "When a person sleeps, his soul rises up out of his body and does not return until all the transgressions the person committed on that day have been requited. This is why the celestial court takes the soul as security, for the accuser climbs up behind it in order to demand its proper punishment in keeping with the four types of execution. . . . If the sins should gain the upper hand, the person heaps sins upon the security, and the security, which is his soul, perishes and never returns to his body again. And all of this takes place in the great court where the soul is judged every night . . ." In what follows in later chapters of this study, even the shekinah acts as an accuser against man.
3. A portion of a prayer inserted into the seventeenth blessing of the eighteen prayers recited upon the advent of the new moon and during the intermediate

days of Passover and Sukkot. cf. Elbogen (1967), 57 and, for example, *Siddur Safa Berura*, 46, 186

Chapter 11 "Women Have a Great Power"—The Feminine Element in the Hierarchies of the Court

1. Cf. Scholem, *Godhead*, chap. 2.
2. Cf. also the diary entry of September 30, 1911.
3. Cf. Scholem, *Idea*, 78–141.
4. Cf. Piekarz, 176.
5. *Megillat Jochsen*, Lemberg (n.d.), II:38.

Chapter 12 The Judgment Theme in Eastern Jewish Folktales—Kabbalah as Narrative

1. In fact, Kafka's opinion of the quality of the stories in question holds true for most of the Yiddish and Hebrew originals. They belong to the simple, at times primitive folktale tradition, a fact which only increases their value for scholarship.

2. ". . . The Rabbi of Belz is here. I have joined in twice already with his followers during their evening walks. He alone makes the trip from Karlsbad to Marienbad worthwhile," (*Letters*, 141ff).

3. October 6, 1915; *Diaries*, 300. Kafka heard these tales from his friend Georg Mordechai Langer, who later collected them in his anthology of hasidic stories called *Neun Tore*. The stories repeated by Kafka as well as the ones in Langer's anthology have been traced back to the sources I cite in the text. Even though Langer comes much closer to hasidic reality in his retelling of the tales than do the philosophically and romantically tinged renditions of Martin Buber or Elie Wiesel, he still could not completely resist certain rationalisations and attempts at polishing.

4. Cf. Grözinger, "Erzählungen", 91–114

5. From the anthology *Sippurim nora'im*, Lemberg, 1875, 46

6. From the anthology *Sippure Ja'akov*, "Husiatin" 1904, 1

7. In the anthology *Kehal Hasidim*, no date and no place, between 1864 and 1912, 33 a/b. Deviating version in Mintz, 162f, *Praise*, 260.

8. Cf. *Nifle'ot Elimelekh*, Pietrkow 1910, 27

9. 1773–1827

10. *Sippurim Nora'im*, 46

11. *Nifle'ot Elimelekh*, 30

12. Mintz, 127f; *Praise*, 87f. Here I am following the Yiddish version in Korez, 1815. When the trial is nullified and the "temporary" acquittal passed, the patient on earth returns to himself: "and then he began to speak again" (Mintz, 127). In the case of Joseph of Hannipoli: "down below his body began to break out in sweat . . . and he was healed of his sickness" (*Kehal Hasidim*, 33b).

13. Cf. Babylonian Talmud, *Megilla* 18b

14. Bardiov, 1925, 21

15. Following the talmudic principle quoted here (bMak. 7a; bBM 91a), Rabbi Akiba and Rabbi Tarfon actually did obstruct the death sentence in trials involving incest, which, according to the biblical commandment, are to be punished by death, by allowing the testimonial statements only if the witnesses of the sex act actually saw how the stick disappeared into its case. cf. Maimonides, *Mishne Torah*, Hilkh. Issure Bi'a, I:19

16. Jewish criminal law presupposes a conscious knowledge of the prohibition and of the stipulated punishment in any condemnation. Cf. *The Principles of Jewish Law*, ed. M. Elon, Jerusalem 1975, 473, = EJ ad voc. Penal Law by H.Cohen; cf. Maimonides, *Mishne Torah*, Hilkh. Issure Bi'a, I:1–3

Chapter 13 The Animal Stories

1. *Sefer Derekh ha-Hokhma*, 32f; *Netiv* 14; likewise *Scha'ar ha-Gilgulim*, Jerusalem 1962/63, c. 22.63a.
2. *Ibid.*
3. *Ibid.*, 32d.
4. Cf. Bloch, 47.
5. *Op. cit.*, 148.
6. Benajahu, 188f.
7. Cf. the argument the two of them had with Moses in Numbers 16.
8. Cf. also the fragment in *Description*, 248–51.
9. *Sefer Minhat Jehuda*, Jerusalem 1989/90, 154.
10. Benajahu, 235.
11. *Scha'ar Ruah ha-Kodesh*, Tikkun 20, 54a; *Minhat Jehuda*, 154
12. Cf. Schechter (1961); Urbach (1979), c. 15, 6.
13. J. Davidson, *Ozar ha-Meshalim weha-Pitgamim*, Jerusalem 1978/79, No. 2813.
14. Diary entry according to Binder, 339.
15. Babylonian Talmud, Berakhot 32b; Zohar II: 92b.
16. The book was found among Kafka's personal library; cf. Zimmermann, 213. These legends were reprinted in 1970 by Salcia Landmann under the title *Sagen der Chasidim*, Frankfurt, Berlin, Vienna.
17. Benajahu, 177f.
18. *Ibid.*, 234.
19. This story was also reprinted in the Eisenberg anthology with which Kafka was acquainted.
20. Cf. *Scha'ar ha-Gilgulim*, c. 22.
21. The *Scha'ar ha-Gilgulim* touches upon this same point in its discussion of animal reincarnations, c. 22, 63a.

Chapter 14 Divine Judgment via the Word—"I Now Sentence You To Death By Drowning"

1. Cf. Binder, *Kommentar E*, 123.
2. Yom Kippur started on the evening of September 20 and continued until September 21; Kafka wrote the story during the night of September 22 to 23; cf. *Diaries*, 183; *Critical Edition*, 293.
3. Binder, *op. cit.*, 132, following E. T. Beck, *Theatre*, 98f.
4. Binder, *op. cit.*, 133; Beck, *op. cit.*, 72ff; cf. also Beck, "Durchbruch," 209f.
5. *Sippurim nora'im*, No. 26, 47
6. Babylonian Talmud, Sanhedrin 100a; *Bereshit Rabba* 79, 18, Albeck 945; *Pesikta de Rav Kahana* 11, 17, Mandelbaum, 193.
7. Cf. Appendix for additional tales.

Chapter 15 Language and Reality—Writing as a Form of Prayer

1. Cf. Grözinger, "Names", JSJT VI (1987).
2. Cf. Grözinger, "Wundermänner" (1991), note 32.

3. Cf. Gowortschow, 48–55; from Schneur Salman of Lyady's *Tanya*, Brooklyn 1979, 152.

4. The reference is to the ancient *Sefer Yetzirah*, according to which God created the world by means of the ten basic numbers and the twenty-two letters of the Hebrew alphabet; c. 2.5.

5. Cf. Grözinger, "Names", note 342; also Grözinger, *Musik*, 291.

6. *Scha'ar* 26, "Scha'ar ha-Otiyot", Bl. 59c.

7. For more information about him, cf. Scholem, *Symbolism*, 286, n. 72; Grözinger, "Wundermänner" 205, 219; Idel, *Golem*.

8. Acronym for Morenu ha-Rav Liva.

9. The dream was considered a prophetic medium. The technique of dream inquiry was developed in the Middle Ages and was used to elicit direct heavenly revelations.

10. The number ten is certainly not coincidental, cf. the Ten Creative Utterances mentioned above.

11. In 1916, the year Kafka was working on his golem story, the 20th of Adar fell on March 13; Kafka's golem fragment was written in April.

12. This version follows the Warsaw editions of 1913 and Pietrkov, 1909.

13. "Scha'ar" 29, Bl. 68c.

14. ibid, Bl. 71b.

15. "Scha'ar" 26, Bl. 59c.

16. Cf. E. Lipner, *Hason ha-Otiyot*, Jerusalem 1989, 403

Chapter 16 "Josephine the Singer, or the Mouse People"

1. Cf. the chapter on Aphorisms.

2. Babylonian Talmud, *Ta'anit* 8a.

3. Cf. Grözinger, "Wundermänner", 201.

4. Cf. Max Brod, *Briefe* in Binder, *Kommentar E*, 327.

5. Cf. Babylonian Talmud, *Megilla* 28b; *Mishna, Avot* 1, 13; 4, 7.

6. Cf. Grözinger, "Wundermänner" (1991).

7. Cf. also J. Jaakov (J. Klapholz), *Kol Sippure Ba'al Shem Tov*, Jerusalem, Bne Brak, no date, I: 236–238; after "Mayyim rabbim."

8. Cf. Grözinger, "Wundermänner", *op. cit.*

9. Cf. Scholem, *Godhead* (1991).

10. For further information on the significance of song as far back as ancient talmudic literature and particularly in early Jewish mysticism, cf. Grözinger, *Musik*; for the Kabbalah, cf. Idel, "Music and Kabbalah" in: Mendes-Flohr and Cohen (1987); Grözinger, "Tradition und Neuerung in der Musikauffassung des Sohar (hebr.)" in: J. Dan, editor, *The Age of the Zohar, Jerusalem Studies in Jewish Thought*, Jerusalem 1989; Moshe Idel, *The Mystical Experience in Abraham Abulafia*, Albany 1988, the chapter on "Music and Ecstatic Kabbalah."

11. Cf. M. Idel in: *Mystical Experience*, 64.

12. *Megillat Yuhasin*, 31; cf. also Grözinger, "Gegenwart" (1988).

13. Cf. Grözinger, "Neoplatonisches Denken", 86ff.

14. Cf. Israel Adler, "Synagogale Kunstmusik in Europa aus der Zeit vor der Emanzipation" in: Grözinger, *Judentum* (1991).

15. Cf. Grözinger, *Musik*, 240ff; also Adler, *op. cit.* 237.

16. Cf. Nigal, I. 118.

17. *Ibid.*, I. 118f.

18. *Ibid*, 38.

19. *Ibid.*, 23. cf. also Nigal, G. *Mishnat ha-Hasidut be-Kitve R. Elimelech mi-Lisensk u-Bet Midrasho*, dissertation, Jerusalem 1971/72, 80.

20. Cf. Martin Buber, *Der Jude und sein Judentum*, 239; also Grözinger, "Chassidismus," 281–94, particularly 290ff.
21. Ja'akov Josef *Sefer Toledot Ja'akov Josef*, reprint of an earlier (Eastern European edition), Brooklyn, n.d., Bl. 44d.
22. *Ibid.*, Bl. 75d; cf. also *Ben Porat Josef*, Bl. 54b; cf. also Grözinger, article on "Hasidismus" in: *Theologische Realenzyklopädie*, Berlin, New York , XVII:377ff, especially 383f.

Chapter 17 The Aphorisms—Between the Two Trees of Paradise

1. Cf. Langer, *Neun Tore*, Introduction, 29.
2. This process of the self-withdrawal of the Godhead into a void, which the Maggid called "tzimtzum" and which signified a dimunition of the plethora of light or a concentration to one point, is not to be confused with the identically labelled "tzimtzum" of Lurianic Kabbalah (cf. Scholem, *Die jüdische Mystik in ihren Hauptströmungen*, 285ff; *Major Trends*). Luria understood "tzimtzum" primarily as the creation of a space emptied of God, out of which the Godhead, which originally permeated everything, had retreated.
3. Cf. Joseph Weiss, "Via Passiva in Early Hasidism", in: Weiss, J. *Studies in Eastern European Jewish Mysticism*, Oxford 1958, 69ff, also in *Journal of Jewish Studies* 11, 3-4(1958), 163–192.
4. Buber, *Chassidim*, 326f.
5. Cf. Grözinger, "Neoplatonisches Denken", 57ff; "Hasidim und Hasidismus", 131ff; "Martin Bubers Hassidismus-Deutung" (1982).
6. ed. C. Gebhardt, Heidelberg, London, Paris, Amsterdam 1929, 130a and 28b. The Hebrew translation by Jehuda da Modena (1571–1648), Lyck 1871 under the title *Wikkuah 'al ha-Ahava*, 87a and 10a.
7. *Ziw'at ha-Rivasch*, Brooklyn 1975, paragraph 90, 30; also in: *Or Tora*, Brooklyn 1972, 206, 133a.
8. I am translating the biblical text here in the sense required by the homily—author's note.
9. The passages enclosed within parentheses are indicated in the edition as an alternative reading and correspond to the *Or Torah* to a considerable degree.
10. Benjamin, *Briefe*, 611.

Chapter 18 Kafka Without End—Yet Another Interpretation

1. W. H. Auden in his book of the same name, New York 1947; also according to H. Politzer in his "Einleitung zu Franz Kafka", *Wege der Forschung* 322, Darmstadt 1973, 2.
2. Anders, 84.
3. I. Zangerle, "Die Bestimmung des Dichters" in: *Der Brenner*, Innsbruck XVI (1946), 155–161, according to Politzer, *WdF*, 219.
4. Collected in Brod, *Über*, 1966.
5. Munich, 1982.
6. The following works are worthy of note in this regard: Ritchie Robertson: *Kafka, Judaism, Politics and Literature*, Oxford, 1985 and Frank Schirrmacher: *Verteidigung der Schrift in Kafkas Prozeß*, Frankfurt a.M. 1987.
7. W. Kraft, 1968.
8. Benjamin, *Briefe*, 611f.
9. Politzer, *Kafka*, *WdF*, 217, n. 5.
10. Benjamin, *Briefe*, 612.

APPENDIX

1. "Scha'ar" 24, c. 1ff, 45cff.
2. Regarding this talmudic idea, cf. Grözinger, *Ich bin der Herr Dein Gott* (1976), 159ff.
3. This is to say that the judicial authorities described here are the emanations of the divine powers of grace (love), justice and compassion as well as those charged with these assignments and that the judicial system, therefore, proceeds from the Godhead and its inner forces. These divine forces are themselves the highest part of the judicial hierarchies.
4. *I.e.*, the Halls of the Other Side, which are described below.
5. See below, the Fifth Hall.
6. Cf. Prov. 3:12: "For whom the Lord loveth, He correcteth."
7. Sandalfon, ordinarily described as the angel who weaves prayers into crowns and lets them ascend to the head of God, is here described, by way of exception, as the angel of death, or at least as his heavenly counterpart.
8. "Scha'ar" 25.53bff and "Scha'ar" 26.57aff.
9. What follows are only the opening words of "Scha'ar" 25.
10. "Scha'ar" 26, Hekhalot ha-Klippot.
11. See above, the First Holy Hall.
12. Among the Kabbalists, the shekinah is the tenth spiritual force or manifestation of God, the one closest to the world which also serves as the mother of Israel. This is where entry to the divine sefirotic world begins, and this entry is the highest goal of the mystic as well as of all mankind.
13. The Talmud already identifies man's evil instinct with the accuser and the angel of death, Babylonian Talmud, *Baba Batra* 16a; cf. Schechter, 244.
14. Jer. 3:14; Babylonian Talmud, *Hagiga* 14b, 15a-b; *Kidduschin* 39b; Palestinian Talmud, *Hagiga* 2, 1 (77b).
15. *H*, 237; *Praise*, 218. This story is also included in *Sagen polnischer Juden*, an anthology with which Kafka was familiar. It appeared there as Number 5, although it bears the misleading title of "A Bewitched Horse".
16. Babylonian Talmud, *Sanhedrin* 7a.
17. All of these are prayers that may only be recited by a minyan or else may open the main worship service.
18. "And cut off the idols" from the Alenu prayer.
19. Nigal, G., editor, *Gedolim Ma'ase Tzaddikim*, Jerusalem 1991, 26.

BIBLIOGRAPHY

Note: All page references in the text refer to the original German language bibliographic entries and not to the English version of the work unless this is specifically stated. References in the text refer to the author of the work cited unless that author has a number of books or articles included in this bibliography, in which case the notation in the text will refer directly to the work being cited. All quotes taken from the works of Franz Kafka are my own translations taken from the original texts; for this reason, no English translations of Kafka's works are included in this bibliography. These original German language texts are listed below under "Primary Sources"; the words in square brackets indicate the English translation of the title, while the words in parentheses indicate the reference used in the text to identify the source. All other works are listed under "Secondary Sources"; again, the words in parentheses indicate the reference used in the text to identify the source.

PRIMARY SOURCES

Kafka, Franz. *Beschreibung eines Kampfes*, edited by Max Brod, Frankfurt a.M. 1980 [*Description of a Battle*] (*Description*)

——. *Briefe 1902 – 1924*, Frankfurt a.M. 1975 [*Letters 1902–1924*] (*Letters*)

——. *Briefe an Felice*, edited by E. Heller and J. Born, Frankfurt a.M. 1976 [*Letters to Felice*] (*Felice*)

——. *Briefe an Milena*, edited by W. Haas, Frankfurt a.M. 1970 [*Letters to Milena*] (*Milena*)

——. *Briefe an Ottla und die Familie*, edited by H. Binder and K. Wagenbach, Frankfurt a.M. 1981 [*Letters to Ottla and the Family*] (*Ottla*)

——. *Die Erzählungen*, Frankfurt a.M. 1961 [*Stories*] (*Stories*)

——. *Hochzeitsvorbereitungen auf dem Lande*, edited by M. Brod, Frankfurt a.M. 1980 [*Wedding Preparations in the Country*] (*Wedding*)
——. *Der Proceß*, edited by M. Pasley, Frankfurt a.M. 1990 [*The Trial* in Kafka's original spelling] (*Trial*)
——. *Das Schloß*, Frankfurt a.M. 1971 [*The Castle*] (*Castle*)
——. *Tagebücher 1910 - 1923*, edited by Max Brod, Frankfurt a.M. 1973 [*Diaries 1910-1923*] (*Diaries*)
——. *Tagebücher 1910 - 1923*, Kritische Ausgabe, edited by H. G. Koch, M. Müller and M. Pasley, Frankfurt a.M. 1990 [*Diaries 1910-1923, Critical Edition*] (*Critical Edition*)

SECONDARY SOURCES

Anders, G. *Kafka, Pro und Contra, Die Prozeß-Unterlagen*, Munich 1951
Beck, E. T. "Kafkas 'Durchbruch', der Einfluß des jiddischen Theaters auf sein Schaffen" in: *Basis, Jahrbuch für deutsche Gegenwartsliteratur*, 1(1970) ("Durchbruch")
——. *Kafka and the Yiddish Theatre. Its Impact on His Work*, Madison, Milwaukee, London 1971 (*Theatre*)
Ben Amos, Dan and Jerome R. Mintz, editors. *In Praise of the Baal Shem Tov [Shivhei ha-Besht]*, Bloomington 1970 (*Praise*)
Benajahu, M. (editor). *Toledot ha-Ari*, Jerusalem 1967
Benjamin, Walter. *Briefe*, edited by G. Scholem and Th. W. Adorno, Frankfurt a.M. 1966 (*Briefe*)
Benjamin, Walter and Gershom Scholem. *Briefwechsel 1933 - 1940*, Frankfurt a.M. 1985 (*Briefwechsel*)
Benz, E. *Die christliche Kabbala*, [n.p.] 1958
Bernhart, J. *Die philosophische Mystik des Mittelalters*, Munich 1922
Binder, H. *Franz Kafka, Leben und Persönlichkeit*, Stuttgart 1979
——. *Kafka Kommentar*, Munich 1976 (*Kommentar*)
——. *Kafka Kommentar, Erzählungen*, Munich 1975 (*Kommentar E.*)
——. *Kafka Kommentar, Romane*, Munich [no date] (*Kommentar R.*)
Bloch, Chajim. *Der Prager Golem*, Berlin 1920
Brod, Max. *Franz Kafka, Eine Biographie*, Frankfurt a.M. 1954 (*Kafka*)
——. *Über Franz Kafka: Franz Kafka, Eine Biographie; Franz Kafkas Glauben und Lehre; Verzweiflung und Erlösung im Werk Franz Kafkas*, Frankfurt a.M. 1966 (über)
Buber, Martin. *Der Jude und sein Judentum*, Cologne 1963
——. *Die Erzählungen der Chassidim*, Manasse, Zurich 1949
——. "Deutung der jüdischen Geschichte als der Versuch einer Modernisierung des Judentums" in: *Konfrontation und Koexistenz*, edited by N. Altenhofer, in preparation
Cordovero, Moses. *Pardes Rimmonim, Scha'ar ha-Hekhalot*, edited by Munkacz, Jerusalem 1961/62 (*Pardes*)
Danby, H. (translator). *The Mishnah*, Oxford 1933
Davidson, J. *Ozar ha-Meshalim weha-Pitgamim*, Jerusalem 1978/79, No. 2813
de Vidas, Eliahu. *Reshit Hokhma*, reproduction of Munkacz Edition, Brooklyn 1968/69 (*Reshit Hokhma*)
Dov Ber, *Schivhe ha-Besht*, edited by Benjamin Mintz, Jerusalem 1968/69 (Mintz)
Elbogen, Ismar. *Der jüdische Gottesdienst in seiner geschichtlichen Entwicklung*, Hildesheim 1967
Emrich, Wilhelm. *Franz Kafka*, Frankfurt a.M./Bonn 1965 [also available in English: *Franz Kafka. A Critical Study of His Writings*, translated by Sheema Zeben Buehne, New York 1968] (*Critical Study*)

Eschweiler, Ch. *Der verborgene Hintergrund in Kafkas 'Der Proceß'*, Bonn 1990
Fingerhut, K. H. *Die Funktion der Tierfiguren im Werke Franz Kafkas*, Bonn 1969
Flasch, K. *Einführung in die Philosophie des Mittelalters*, Darmstadt 1989
Friedlander, G., (translator). *Pirke de Rabbi Elieser*, Warsaw edition 1851/52, London 1916
Friedmann, (editor). *Pesikta Rabbati*, Vienna 1880
Ganzfried, R. Shelomo. *Kizzur Schulchan Aruch*, Hebrew-German edition by R. Selig Bamberger, Basel 1988
Gowortschow, S. M. M., (editor). *Sefer Ba'al Shem Tov*, reprint, Tel Aviv [no date]
Grözinger, K. E. *Musik und Gesang in der frühen jüdischen Literatur*, Tübingen 1982 (*Musik*)
——. (translator). *Schivhe ha-Besht* (in preparation) [based upon Hebrew and Yiddish first editions, Kopust 1815; Korez 1815] from the Hebrew version (*H*)
——. "Chassidismus und Philosophie—ihre Wechselwirkung im Denken Martin Bubers" in: *Martin Buber (1878 - 1965)*, edited by W. Licharz and H. Schmidt, Frankfurt a.M. 1989 (*Chassidismus*)
——. "Die hasidischen Erzählungen, ihre Formen und Traditionen" in: *Frankfurter Judaistische Beiträge* [FJB] 9(1981) (*Erzählungen*)
——. "Die Gegenwart des Sinai, Erzählungen und kabbalistische Lehrstücke zur Vergegenwärtigung der Sinaioffenbarung" in: FJB 16(1988) (*Gegenwart*)
——. "Die Hasidim und der Hasidismus" in: *Beter und Rebellen*, edited by M. Brocke, Frankfurt a.M. 1983
——. "Himmlische Gerichte, Wiedergänger und Zwischenweltliche in der ostjüdischen Erzählung" in: *Franz Kafka und das Judentum*, see below (*Himmlische Gerichte*)
——. *Ich bin der Herr dein Gott, Eine rabbinische Homilie zum Ersten Gebot*, Frankfurt a.M., Bern 1976
——. "Jüdische Wundermänner in Deutschland" in: Grözinger, K. E., (editor). *Judentum im deutschen Sprachraum*, Frankfurt a.M. 1991 (*Wundermänner*)
——. "Martin Bubers Chassidismus-Deutung" in: *Dialog mit Martin Buber*, edited by Werner Licharz, Frankfurt a.M. 1982
——. "The Names of God and the Celestial Powers: Their Function and Meaning in the Hekhalot Literature" in *Jerusalem Studies in Jewish Thought* VI (1987) (*Names*)
——. "Neoplatonisches Denken in Hasidismus und Kabbala" in: FJB 11(1983)
——. "Osteuropäischer Hasidismus" in: *Theologische Realenzyklopädie*, Vol. XVII
——. "Schuld und Sühne bei Kafka im Lichte jüdischer Theologie" in: W. Kraus and N. Winkler, editors. *Das Schuldproblem bei Franz Kafka*, Schriftenreihe der österreichischen Kafka-Gesellschaft, Vol. 6, 1994 (*Schuld und Sühne*)
——. "Sündenpropheten. Halachaprophetie im Judentum Osteuropas" in: FJB 15(1987) (*Sündenpropheten*)
——. "Theosophie, Historiosophie und 'Anthroposophie' des Kabbalisten Azriel aus Gerona (13. Jh.)" in: FJB 14(1986)
——. "Tradition und Neuerung in der Musikauffassung des Sohar" (Hebrew) in: J. Dan, editor. *The Age of the Zohar, Jerusalem Studies in Jewish Thought*, Jerusalem 1989
——. "'Trübselige Meinung', sagte K." in: M. Voigt (editor). *Franz Kafka "Vor dem Gesetz"*, Würzburg 1994
Grözinger, K. E., S. Mosès, H. D. Zimmermann, editors. *Franz Kafka und das Judentum*, Frankfurt a.M. 1987 (*Judentum*)
Harnischfeger, E. *Mystik im Barock. Das Weltbild der Teinacher Lehrtafel*, Stuttgart 1980
Honig and Sons, editors. *Sefer Gevurot Adonai*, Israel 1980
Horowitz, Isaiah. *Schne Luchot ha-Brit*, Warsaw 1862
Idel, Moshe. *Golem*, Albany 1990

——. *Kabbalah, New Perspectives*, New Haven and London 1988
——. *The Mystical Experience in Abraham Abulafia*, Albany 1988
Jacobs, L. *Hasidic Prayer*, New York 1972
Joseph, Jacob, of Polonnoye. *Ben Porat Josef*, edited by Pietrkov, n.p., 1883/84
Kraft, W. *Franz Kafka, Durchdringung und Geheimnis*, Frankfurt a.M. 1968
Landmann, Salcia, (editor). *Sagen der Chasidim*, Frankfurt a.M., Berlin, Vienna 1970
Langer, G. M. *Neun Tore*, München-Planegg 1959. Reissued as *Die schönsten chassidischen Geschichten*, Frankfurt a.M. 1986 (*Neun Tore*)
Langer, Jiri. *Nine Gates*, London [no date] (*Nine Gates*)
Mendes-Flohr, P. and Cohen, A. A. *Contemporary Essays in Jewish Religious Thought*, New York 1987
Mondshayn, Y. *Shivhei ha-Baal Shem Tov, A Facsimile of a Unique Manuscript*, Jerusalem 1982
Nagel, Bert. *Kafka und die Weltliteratur*, Munich 1983
Nigal, Gedalja. *No'am Elimelech*, Jerusalem 1978 (in Hebrew)
Pasley, M. "Die Handschrift redet" in: *Marbacher Magazin* 52(1990) (*Handschrift*)
Piekarz, Mendel. *Bime Zmihat ha-Hasidut*, Jerusalem 1978
Politzer, Heinz. "Franz Kafka" in: *Wege der Forschung* [WdF] 322, Darmstadt 1973
——. *Franz Kafka, der Künstler*, Frankfurt a.M. 1962 (*Künstler*)
Pollack, H. *Jewish Folkways in Germanic Lands*, Cambridge, Mass., London 1971
Schatz-Uffenheimer, R., (editor). *Maggid Devaraw le-Ja'akov*, Jerusalem 1976 (*Maggid Devaraw*)
Schechter, Solomon. *Some Aspects of Rabbinic Theology*, New York 1961
Scholem, Gershom. *Die jüdische Mystik in ihren Hauptströmungen*, Frankfurt a.M. 1967 [also available in English: *Major Trends in Jewish Mysticism*, New York 1961] (*Major Trends*)
——. *The Messianic Idea in Judaism*, New York 1971 (*Idea*)
——. *Über einige Grundbegriffe des Judentums*, Frankfurt a.M. 1970 (*Grundbegriffe*)
——. *Ursprung und Anfänge der Kabbala*, Berlin 1962 [also available in English: *Origins of the Kabbalah*, translated by Allan Arkush, Princeton University Press 1987]
——. *Von der mystischen Gestalt der Gottheit*, Frankfurt a.M. 1973 [also available in English: *On the Mystical Shape of the Godhead, Basic Concepts in the Kabbalah*, translated by Joachim Neugroschel, New York 1991] (*Godhead*)
——. *Walter Benjamin—Die Geschichte einer Freundschaft*, Frankfurt a.M. 1975 (*Freundschaft*) [also available in English: *Walter Benjamin: The Story of a Friendship*, translated by Harry Zohn, Philadelphia 1981] (*Friendship*)
——. "Zehn unhistorische Sätze über die Kabbalah" in: *Judaica* III, Frankfurt a.M. 1973
——. *Zur Kabbala und ihrer Symbolik*, Zurich 1960 [also available in English: *On the Kabbalah and its Symbolism*, translated by Ralph Manheim, New York 1969] (*Symbolism*)
Schreiber, Michael. *"Ihr Sollt Euch kein Bild ...", Untersuchungen zur Denkform der negativen Theologie im Werk Franz Kafkas*, Frankfurt a.M., Bern, New York 1986
Secret, Francois. *Les Kabbalistes chrétiens de la Renaissance*, Milan 1985
Sfurim, Mendele Moicher. *Fischke der Krumme*, Munich 1967
Steinberg, E. R. "The Judgement in Kafka's 'The Judgement'" in: *Modern Fiction Studies*, 8(1962)
Tishby, Isaiah. *The Wisdom of the Zohar*, Oxford 1988
Urbach, E. E. *The Sages: Their Concepts and Beliefs*, Jerusalem 1979
Vital, H, (editor). *Sefer ha-Kawwanot*, Korez, 1773/74 (reprint Israel 1970/71)
Zimmermann, H. D. *Der babylonische Dolmetscher*, Frankfurt a.M. 1985

Index

Abravanel, Judah. *See* Ebreo, Leone
Adultery, transmigration and, 103, 117–18
"Advocate, The." *See* Kafka, Franz
Amerika. *See* Kafka, Franz
Am ha-aretz, 50
Amulets
  during circumcision, 150
  in Jewish folklore, 146–50
Anders, Günther, 182, 186–87
Angels, 53, 63, 190–92
  advocate, 192, 195
  courier, 191, 192
Angiriyon, 198
"An Animal Lives in the Thamühl Synagogue." *See* Kafka, Franz
Animal stories, 95–120
  Baal Shem Tov legends, 201–5
Asatiria, 197
Asirta, 200
Asiyah, world of, 9, 66
Askara, 200
Askari, Elasar, *Book of the Godfearing*, 90–91
Asriel, 192
Atonement, 79, 80, 108, 202
  redemption through, 113
Atsiluth, world of, 9, 66
Avraham the Angel, legend of, 82
Baal Shem Tov, 88, 98
  letter to Gershon Kutover, 42–43
  as redeemer in gilgul tales, 112
  use of the *Sefer Hasidim*, 152–53
Baal Shem Tov legends, 40–42, 86, 90, 117
  on advocates' prayers, 87–88
  Deadly Perjury before the Court of Rabbi Isaac, 205
  Death by Drowning, 206–7
  demons in the synagogue tale, 119–20
  A Dog and a Fish, 203–4
  An Extraordinary Horse, 202–3
  Fatal Disobedience, 206
  A Frog, 201–2
  The Haughty Rich Woman, 205–6
  The Man Who Struck His Drunken Father, 124–25
  physiognomy in, 57–58
  Rabbi Isaac Warns Quarrelsome Antagonists, 205
  song in, 154–55
  theology of the creative word in, 129–31
Beck, Evelyn Torton, *Kafka and the Yiddish Theater: Its Impact on His Work*, 3
Benjamin, Walter, 65, 88, 180
Berakhot, 132

Beriah, world of, 9, 66
Bezalel, Liva Ben, 132, 134
Binder, Hartmut, 122
  Kafka Kommentar, 77
  on Kafka's Judaism, 2, 121
  on *The Castle*, 104–5
Boiling ejaculation, 197
Book of the Godfearing. See Askari, Elasar
Book of the Pious. See Sefer Hasidim
Book on the Transmigration of the Soul. See Luria, Isaac
Botarel, Moses, 139–40
Brief Marriage, The, 108
Brod, Max, 27, 84
  on the aphorisms, 185
  Franz Kafka, Eine Biographie, 151, 163
  on Kafka's Jewish influences, 180
Buber, Martin, 176
  on evil, 169
  sociological utopias, 160

Careless Shohet, The, 102
Castle, The. See Kafka, Franz
Celestial court
  advocates' prayers, 87
  ascent to, 22–23, 39–45
    divine judgment and, 45
    nightly court, 70–76
  bailiffs, 88
  connections and influences, 89
  Davidian judgment, 86
  description of, 21
  judicial hierarchy, 22–23, 63–64, 66–68, 184, 186, 187, 190–200
    women's roles, 188
  in the Kabbalah, 190–200
  in legends, 83–94
  man's relation to, 54, 89, 93
  post-thirteenth-century conception, 61
  punishments, 24
  pure vs. impure halls, 52, 62–63, 194, 196, 200
  significance of, 17–18
  twice seven layered halls, 64–65
Christian Kabbalah, 5
Circumcision in Russia, 19, 150
Conditio humana, 185
Cordovero, Moses, 53
  on the heavenly halls, 54
  on the Hebrew alphabet, 140
  on the individual understanding of the Torah, 47
  Pardes Rimmonim, 62–63, 134
    celestial court, 62–63, 64, 66–67, 190–200
    on language to attain the divine, 137
  on women's roles, 78
Creation
  in mystical theology, 166–69
  via the word, 127–28, 131, 133–34

Dahariel, 194
Deadly Perjury before the Court of Rabbi Isaac. See Baal Shem Tov legends
Death by Drowning. See Baal Shem Tov legends
"Death in a kiss," 156
Den of Iniquity, 197, 198
"Description of a Battle." *See* Kafka, Franz
Deus absconditus, 187
Deus revelatus, 187
De Vidas, Eliahu
  on the Final Judgment, 24–25
  gatekeeper tradition in writings of, 20–21, 23, 51
  Reshit Hokhma, 16–22, 29
Dialectic of temporal existence, 169–71
Dialoghi d'amore. See Ebreo, Leone
Din, 19
Divestment of corporeality, 172
Divine judgment, 95
  High Holy Days, 35–45
  in Kafka's work, 15
  via the Word, 205–7
Divine love vs. sensuous love, 174, 177
Divine Names, 129, 188
Divine punishment, 20
Divine Throne of Judgment, 183
Dog and a Fish, A. See Baal Shem Tov legends
Dov Ber, the Maggid of Mezhirich, 11, 13
  on the building of the ark, 133
  creation story, 166–69
  description of, 173
  on man's evil eye, 169

on the Oneness of God, 167, 168–69
on sensuous vs. divine love, 174–75
Dr. Bucephalus character, 101, 115–16
Dreams and ascent to celestial court, 70–76
Dualism in the Kabbalah, 186, 187
Duma, 196–97

Eastern Jewish literature
influence on Kafka's writings, 117
rebellion against authority theme, 125–26
Ebreo, Leone, *Dialoghi d'amore*, 172–73
Eliasberg, Alexander, *Sagen polnischer Juden*, 106–7
Elimelech of Lizensk, 89
on man's temporal existence, 170
No'am Elimelech, 166
tzaddikim folk tales, 146
on the tzaddik's power, 158–59
Elisha's curse, 122
Emrich, Wilhelm, 105–6
Franz Kafka, 180–81
En-Sof, 95, 132, 187
Ephraim of Sodilkov, 133
Evil
dialectic of temporal existence, 169–71
Kafka's view of, 168, 169
man's awareness of, 173–74
Evil eye, 169
Evil instinct, 104
seven names of, 200
Extraordinary Horse, An. See Baal Shem Tov legends
Ezem ha-Shamayimk, 191–92

Fatal Disobedience. See Baal Shem Tov legends
Feast of the Tabernacles, 27
Final Judgment, 24–25
Fingerhut, Karl-Heinz
on Gregor Samsa's metamorphosis, 116
on Kafka's animal figures, 113–15
on Kafka's language and reality, 127, 134, 139, 140
on the mouse people, 141–42
Frankfurt Fettmilch Uprising of 1614, 145
Franz Kafka. See Emrich, Wilhelm
Franz Kafka, Ein Schriftstellerleben. See Unseld, Joachim
Free will, 53–55
Frog, A. See Baal Shem Tov legends

Gabriel, 196
Gadiel, 195
Gaon, Rav Saadyah, 98
Gasriel, 192, 194
Gatekeeper legend, 20–21, 29, 30, 51–52, 188
individualization of the Law, 46
interpretation of, 181
Gate of the Law, 50
individual path to, 49
Gebura, 196
Gehinnom, 33, 71, 74–75, 100, 190
seven chambers, 200
Gematria, 139
Gikatilla, Joseph, 90–91
Gilgul, 47, 49, 71, 95, 202, 203, 204
Gilgul stories, 97, 100, 201–5
animal-man in, 113, 115
dogs, 103
Eastern Jewish, 101, 114
ethical moral realm, 101
Lurianic, 105
redemption theme, 112, 113
relation to Kafka's animal stories, 109–12
sexuality theme, 103–4
types of, 106–9
Golem, 99, 124
creation of, 134–37
Good instinct. *See Good yezer*
Good yezer, 104
Gordin, Jacob, *Gott, Mensch und Teufel*, 121
Gott, Mensch und Teufel. See Gordin, Jacob
"Great Man of the Generation," 145–46

Halakhah, 15
Half-cat, half-lamb creature, 101–2, 109, 110–11
symbolism, 115
Hall of Delight, 195–96
Hall of Justice, 193–95

Hall of Love, 195
Hall of the Shells, 196
Hall of Splendor, 192–93
Hall of the Wine Dregs, 200
Hasidic folk tales, 83
  hero stories, 162
  in Kafka's work, 4–5, 16, 18–19, 84, 118–20
  location of celestial court in, 87
  narrative form, 85
  song in, 154
  tzaddik ha-dor in, 146–50
Hasidic mysticism, parallels to Kafka's aphorisms, 176
Hasidic rebbe, 14, 189
  ascent to celestial court, 39–43
Hasidism
  renunciation of theurgy, 11
  unio-mystical thought, 142
Haughty Rich Woman, The. See Baal Shem Tov legends
Heaven, Jewish view of, 84
Heavenly halls. *See* Celestial court
Hebrew alphabet
  shape of letters, 139
  spiritual significance of, 140
Hekhalot ha-Klippot, 64–65
Hekhalot mysticism
  Divine Names, 129
  passage through heavenly halls, 22
Hero stories, 143–44
  hasidic, 162
  post-classical period, 143
  relations between hero and community, 163–64
Hesed, 52
Hevra Kaddisha, 70
Hibbut ha-kever, 33
High Holy Days
  divine judgment theme, 30–32, 42–45
  in Kafka's works, 183–84
  sermon, 35
Holy of Holies, 196
Holy Names of God, 152–53
"How the Maharal Made the Golem." *See* Rosenberg, Yehudah Yudel
Human court, 27
"Hybrid, A." *See* Kafka, Franz

Ignorance of the law, principle of, 91
Impartial justice principle, 52
Infinite Oneness of Being, 186
Infinite Oneness of the Divine, 168–69, 171–73
  dissolution of, 166–67
"In the Penal Colony." *See* Kafka, Franz
"Investigations of a Dog, The." *See* Kafka, Franz
Isaac of Drohobycz, curses of, 123–24

Jacob Joseph of Polonnoye
  hasidic teachings, 159–60
  Toledot Yaakov Yoseph, 73
Jofiel, 191
Joseph of Hannipoli, 87, 88
Josephine the Singer, 11, 59, 60, 141, 152, 160
  Eastern Jewish influence, 161–62
  religious significance, 158–59
Joseph K. character, 10–11, 14, 23, 25, 80
  climb to courthouse attic, 45
  conversation with merchant Block, 55, 58–59
  court judgment, 86–87
Judaism
  annual judgment periods, 33–36
  ascetic form, 13
  Christian influences, 5
  Eastern European
    folk tales, 83–84
    view of sexual temptation, 79–80
  historical awareness, 142–43
  judgment theology, 26–27, 184
  post-biblical history, 2–3
  women's roles, 77–82
Judgment, 31
  incursion into temporal life, 69–76
  kabbalistic interpretation, 62
  theme in Kafka's works, 183–84
Judgment Day, 32
"Judgment in Paradise" tale, 73–74
"Judgment, The." *See* Kafka, Franz
Jüdisches Echo, 84

Kabbalah
  celestial court, 184
  doctrine of parallels, 65
  hierarchy of the worlds, 9, 10–12
  history, 7
  interpretation of judgment, 62
  judicial hierarchies in, 186

letter games, 137–38
Lurianic, 47–49, 77, 187
gilgul stories, 95, 97, 105, 114
reincarnation, 13
transmigration theme, 101
medieval philosophical elements, 9
popularized folkloric form, 15–16
practical application, 9–10
unio-mystical thought, 142
unity of all being, 8
view of God, 187
women's roles, 77
Zoharic, 62, 187
Kabbalistic tradition in literature, 7–8
Kafka and the Yiddish Theater: Its Impact on His Work. See Beck, Evelyn Torton
Kafka, Franz. *See also* Dr. Bucephalus character; Josephine the Singer; Joseph K. character; Mouse People
"The Advocate," 98
Amerika, 77
Karl Rossmann character, 80
on amulets, 150
"An Animal Lives in the Thamühl Synagogue," 116–17
hasidic counterpart, 118–20
animal stories
gilgul tales and, 109–12
Isabella, the dapple-gray horse, 101, 116
reality vs. unreality in, 114–15
aphorisms, 13–14, 165–78
hasidic mysticism and, 176
kabbalistic themes, 187–88
No. 50, 176
No. 54, 83, 166, 167
No. 62, 168, 177
No. 79, 174
No. 83, 167, 171
No. 85, 168
No. 90, 168
No. 105, 173–74
relation to narratives, 185–86
on the Trees of Life and of Knowledge, 171–72
asceticism, 82
belief in personal God, 177
The Castle, 10–11
agencies, 68
bachelor characters, 104–5
interpretation of, 181
conception of language, 188
"Description of a Battle," 127–28
diaries, 4, 6, 23, 28, 39, 79
on evil, 168, 169
female characters, 77–82, 116–17, 188
fictional texts, 6
gatekeeper legend, 53–54
golem story, 99, 135
Gracchus story, 99–100
hasidic legend in works of, 16, 18–19
on his Judaism, 3
"A Hybrid," 95, 101
"In the Penal Colony," 2
judgment theme, 183
"Investigations of a Dog," 104, 153
Jewish influences, 1–14, 181–89
Eastern Jewish tradition, 6, 117
in hero stories, 151
Yiddish theater, 121
"Josephine the Singer; or, the Mouse People," 141–64
"The Judgment," 29, 183
Georg Bendemann's curse, 121, 123, 138
kabbalistic influences
High Holy Days, 35
use of language, 188
Yiddish theater, 3
kinship with Jewish literary tradition, 84, 94
letter to Grete Bloch, 132
letter to Max Brod, 27–28, 84
Letter to My Father, 3, 26–27, 126
"man from the country," 50, 53
"The Metamorphosis," 102, 106, 116, 120
"nihilistic" and "confident" statements, 187
rabbi-priest story, 92–93
on reincarnation, 105
"Report to an Academy," 97
self-representation as a dog-like man, 105
The Trial, 2, 10–11, 16
cleric's words, 54
condition of judicial chambers, 65
gatekeeper legend, 46–50, 51–52

    interpretation, 185
    judgment theme, 183
    judicial hierarchy, 67–68
    kabbalistic themes, 6–7, 187–88
    Kafka on writing of, 31–32
  tzaddik ha-dor story, 146–47
  visit with Rebbe of Belz, 163
  visits to synagogue, 28
  visit to Zizkover Rabbi, 151–52
  "Writing as a Form of Prayer," 134
Kafka Kommentar. See Binder, H.
Kafziel, 193
Kaidanover, Aaron Samuel, *Olelot Efraim*, 79–80
Kaidanover, Tzevi Hirsch, *Kav ha-Yashar*, 25–26, 62, 69–70, 138–39
Kapparah, 34
Katritia, 197
Kav ha-Yashar. See Kaidanover, Tzevi Hirsch
Kemuel, 192
Kirchheim, Liva, "The Great Man of the Generation," 145–46
Kol Nidre (play). *See* Scharansky, Abraham
Kol Nidre, 28
Kraft, Werner, 182
Kurz, Gerhard, 46, 51
Kutover, Gershon, 42

Landau, Ezekiel, judicial sermon, 44–45
Langer, Frantislek, 29
Langer, Georg, 151, 158, 166, 176, 182
  Kafka and, 29–30
  move towards orthodox Judaism, 29–30
  Neun Tore, 16
  tzaddik ha-dor story, 147–50
Language
  Kafka's use of, 188
  mystical power of, 133, 137
  in prayer, 133–34
Letter games
  kabbalistic, 137–38
  in Kafka's diaries, 138
  shape of letters, 139–40
Letter to My Father. See Kafka, Franz
Light of Life, 50
Lilith, 63–64, 78, 200
Löw ben Bezalel, Judah, Chief Rabbi of Prague, 19–20, 53, 98, 184
  curses of, 124
Löwy, Isaac, 30
Löwy, Jizchak, 182
Lunchitz, Ephraim, 80
Luria, Isaac, 12, 130, 201
  ascetic Judaism, 13
  Book on the Transmigration of the Soul, 47–49
  death, 96–97
  gilgul stories, 95, 99, 102, 106–7, 109
  on transmigration, 98

Maggid of Mezhirich. *See* Dov Ber, the Maggid of Mezhirich
Maharal. *See* Löw ben Bezalel, Judah, Chief Rabbi of Prague
Major Trends in Jewish Mysticism. See Scholem, Gershom
Malkiel, 192
Man-ape character, 97, 101
Man from the country, 50, 53, 188
Man Who Struck His Drunken Father, The. See Baal Shem Tov legends
Man Who Was Lost Sight of, The. See Kafka, Franz, *Amerika*
Martyriologies, 143
Massal, 195
Mendele the Bookseller, 84
Messiah's coming, 96
Mezuzah, 4
Michael, the Advocate of Israel, 195
Michel of Zolochev, 87
Mif'alot ha-Tzaddikim, 147–50
Mirror, 199–200
Mosche, Perez Ben, 80
Mouse people, 141, 152, 155
Music. *See also* Song
  rabbinical prohibitions, 158
  synagogal, 158
Mysticism, Jewish, dualistic-dialectical aspects, 186

Nagdiel, 198
Nagel, Ben, on Kafka's Judaism, 2
Names of God, theology of, 129, 131

Naming
  creation through, 127–28, 131
  in gilgul stories, 114
Neun Tore. *See* Langer, Georg
New Year's judgment, 34–36, 38, 198
Nifleot ha-Shem, 70–72
No'am Elimelech. *See* Elimelech of Lizensk

Ofel, 197–98
Olelot Efraim. *See* Kaidanover, Aaron Samuel
Oral Law, 21
Orpaniel, 191
Other-God, 198

Padael, 194
Pardes Rimmonim. *See* Cordovero, Moses
Pasley, Malcolm, 28
Patia, Yehuday Ben Moshe, 100
Personal God, belief in, 59
Physiognomy, 60
  in legend, 57–58
Pircha, Rosa Bat, in gilgul stories, 100
Pit, 196–97, 198
Politzer, Heinz, 50, 180, 181
  on Kafka's aphorisms, 185–86
Prayers
  divine creative power of language, 133–34
  fate of, 87, 193
Prophet of sin in legend, 57
Prosopomancy, 56–57
Protocols of the Elders of Zion, 2
Purim celebrations, 144

Rabbi Isaac Warns Quarrelsome Antagonists. *See* Baal Shem Tov legends
Raja Mehemna, 37–38
Rashi of Troyes, 31
Rav Dov Ber of Lubavitch, 89
Reading faces. *See* Physiognomy
Rebbe. *See* Hasidic rebbe
Rebellion against authority theme, 122, 123
Redeemer stories, 143–44
Redemption
  death as, 108
  in gilgul tales, 112
Reincarnation, 12–13. *See also* Transmigration
  as an animal, 98, 118
  of Cain and Abel, 99
  in Kafka's writings, 100
  Lurianic tales, 188
  sexuality theme, 103–4, 117–18
"Report to an Academy." *See* Kafka, Franz
Reshit Hokhma. *See* De Vidas, Eliahu
Rosenberg, Yehudah Yudel, "How the Maharal Made the Golem," 135–37
Rosh ha-Shanah, 26, 43, 44
  judgment theme, 28–32

Sagen polnischer Juden. *See* Eliasberg, Alexander
Sahadiel, 191
Saktofa, 199
Sandalfon, 190, 196
Sanegoria, 195
Sangadiel, 192, 197
Sansinia, 193
Sapphire, 190–91
Sarsaris, 197
Scape-goat theology, 113
Scharansky, Abraham, *Kol Nidre*, 28, 121
Scholem, Gershom, 65–66
  dissident thoughts, 3
  on the individualization of the Law, 46
  on judicial hierarchies, 66
  on Kafka, 15, 95
  Kafka-poem, 178, 183, 186, 188
  Major Trends in Jewish Mysticism, 144–45
  The Story of a Friendship, 1–2
  "Ten Unhistorical Statements about the Kabbalah," 1, 182–83
Schreiber, Michael, 165
Sechutel, 193, 195
Sechut Hall, 196
Sefer ha-Peli'a, 154
Sefer Hasidim, Holy Names of God, 152–53
Sefer Hokhmat ha-Parzuf, 56
Sefira, 20, 21
  of grace, 194
  of judgment, 194, 196
  of mercy, 194
Sefira tiferet, 49

Sefirot, 8–9, 61, 64, 65, 184, 200
anti-sefirot powers of women, 78, 81
Separation of God from man, 54
Sexual temptation, 79–80, 199
judgment and, 198
reincarnation and, 117–18
Sha'ar ha-Gilgulim. See Vital, Hayyim
Shadow of Death, 199–200
Shamshiel, 192
Shekinah, 80, 81–82, 197
Sheol, 199
Shofar, 34, 35
Shulchan Arukh, 34–35
Sin
consequences of, in Kafka's works, 122–26
Hall of, 198–99
judgment of, 186
Sola gratia, 37–38
Song
in hasidic folk tales, 154
kabbalistic, 153–54
power of, 154–58
Story of a Friendship, The. See Scholem, Gershom
Sub specie aeternitatis, 10

Talmud
Babylonian, reincarnation into animals, 118
Berakhot, 132
Hasid ha-Dor, 145
on justice and grace, 184
New Year's judgment, 35–36
"Tame Ram, The," 109–10
Tashlikh, 34
Tax Collector's Disobedient Wife, The, 123–24
Tefillin, 4, 90
Temptation, 174–76. *See also* Sexual temptation
judgment and, 63–64
in *The Trial*, 65
Ten Creative Utterances of the Torah, 130–31
Ten Days of Penitence, 44–45
"Ten Unhistorical Statements about the Kabbalah." *See* Scholem, Gershom
Terrestrial Mire, 198–99
Theurgy, 9–10, 188
Hasidic renunciation of, 11
Lurianic view, 12

Tikkun, 96, 110, 201, 202, 204
in Jewish folk tales, 95–96
Tohariel, 190, 196
Toledot Yaakov Yoseph, 73
Torah
chantings, 157
four levels of, 47, 49–50
individual understanding of, 46–47
letters of, 139
Oral, 21
study of, 133
Ten Creative Utterances, 130–31
Written, 21, 49
Transmigration, 99, 188. *See also* Reincarnation
in animal stories, 95–120
as a sign of sin, 116
Tree of Knowledge of Good and Evil, 21, 170
aphorisms, 171–72, 173–74
Tree of Life, 21, 23, 170
aphorisms, 171–72, 173–74
Trial, The. See Kafka, Franz
"Two Demons in the Synagogue in Izbors," 118–19
Two trees of paradise, 165–66
Tzaddik, 11
powers of, 153, 158–59
relations with community, 160–61, 163–64
talmudic vs. kabbalistic, 153
Tzaddik ha-Dor. See also Isaac of Drohobycz
in Jewish folklore, 145–50
Tzaddikism, 146

Unio mystica, 142, 156, 161, 165
Unseld, Joachim, *Franz Kafka, Ein Schriftstellerleben*, 182

"Visit to Hell" tale, 74–75
Vital, Hayyim, 102
gilgul stories, 109
on reincarnation, 100–101
Sha'ar ha-Gilgulim, 99

Whip and Rod, 67
Women in Kafka's writings, 77–82, 116–17, 188
Wonder rabbi, 84
"Writing as a Form of Prayer." *See* Kafka, Franz
Written Law, 21

Yasid ha-Dor, 145
Yetsirah, world of, 9, 66
Yezer ha-Ra, 104
Yiddish theater, influence on Kafka's work, 3, 121
Yom Kippur, 26, 192
  judgment theme, 28–32, 43–44
  Kafka on, 28–29
Zadkiel, 191
Zangerle, Ignaz, on Kafka, 179
Zimmermann, D. H., 141
Zohar, 20–21, 37–38, 187
  on the celestial court, 52
  celestial world of judgment in, 62
  gatekeeper theme, 21
  images of women, 78–79, 81

129 [illegible] λόγος: the object as mere embodiment of the Word, which is the essence/the object.

133 prayer seen not as beseeching God but as restoring/putting in the creative process!

113 animals as humans-in-judgment via metamorphosis

48 emphasis on good deeds

49 cf. analogy of reincarnation belief in Buddhism. 2/81

p. 11 Maggid of Mezhirich's Kabbalism & Joseph K's renunciation & surrender to Oneness

216n. 5185 dream as prophetic medium

136 Golem made of the 4 elements: Earth Air Fire Water.

107 incredible ways of rationalizing tragedy via gilgul belief! (amounting to a denial of evil)

Pardes (garden) made acronym for Peshat - literal level/meaning, Remez - allegorical, Derash - moral, Sod - mystical

56 prosopomancy Προσωπο[illegible] reading the signs of the human face

Monotheism: a yearning for smth. indestructible in us → belief in a personal god

105 gilgul belief helps ordinary people endure suffering — as tho it were warranted by sins in a previous gilgul, not atoned for then but being atoned in the new gilgul

52 Free will is an attribute of man & is what is the cause of his ability to sin. The degree of divergence from the divine path is then mediated by the Law; human life is a life-in-judgment

63 Lilith — queen/seductress

Kab. psychology: judicial hierarchy of pure & impure courts = mirror of human behavior & the psyche & concerns conflict betw good & evil impulses

70 Kab. view of dreaming

72 The dream — cure of a cheapskate!

78 the ascetic's struggle ag. sexuality.

98 Gilgul: arrogant people were probably wild beasts in a previous [illegible]

102 Gregor Samsa changed into a bug remains in his family (reincarnation story)

[The Metamorphosis also p. 100]

96 The Messiah will only come when he is no longer needed...

90 [illegible] rabbis, holy men as intercessors & advocates for lightening one's "sentence"